DEMOCRACY ENCHAINED NATION DISGRACED

DEMOCRACY ENCHAINED NATION DISGRACED

DARK DAYS OF INDIA'S EMERGENCY

P.S. SREEDHARAN PILLAI

Konark Publishers Pvt. Ltd
206, First Floor,
Peacock Lane, Shahpur Jat,
New Delhi - 110 049
+91-11-4105 5065
india@konarkpublishers.com, us@konarkpublishers.com
www.konarkpublishers.com

The photographs used in this book are from the personal collection of the author.

ISBN: 978-81-987405-2-6

Edited by M.R. Narayan Swamy
Jacket design by Sourish Mitra
Typeset by Saanvi Graphics, Noida
Printed and bound in India by Thomson Press India Ltd.

Dedicated to

All those who suffered beyond imagination
and sacrificed their own lives during the Emergency.

Declaration

I was appointed as the Governor of Mizoram on 5 November 2019. Before assuming this gubernatorial position, I had the opportunity to publish two books on the Emergency: *Adiyanthiravastha – Irutinte Nilavilikal* in Malayalam (2017) and *Dark Days of Democracy* in English (2017). Both books were based on my studies on the Emergency period and my experiences as an underground activist of the Lok Sangharsh Samiti. They reflect my political perspectives, with a particular focus on the situation in Kerala.

I hereby declare that this book also includes certain portions from my previously published works.

P.S. Sreedharan Pillai

प्रधान मंत्री
Prime Minister

MESSAGE

It is a pleasure to know that the book "Dark Days of Democracy" authored by Sh. P.S. Sreedharan Pillai is being released.

Emergency remains the darkest chapter in Indian history when democratic rights of citizens were taken away overnight. During those days we witnessed the indefatigable spirit and the sacrifices of the people of India, who were relentless in fight against the authoritarianism.

Sh. Sreedharan Pillai who had been in the front of those struggles as a student activist has penned down this important book to remind everyone about the dark days of the Emergency. His experiences have made this book a powerful document about those months.

I am sure that the book will be warmly received by readers.

(Narendra Modi)

New Delhi
26 February, 2018

Shri P. S. Sreedharan Pillai
Mararji Smrithi Mandiram
K. G. Marar Road
Post- Thycaud
Thiruvananthapuram
Kerala- 695014

PRIME MINISTER
INDIA

Message from Hon'ble Prime Minister Narendra Modi for the author's book *Dark Days of Democracy*

Hon'ble Prime Minister Narendra Modi releasing the author's book, *Dark Days of Democracy*, by presenting a copy to Rt. Rev. Gregorios Mar Stephanos Episcopa, head of the Mar Thoma Delhi Diocese, in New Delhi on 21 March 2018. Also seen (from left) are Adv. Arjun Sreedhar (author's son), Ramachandran (author's brother), Adv. Reetha (author's wife), Adv. Arun Krishna Dhan (author's son-in-law), Kerala BJP president Kummanam Rajasekharan and BJP national executive member P.K. Krishnadas (second from right)

Contents

Preface xiii

PART- I: Emergency: History – Views – Experience

1. What was Emergency? 3
2. Emergency: A Critical Evaluation 6
3. The Dark Days of Emergency 11
4. Emergency: Unwarranted and Illegal 18
5. Muzzling the Media 24
6. Total Revolution 31
7. People's Declaration of Rights 36
8. Emergency: A Background 40
9. Timeline of Emergency 43
10. Constitutional Autocracy 51
11. Emergency Excesses 54
12. Inhuman Atrocities 58
13. Heroes in the Shadows 69
14. Diverse Ways of Agitation 72
15. The Days When the Constitution Collapsed 76
16. The Shah Commission Report Vanishes 82

17. Relevance of A Missing Chapter 84

18. The Role of Judiciary 87

19. The Dual Faces of Emergency 90

PART - II: The Shah Commission Report

20. The Shah Commission's Findings on Circumstances Leading to Declaration of Emergency 97

PART - III: Prominent Leaders on Emergency

21. M. Venkaiah Naidu 143

22. Pinarayi Vijayan 146

23. K. Karunakaran 153

24. Cherian Philip on A.K. Antony 155

25. P.K. Vasudevan Nair 159

26. Arangil Sreedharan 161

27. P. Parameswaran 163

28. Prof. T.V. Eachara Warrier 166

29. U. Dattatreya Rao 168

30. M.P. Veerendra Kumar 170

Part- IV: Annexures

Annexure I: The Shah Commission Final Report: Summary of Findings, Observations and Recommendations 181

Annexure II: The Shah Commission Report 259

Annexure III: Mar Thoma Sabha – The Only Church That Dared to Oppose the Emergency 274

About the Author 277

Preface

India's great history and culture have always helped us to stand tall with pride before the rest of the world. Freedom and democracy are two enduring facets of our ancient and evergreen civilisation—values we continue to uphold and cherish. As the world's largest democracy, India represents a unique confluence of sovereignty, humanity and equality.

Our forefathers often referred to our nation as Bharat, meaning "the land that seeks light". Yet, even in our proud democratic journey, we have faced moments of profound challenges. One such moment was the 21-month period between 1975 and 1977, known as the Emergency, when the absolute power constitutionally that resided with the people of India was taken away by Prime Minister Indira Gandhi and her family. During this time—from 25 June 1975 to 21 March 1977—India was slowly transformed into what many described as "an open prison", with citizens being denied their fundamental rights.

All constitutionally guaranteed rights were frozen, and media censorship was enforced, dragging the nation back into a dark era of human history. Draconian laws were used to detain people without valid reasons, and even grave acts such as police killings went unquestioned by the judiciary during that period. By banning numerous organisations, citizens were deprived of access to information, plunging society into darkness at the hands of the government.

Those who stood up, protested and resisted the Emergency are true warriors of our nation's second freedom struggle. But the sad truth is that the collective memories of this historic struggle are fading. Even more troubling is the fact that the Emergency, as portrayed in available historical narratives, is largely twisted and manipulated.

The Shah Commission Report, which named those who misused the constitutional machineries and indicted them for the chaos during the Emergency, was tactfully rejected and destroyed by Indira Gandhi's regime between 1980 and 1984. Similarly, the Jivanlal Kapur Commission Report on Mahatma Gandhi's assassination was suppressed and remains largely inaccessible to the public. Even the Shah Commission Report, running into three volumes, is not easily available in our country today.

As a result, the present generation—including young politicians in our country—does not know the actual gravity and seriousness of the Emergency. This is an alarming situation. Disturbingly, several individuals who openly supported the Emergency now present themselves as champions of freedom of speech and expression!

A vigilant society is indispensable to the functioning of a healthy democracy. It is crucial that we raise awareness about the dangers of authoritarianism and the long-term damage an Emergency can inflict on a nation. The primary motivation behind writing this book is to awaken public consciousness and to shed light on one of the darkest chapters in the history of independent India.

Before the Emergency, I held various responsibilities that shaped my early political and social journey. I served as the Jana Sangh Pradheshika Sthaneeya Samithi Karyadarshi, college Unit secretary of the Akhil Bharatiya Vidyarthi Parishad (ABVP), convener of the Bharatiya Yuva Sangh Assembly Committee, Kesari agent, Sangh Parivar worker, Malayalam Association Secretary of the Pandalam NSS College Union and General Secretary of ABVP Kerala State.

The anti-Emergency movement brought the social worker in me to the forefront, giving me an opportunity to engage in state-wide activities. Even today, there are many anti-Emergency activists who continue with the principle-based mode of politics. These brave warriors did not dive into protests with any desire to acquire a position or power. But the pertinent question is: do we remember these warriors and do we give them the respect and honour they so rightfully deserve?

Today, we see many new-age politicians who are driven by a hunger for power and, in the process, diminish themselves to mere individuals, disconnected from the greater purpose of serving the nation. It is during such testing times that we must remind ourselves of the sacrifices made by leaders like Jayaprakash Narayan (JP) and try to redeem and motivate ourselves.

When the Emergency was declared, I was a first-year student at Kozhikode Law College, recently elected as the college magazine editor. The following year, I was elected Vice Chairman of the College Union. Later, I was elected to the University Senate from the Registered Graduate Mandal for three consecutive terms. It was during those vibrant college days that I was drawn to JP's youth movement and his call for "Total Revolution".

During the nationwide Satyagraha movement launched by the Lok Sangarsh Samithi, I actively participated as a law student. This movement gave me

The controversial cover page of the Kozhikode Government Law College magazine (1975–76), published during the Emergency, depicted the country in the clutches of tyranny. The author was the magazine's elected student editor at the time.

ample chances to lead and mobilise fellow students. As editor of the Government Law College (Kozhikode) magazine in 1975–76, I chose a bold cover illustration—an image showing our country in chains, symbolically shackled by Indira Gandhi's authoritarian rule. This act of defiance did not go unnoticed. Serious actions were taken against me for that cover, which pushed me into embarrassing situations.

In protest against the Emergency, the youth wings of the Jana Sangh, the Congress Socialist Party and other independent groups came together to form the Loktantrik Yuva Morcha, with Arun Jaitley as the national convener. I was the state convener.

I have attempted to approach this book in most honest and unbiased manner, and I am always open to constructive criticism. To present a balanced view, I have included the speech of former Kerala Chief Minister K. Karunakaran, in which he justified the Emergency on its 25th anniversary, as an annexure. I have also annexed the dissenting voice of A.K. Antony, expressed in the presence of Indira Gandhi and Sanjay Gandhi at the Guwahati AICC session, as well as the opinion of the late Eachra Warrier.

This is my 260th book, and I am delighted that my works in Malayalam and English are being translated into 11 Indian languages. I would like to express my heartfelt gratitude to all those who supported me throughout the journey of this book. I extend my heartfelt thanks to Mr K.P.R. Nair, Managing Director of Konark Publishers, for readily agreeing to publish this book and for ensuring its timely release. I am especially grateful to my family and colleagues for their encouragement, and to the readers whose continued interest inspires me to keep writing. Without their support, this book would not have been possible.

Kozhikode
2 April 2025

P.S. Sreedharan Pillai

PART- I

EMERGENCY:
HISTORY – VIEWS – EXPERIENCE

1

What was Emergency?

For 21 months in independent India, it seemed as though the country no longer belonged to its people. This dark period in history is known as *The Emergency*. According to the democratic system and the Constitution we adopted, the people are the true sovereigns of India. Ministers, bureaucrats and politicians are meant to be their servants—beacons of hope, not masters. That is why, during the freedom struggle, Gandhiji led from the front, yet stepped back and stood alongside the poor at the farthest end when the transfer of power took place. That gesture symbolised the ideal that leadership is service. But during the Emergency, the nation veered completely away from this Gandhian ideal.

The Emergency was a time when the then Prime Minister, Indira Gandhi, imposed a de facto dictatorship, effectively reducing the Indian state to her private domain. For 21 months—from 25 June 1975 to 21 March 1977—the nation endured what can only be described as lawless rule. The foundational idea that the state belonged to the people was dismantled, and the entire democratic machinery was reduced to a tool of oppression. It was a time when the country became a vast prison, with fear and coercion reigning supreme.

All power was concentrated in the hands of Indira Gandhi and her son, Sanjay Gandhi. The entire administrative apparatus collapsed into moral and institutional decay. The Constitution was misused, fundamental rights were suspended, and the voice of the people was brutally suppressed. The Emergency was marked by widespread state violence, arbitrary arrests, and blatant violations of human rights. It was not just an error—it was a crime against democracy. A crime that later pushed the nation to the brink of destruction.

During this dark chapter, many towering leaders of Indian politics—including Jayaprakash Narayan, Morarji Desai, Atal Bihari Vajpayee, L.K. Advani and Raj Narain—were imprisoned without reason under draconian laws such as MISA (Maintenance of Internal Security Act). On 4 July 1975, the Central government banned several organisations including the RSS, Jamaat-e-Islami, and various Naxalite movements. Balasaheb Deoras, then *Sarsanghchalak* of the RSS, spent the entire Emergency period as a MISA detainee.

The Emergency inflicted deep wounds on Indian democracy and its constitutional institutions. A dangerous blend of fascism and authoritarianism was unleashed upon the people. Basic freedoms—including the freedom of the press, often described as the lifeblood of democracy—were brutally crushed. Nearly 3,000 media outlets were shut down due to censorship, threats, repression, and financial strangulation.

Arbitrary arrests and disproportionate detentions were common. According to the Justice Shah Commission—a judicial body established after the restoration of democracy—1,12,890 people were arrested under draconian laws such as MISA, DIR, and COFEPOSA. Even more horrifying were the forced sterilisations: 26.2 lakhs people were sterilised in 1975-76 and a staggering 81.3 lakhs in 1976-77. Most of the victims were poor, including many from the Muslim community in Delhi.

All six fundamental rights guaranteed by the Constitution were suspended. Citizens could no longer approach the courts to protect their lives or assert their freedoms. The judiciary, meant to be the guardian of these rights, was manipulated. In 1973, when the Supreme Court, in the Kesavananda Bharati Case, ruled that the basic structure of the Constitution could not be altered, the government retaliated by bypassing the three senior-most judges and appointing Justice A.N. Ray as the Chief Justice. This move shattered judicial independence. In protest, senior judges J.M. Shelat, A.N. Grover, and K.S. Hegde resigned.

The Congress-CPI alliance went so far as to demand a "committed judiciary"—one loyal to the government rather than the Constitution. Meanwhile, public outrage was mounting. By June 1975, widespread protests led by Jayaprakash Narayan called for Indira Gandhi's resignation over allegations of corruption. On 12 June 1975, the Allahabad High Court declared her election invalid due to electoral malpractices. That same day, the Congress lost the Gujarat Assembly elections to the opposition led by Morarji Desai.

In response to these political threats, the Emergency was declared at midnight on 25 June 251975, ushering in a period where dissent was crushed and power was abused. Parliamentary debates were stifled, court rulings censored, and opposition voices silenced.

Yet, many stood against this tyranny, guided by their faith in democracy and non-violence. Their courage has not been adequately remembered in mainstream history. During the Emergency, Indira Gandhi inflicted more vengeance and repression on her political opponents than even the British colonial rulers had during the freedom struggle.

In essence, the Emergency was a time when dictatorship reigned, fear dominated, and the people were trampled by those in power. Yet, the spirit of the people remained unbroken. What followed was a second freedom struggle—some call it the third—anchored in peaceful resistance. In 1977, democracy triumphed once more as the people voted overwhelmingly to end the authoritarian regime.

The Emergency, declared at midnight on 25 June 1975, was not just unconstitutional—it was immoral and anti-people. On 21 March 1977, it was officially lifted. India, reborn as a democracy, proved to the world that even from the ashes of repression, it could rise again, like a phoenix.

As the poet once wrote in memory of a lost civilisation:

**"I will rise from the pyre.
The wings will bloom and rise."**

And rise India did—stronger, wiser, and ever more vigilant.

2

Emergency: A Critical Evaluation

It is the sacred duty of a nation—*Rajdharma*—to record its historical events with complete honesty and pass them on to future generations without distortion. Unearthing the truth and documenting it faithfully is not just a responsibility of the present but also a guide for the future. The Emergency of 1975–77 remains deeply etched in the memory of my generation and must be remembered by those yet to come. The testimonies, the trauma and the torture endured during that time are not just episodes of the past—they are warnings that must never be forgotten or buried in ignorance.

The Emergency represents a dark chapter in the history of independent India—a time when the country was plunged into dictatorship and civil liberties were either suspended or eliminated by law. Censorship placed the entire propaganda apparatus, including the media, under State control. With the freedoms of expression and assembly effectively outlawed, independent India was reduced to a silenced nation, where fear stifled dissent and democracy stood paralysed. Amid this repression, the Lok Sangharsh Samiti emerged as a powerful force. Through non-violent struggle, it played a crucial role in helping restore freedom to the nation.

Formed by political parties such as the Jana Sangh, the Socialist Party, the Congress (O) and Sarvodaya leaders, the Lok Sangharsh Samiti resisted the dictatorship with determination. Although banned during the Emergency, the movement drew much of its strength from the Rashtriya Swayamsevak Sangh (RSS), which formed its backbone.

Tragically, the failures and excesses of the regime that pushed the country to the brink of dictatorship remain inadequately documented in our history books. It is a national tragedy that the horrors of the Emergency have been consigned to the margins of history. History flows ceaselessly, and it is our collective duty to gather, preserve and pass on its vital fragments to future generations.

Many of those who resisted the Emergency often did not pursue this responsibility with the urgency it required. I, like many others, carry the burden of not having done full justice to that critical chapter of our past. Yet, through annual commemorations organised by Vigil Human Rights, we strive to keep that memory alive and to dispel the darkness the Emergency brought, especially in Kerala. On the 50th anniversary of the Emergency, I take solace in knowing that Vigil's efforts have continued to grow in strength and reach.

It was at midnight on 25 June 1975 that Prime Minister Indira Gandhi recommended the imposition of Emergency to President Fakhruddin Ali Ahmed, marking the matter "Top Secret". The President approved the recommendation without adequate examination, invoking Article 352 of the Constitution. In his memoir *The Dramatic Decades: The Indira Gandhi Years*, former President Pranab Mukherjee noted that Fakhruddin Ali Ahmed exercised his constitutional powers automatically and without scrutiny. Indira Gandhi herself later admitted that the decision lacked proper legal procedure and careful study. This abuse of executive power laid the foundation for a decision that would cast a long, dark shadow over Indian democracy.

The Shah Commission, established to investigate Emergency-era abuses, clearly documented how the Constitution and the rule of law were systematically subverted. According to V.D. Pandey, the then Cabinet Secretary, the Emergency was declared without consulting the Cabinet or senior officials. He learnt of it when summoned to a Cabinet meeting at 4.30 a.m. on 26 June. Intelligence Bureau

Director Atma Jayaram, Home Secretary S.L. Khurana, and even the Law Minister were kept in the dark. On 25 June 1975, the Prime Minister circumvented democratic processes, effectively stripping the people of their rights through the back door.

Indira Gandhi's decision to declare the Emergency without consulting her Cabinet was both undemocratic and unconstitutional. Her decision was heavily influenced by power-hungry sycophants and external forces, including the Soviet Union and the Communist Party of India (CPI). In the wake of the Bangladesh War and riding the wave of her "Garibi Hatao" slogan, she had secured a sweeping electoral mandate in 1971. However, by centralising power, sidelining senior Congress leaders and manipulating the presidential election, she cut herself off from internal checks and balances. The country was already grappling with widespread corruption, and scandals like the Nagarwala case further tarnished her reputation.

Student-led anti-corruption protests in Gujarat and Bihar, especially under the leadership of Jayaprakash Narayan, shook the Congress to its core. Between 18 and 27 March 1974, official records reported 27 student deaths due to police action in Bihar, though Opposition parties claimed the number was as high as 236. Jayaprakash Narayan's call for a "Total Revolution" galvanised the masses and unnerved the Congress-Left alliance, which responded by branding him a fascist. Even in Kerala, his visit was met with resistance from both the Left and the Congress. Yet, at a meeting in Kozhikode addressing RSS volunteers at the Thali Samoothiri Higher Secondary School ground, he defiantly declared, "If you are fascists, then I too am a fascist".

After the Allahabad High Court invalidated Indira Gandhi's election on charges of electoral malpractice, she should have resigned. Instead, she chose the path of authoritarianism. Scandals such as the Nagarwala and the Pondicherry scams further implicated her government. Declaring the Emergency, she jailed opposition leaders, froze civil liberties, and imposed draconian censorship laws. Upon his imprisonment, Jayaprakash Narayan aptly remarked, *Vinash Kale*

Viprit Buddhi, meaning "when destruction nears, the mind works against reason".

The 1977 general elections became a referendum against this authoritarianism. Indira Gandhi and the Congress were resoundingly defeated across North India. Yet, in Kerala and other southern states, the electorate largely continued to support her, reflecting a regional endorsement of autocracy and sparking accusations of democratic betrayal. Despite this, the verdict in almost all northern states was decisively against autocratic rule during the Emergency.

Marxist veteran A.K. Gopalan issued a strong call to resist fascism, even comparing Indira Gandhi to "a female Hitler". However, this call was not fully embraced, as the Communist Party of India (Marxist) (CPM) adopted a strategy of avoiding confrontation. Later, E.M.S. Namboodiripad admitted that the decision to stay away from protests was a mistake.

National leaders like Jayaprakash Narayan, A.B. Vajpayee, Morarji Desai and L.K. Advani were imprisoned without due process. Meanwhile, the CPI and the Revolutionary Socialist Party (RSP) openly supported the Emergency and its controversial 20-point programme. In Kerala, Chief Minister Achutha Menon convened special meetings to implement his harsh measures, while media outlets like *Janayugam*, *Patriot*, and *Link* actively supported the regime. On 15 July 1975, Achutha Menon declared that the Emergency was targeted solely at right-wing forces.

It is ironic and disheartening that some political prisoners later became staunch Indira Gandhi supporters, even serving as ministers. History must never be distorted to serve political interests.

The RSS, under the banner of the Lok Sangharsh Samiti, bore the brunt of state repression and led a disciplined, non-violent struggle inspired by Gandhian ideals. In Kerala, activists like M.P. Manmathan were betrayed by the ruling opposition parties. Despite severe beatings and widespread human rights violations, the movement persevered.

The RSS believed that the sacrifices made for the nation should never be exploited for propaganda. But, as we mark 50 years since that fateful period, it is imperative to expose those who distort or manipulate the truth of the Emergency for political gain. Let the shadows of the past be remembered not as folklore, but as a solemn reminder—and a warning—for generations to come.

3

The Dark Days of Emergency

The Emergency—often referred to as the dark age in India's post-independence history—still haunts the memories of thousands who suffered its cruelties and brutal excesses. Declared on 25 June 1975, and lasting for 21 months, it marked a period of tyranny that left a deep scar on the conscience of a nation. On the international stage, it was a moment of great shame for a country that had given the world an unparalleled leader in Mahatma Gandhi, the torchbearer of non-violence. The autocracy and dictatorship of Indira Gandhi, the then Prime Minister, revealed her barbarous face when her political opponents were mercilessly put behind bars without trial. Silencing all dissenting voices, the reins of power were concentrated in the hands of Indira Gandhi and her younger son Sanjay Gandhi, widely regarded as her heir apparent.

Constitutional rights of the people were suspended, and an atmosphere of fear and state-sponsored violence became the order of the day. The Emergency days were not just a time of torture and oppression for politicians and opponents of the establishment but also for the common man, whose basic freedoms were mercilessly stripped away. Yet, the spontaneous uprising that arose from the nation's conscience revealed its strength through icons of vigour and valour—JP, Morarji Desai, Balasaheb Deoras, A.B. Vajpayee, L.K. Advani, George Fernandes, Raj Narain and others—who were imprisoned for their defiance. Organisations such as the RSS

(Rashtriya Swayamsevak Sangh), Jamaat-e-Islami, Ananda Marga, and Naxalite groups were banned. One of the noblest pillars of the Indian Constitution—"The Fourth Estate"—was completely pounded with the hawkish aggression of an autocratic regime.

With scant regard for human rights, black laws like Maintenance of Internal Security Act (MISA) and Defence of India Act (DIR) were widely enforced. According to the Shah Commission Report, which investigated the atrocities committed during the Emergency, nearly 1,12,000 people were arrested or detained under these rules. Even more disturbing was the number of poor, unfortunate men who were forcefully subjected to sterilisation—a gruesome campaign spearheaded by Sanjay Gandhi. Citizens of the nation were deprived of their rights to seek justice, with the judiciary effectively silenced and civil liberties suspended. The right to life, freedom of expression and protection under the law were gravely compromised.

In a disturbing attack on judicial independence, three senior judges of the Supreme Court of India were superseded in 1973 in the appointment process of the Chief Justice because they were not considered "committed" to the government; all three subsequently resigned. Then, on 12 June 1975, the Allahabad High Court declared Prime Minister Indira Gandhi's election null and void on grounds of electoral malpractices and misuse of power. When Indira Gandhi sought an unconditional stay from the Supreme Court, her plea was allowed in parts. All these events became reasons for the proclamation of the Emergency.

Under the guise of the Emergency, both the Union and state governments engaged in unlawful acts of persecution against their political rivals. News about such incidents often vanished into oblivion owing to the eagle-eyed press censorship policies. The fate of court judgments and Parliament debates was no different. The second struggle for independence—against dictatorship and the demolition of democracy—emerged victorious in 1977. The autocratic ruling apparatus lost a critical parliamentary election. The Emergency was then withdrawn, the ban on the organisations was lifted, and democracy was restored. Surviving the darkest phase of a tumultuous eclipse, the dreams of a nation started to blossom in the valley of democracy. Following the peaceful struggle deeply rooted in the principles of non-violence, the entire nation rose like a phoenix with exquisite effulgence.

Independent India witnessed 21 dark months between 1975 and 1977 when her citizens were subjected to untold repression and denied the basic rights guaranteed by the Constitution. That was the Emergency. As per the democratic setup and the Constitution, the supreme authority of the country is vested in its people. Ministers, bureaucrats and politicians are expected to serve the people, giving them hope for a better tomorrow. Mahatma Gandhi, who led the freedom struggle, continued to work among the poor and the needy, even during the transfer of governance from the British to the Indians. The Emergency was a betrayal of this Gandhian legacy.

By imposing autocracy, Indira Gandhi sought to establish that India was her private property, rather than a nation belonging to its people. For a period of 21 months, the law of the jungle prevailed. The atmosphere of fear spawned by the power-hungry ruling dispensation etched gory chapters in the annals of history. During those days, Indira Gandhi and Sanjay Gandhi wielded unbridled authority. The entire administrative machinery was reduced to a tool of oppression. Constitutional provisions and powers were brazenly misused. It was the darkest hour in the history of independent India.

The real trigger behind the declaration of Internal Emergency was the court verdict by the Allahabad High Court in the Raj Narain vs. Indira Gandhi case. Justice Jagmohan Lal Sinha found Indira Gandhi guilty of electoral malpractices and set aside her election to the Lok Sabha. At the time, the Supreme Court was on its annual summer recess. Following the High Court judgment, Law Minister H.R. Gokhale tried to call on Justice V.R. Krishna Iyer, the vacation judge. However, Justice Krishna Iyer declined the meeting after learning that the request pertained to the verdict in the Prime Minister's case. Subsequently, Indira Gandhi filed an appeal before the Supreme Court, seeking an early hearing. On 24 June 1975, her counsel, Nani Palkhiwala, tried his best to get a stay, but the court, reluctant to accept the interim prayer, granted only a limited stay. This judicial setback further contributed to the proclamation of the Emergency on 25 June 1975.

The Shah Commission Report, along with various books on the subject, reveals that the preparations for an Internal Emergency had begun much earlier than officially stated. Indira Gandhi's close advisers—Siddhartha Shankar Ray, the Chief Minister of West Bengal; D.K. Barooah, the Congress President; Rajni Patel, President of the Bombay Pradesh Congress Committee; and Law Minister H.R. Gokhale—formed the core group responsible for these early preparations. It is now known that the list of the proposed detenus was being compiled as early as January 1975. The so-called imminent threat to national security cited by Indira Gandhi as the reason for imposing the Emergency has since been exposed as an outright lie.

The Emergency was a monumental blunder—an error in judgment that proved politically disastrous for the Congress Party. During those days of tyranny, even iconic leaders of the stature of JP, Morarji Desai, A.B. Vajpayee, L.K. Advani and Raj Narain were imprisoned under MISA without any formal charge or show-cause notice. On 4 July 1975, the Central government banned 21 organisations, including the RSS and Jamaat-e-Islami. RSS chief Balasaheb Deoras was jailed for 21 months under MISA. In Kerala, both RSS members and Naxalite activists were subjected to some of the most brutal forms of torture by the Congress government.

The fascist rule during the Emergency caused incalculable damage to Indian democracy and its constitutional institutions. The very foundations of freedom and democracy were badly shaken as a result of unbridled oppression and draconian laws. Freedom of the press, one of the pillars of a healthy democracy, was curbed and censorship laws rendered publications impotent. Almost 3,000 publications had to close down, unable to withstand threats, oppression and financial strangulation. The authorities unleashed terror, arrested opponents of the Emergency at will and ruled the country through ordinances that were anti-people.

During the Emergency, people were put behind bars under draconian laws without proper charges and arrested without warrants. The Judicial Enquiry Commission on Emergency, constituted after the Emergency under Justice J.C. Shah, a former Chief Justice of the Supreme Court, reported that a total of 1,12,850 people were jailed under MISA, DIR and COFEPOSA Act (Conservation of Foreign Exchange and Prevention of Smuggling Activities Act, 1974). Furthermore, as many as 26,24,755 people were vasectomised during 1975-76 under the guise of family planning, through sheer institutional force, and 81,32,209 more during 1976-77. A large number of these were poor people from Delhi.

All the fundamental rights granted by the Constitution of India were suspended during this period. Citizens were denied the right to approach the courts to secure human rights, the right to protection of life, the right to voice their opinion and to propagate ideas on matters of public importance. The world watched the ineffectual and acquiescent role of the judiciary in silence. After gaining absolute control over the legislature, executive and the ruling party, Indira Gandhi got the unstinted support of the USSR. So powerful was her position that she succeeded in rendering the judicial establishment subservient to the government.

In 1973, the majority of the Constitution Bench of the Supreme Court of India held that Parliament had no power to amend the basic structure of the Constitution. Aggrieved by the verdict, Indira Gandhi turned against the judges of the Supreme Court. In a retaliatory move, the Congress government appointed Justice J.N. Ray as the Chief Justice of the Supreme Court, superseding three senior judges—Justice J.M. Shelat, Justice A.N. Grover and Justice K.S. Hegde. In protest, the superseded judges resigned from their posts. The Congress and CPI MPs brazenly raised their voice in favour of a "committed judiciary".

Political history shows that the Congress Party embraced an authoritarian trend from 1969. In June 1975, civil society and the general public launched a mass movement under the leadership of JP, the man who could rightfully claim the legacy of Mahatma Gandhi, against the corrupt Central government. On 12 June 1975, the Allahabad High Court annulled the electoral victory of Indira Gandhi. On the same day, in the Gujarat Assembly election, the combined Opposition parties, under the leadership of Morarji Desai, trounced the Congress.

During the Emergency, the Central and the Kerala governments stood out as the worst oppressors. The misuse of power and the victimisation of political opponents resulted in the death and torture of many. Even parliamentary debates and court decrees were subject to censorship during those days. Nevertheless, a large number of people persevered in resisting the tyranny in a non-violent manner, hoping to put an end to despotism and restore democracy. Unfortunately, most such grassroots efforts have not been documented. Repression under Indira Gandhi was, in many ways, more brutal and vengeful than even the British actions against Indian freedom fighters.

Though the government continued to trample upon the citizens' rights, the resistance to the Emergency was rooted in the principle of *ahimsa* (non-violence) and could rightfully be described as the second freedom struggle. It was a struggle by the common man to reclaim democratic ideals, liberty and human rights. Although the people of North India suffered the most, they had the foresight to recognise the value of democracy and human rights and exert the will to fight against autocracy. The year 1977 undoubtedly proved that Indian society has the intrinsic strength to stand up against tyranny. The people were not willing to accept the Emergency, which was illegal, anti-people, and immoral. It is important to note that while northern states of India stood up against autocracy through the ballot, Kerala voted in favour of Indira Gandhi in the 1977 election.

On 21 March 1977, India once again earned the distinction of being a nation that ended despotic rule through a non-violent struggle. It was on this day that the Emergency was officially withdrawn. Democracy was reborn with renewed energy and vigour. Bharat emerged victorious in the second freedom struggle in a way reminiscent of the lines celebrating the Greek triumph:

From ashes I shall resurrect myself
With wings opening up like flowers.

4

Emergency: Unwarranted and Illegal

The Justice J.C. Shah Commission devoted several days and nights meticulously examining documents, evidence, and witness testimonies. The Commission ultimately concluded that the declaration of the Emergency was unwarranted. Its report asserted that neither the economic situation under Indira Gandhi's leadership was in disarray nor was there a breakdown in law and order or any threat to national security that warranted the invocation of Article 352 of the Constitution.

None of the official authorities or agencies—including the state governments, intelligence agencies, government dossiers or the media—had indicated the presence of any crisis severe enough to merit such drastic action. It becomes abundantly clear to anyone who reads the Commission report that the Emergency was a conspiracy orchestrated by Indira Gandhi and her accomplices to destroy the Opposition and prolong her rule under the false pretext of the country undergoing a grave crisis.

Not even Jawaharlal Nehru would have forgiven the undemocratic actions of his daughter. In a speech delivered in Thiruvananthapuram (then Trivandrum) on 2 June 1950, Nehru had said: "I am not fearful of the Opposition parties of this country. I have no dislike for any Opposition group growing stronger based on any ideology, political practice or creative plan of action. I abhor the idea of India as a place where lakhs of servile people blindly go behind a single leader. I need a strong Opposition." In the mid-1950s, when no political party had enough seats to be the principal Opposition party, Nehru extended the status and perks of the Leader of the Opposition to A.K. Gopalan, the Communist Party leader in the Lok Sabha. But Indira Gandhi's approach, however, was in stark contrast to her father's democratic values.

In an interview with the *New York Times* in 1975, Indira Gandhi made her attitude towards the Opposition unmistakably clear. She said: "Many countries are relinquishing the democratic form of governance for the speedy implementation of programmes and policies. To lay the foundation for progress, this is absolutely necessary." She did not hesitate to express her approval of Bangladesh leader Sheikh Mujibur Rahman's decision to abandon democracy and embrace dictatorship. The Emergency only confirmed to the world that Jawaharlal Nehru, who upheld democratic values and respected the Opposition, had a daughter who showed scant regard to those very ideals. For instance, as early as 1957, Indira Gandhi, then serving as Congress president, made the controversial decision to dismiss the democratically elected Communist government of Kerala.

The declaration of the Emergency was widely judged by both the courts and the general public as ill-motivated and unjustified. Moreover, the Judicial Enquiry Commission categorically stated that the Prime Minister's recommendation for Emergency and its subsequent approval by the President were both illegal and unconstitutional. Crucial documents relating to the recommendation and declaration, which had been marked "Top Secret", have disappeared from public access—courtesy of the successive Congress governments that returned to power. Even the Shah Commission Report, which exposed the illegality of the Emergency, was suppressed and kept classified by Indira Gandhi's government after it regained power in 1980. It was not until 2010 that the public came to know the contents of these suppressed documents, thanks to the book titled *Shah Commission: Lost and Regained,* authored by Era Sezhiyan—one of the founding leaders of the Dravida Munnetra Kazhagam (DMK) and a distinguished parliamentarian.

Following is the letter of recommendation for the Emergency, along with the one-line order passed by the President:

"TOP SECRET"

PRIME MINISTER, INDIA
NEW DELHI June 25, 1975.

"Dear Rashtrapatiji,

As already explained to you, a little while ago, information has reached us which indicates that there is an imminent danger to the security of India being threatened by internal disturbance. The matter is extremely urgent. I would have liked to have taken this to Cabinet but unfortunately this is not possible tonight. I am, therefore, condoning or permitting a departure from the Government of India (Transaction of Business) Rule 1961, as amended up-to-date by virtue of my powers under Rule 12 thereof. I shall mention the matter to the Cabinet first thing tomorrow morning. In the circumstances, and in case you are so satisfied, a requisite proclamation under Article 352(1) has become necessary. I am enclosing a copy of the draft proclamation for your consideration. As you are aware, under Article 352(3) even when there is an imminent danger of such a threat, as mentioned by me, the necessary proclamation under Article 352(1) can be issued.

I recommend that such a proclamation should be issued tonight, however late it may be, and all arrangements will be made to make it public as early as possible thereafter.

With kind regards,
Yours Sincerely
(Sd/- Indira Gandhi)

President Fakhruddin Ali Ahmed's One-line Declaration of the Emergency is as follows:

"In exercise of the powers conferred by clause 1 of Article 352 of the Constitution, I, Fakhruddin Ali Ahmed, President of India, by this proclamation declare that a grave emergency exists whereby the security of India is threatened by internal disturbance."

PRESIDENT
New Delhi 25th June, 1975.

It is imperative, according to the Indian Constitution, that the President can declare an Emergency only after receiving the recommendation of the Cabinet. The Union Constitution Committee, in a meeting on 8 and 9 June 1947, chaired by Jawaharlal Nehru, had unanimously approved this prerequisite for the declaration of an Emergency. The President, as the head of the Central government, can only act with the knowledge and recommendation of the Council of Ministers, as India follows a parliamentary system of government. The Constitution does not permit the President to make unilateral decisions. This general principle is also applicable in the case of Article 352. A detailed administrative legal framework has been laid out for the declaration of an Emergency. However, this framework was flouted *in toto* by the Congress government in 1975.

The Shah Commission found that the decision to impose the Emergency had been made before the formal declaration on 25 June 1975. Siddhartha Shankar Ray from Bengal—a classmate and close confidant of Indira Gandhi—had advised her to declare the Emergency much earlier. Ray had even accompanied the Prime Minister when she visited the President at 5.30 p.m. on 25 June. As mentioned earlier, without informing the Cabinet, let alone discussing it, the Prime Minister prepared the recommendation letter and sent it to the President at 10 p.m. She did not take even her senior Cabinet colleagues into confidence. It is worth mentioning that on 25 June, nothing untoward happened, nor was there any event that could have raised serious concerns.

The Cabinet Secretary, Law Minister and Home Minister were not immediately informed about the declaration of the Emergency. On the morning on 26 June, a notice was sent to the Cabinet members just one and a half hours before the scheduled meeting. The Judicial Commission questioned whether a Cabinet meeting could have been scheduled between 5.30 and 11.30 p.m. the previous day. No valid reason was provided for why such a meeting was not held. In short, the Commission concluded that the declaration of the Emergency, made without Cabinet approval, was entirely illegal.

When the Cabinet finally met on the morning of 26 June, the reservations expressed by the longest-serving Union Cabinet minister, Swaran Singh, were met with displeasure, and it took only hours for him to be replaced. The secretary to the President, in his statement to the Commission, mentioned that he had advised against the President's declaration of the Emergency without Cabinet approval. However, due to Indira Gandhi's insistence, the President had no choice but to acquiesce. This compliance by President Ahmed may be seen by some as a quid pro quo for his appointment as the country's President. He signed the papers when they were brought to him by R.K. Dhawan, Indira Gandhi's personal secretary. The time was 11.45 p.m.

It is ironic that Siddhartha Shankar Ray later testified to the Shah Commission that whatever Indira Gandhi did during the Emergency was illegal. The Commission identified three people as primarily responsible for the excesses during the Emergency. In 1977, the enlightened Indian voter dispelled the myth that if the Opposition is put behind bars and persecuted, the people will be powerless. Indira Gandhi and her supporters were decisively routed in the 1977 elections. This victory was celebrated by the media worldwide, except in the USSR, her staunch ally. Unfortunately, the people of Kerala and other southern states, by and large, supported Indira Gandhi's despotic reign and returned the Congress to power in Kerala. Nevertheless, the 1977 elections are considered a watershed moment in Indian history, marking the victory of democracy.

5

Muzzling the Media

Though freedom of the press is not explicitly stated as a fundamental right in the Indian Constitution, India is among those nations where freedom of expression is held in high esteem. The media was the first victim of the Emergency, and Congress leader Balram Jhakar had the temerity to ask in Parliament why the media should not be nationalised. The committee that designed our Constitution had warned that curtailing press freedom would rob parliamentary democracy of its very breath of life. But the national leaders of the time were optimistic that in a great nation like India such tragedies were quite unlikely. This optimism was justified by the fact that, despite the absence of specific clauses ensuring press freedom, various court rulings and constitutional interpretations had always guaranteed a free press in the country. However, during the Emergency, concerted efforts were made to bring the press under state control by curtailing its independence and freedom of operation.

In an effort to silence the media, several journalists were arrested and publication activities were stopped by disconnecting electricity to the press in Delhi on 25 June 1975. Newspapers were brought under censorship regulations, further restricting press freedom. Chapter 6 of the Shah Commission Report provides a disturbing account of the various measures adopted by the government to suppress the media, including bringing even parliamentary speeches under the scope of censorship laws.

Newspapers were categorised into A, B and C, representing friendly, hostile and neutral outlets, respectively. Each category was further subdivided. Government advertisements were distributed solely based on this categorisation. This classification system was also the basis for pleasing and promoting newspapers deemed friendly, while intimidating and marginalising those considered hostile.

The following is a list of newspapers that were classified as friendly and placed in the A-list:

1. *Nathun Assamia* (Assamese)
2. *Amrita Bazar Patrika* (English)
3. *Nagrika* (Bengali)
4. *Indian Nation* (English)
5. *The Hindu* (English)
6. *Nai Duniya* (Hindi)
7. *Hindustan* (Hindi) and 3 other dailies

The following newspapers were classified as hostile to the government and were included in the B-list:

1. *Dainik Asom* (Assamese)
2. *Dainik Sambad* (Bengali)
3. *Poona Daily* (English)
4. *The Indian Express* (English)
5. *Sandesh* (Gujarati)
6. *Pradip* (Hindi)
7. *Veer Pradip* (Hindi)
8. *Deshabhimani* (Malayalam)
9. *Kannada Prabha* (Kannada)
10. *NavBharat* (Marathi)

The C-list included various smaller news outlets from across India. These are only a representative list, as a large number of newspapers and journals, published in virtually all languages, were classified under categories B or C.

During the Emergency, a number of Indian newspapers ceased publication, and some were forcibly shut down. The following is what the Shah Commission had to say about the dangers of daily censorship, citing entries from the Indian Censorship logbook:

> The actual work of censorship on a day-to-day basis went even beyond the scope of the guidelines. Orders were arbitrary in nature, capricious and often issued orally without any reference to the provisions of Rule 48. Issuing oral orders had been expressly forbidden by Chief Censor H. J. D'Penha in the guidelines issued on 13 July 1975.

D'Penha explained that, in view of the tight deadlines and round-the-clock operations of daily newspapers and news agencies, putting orders in writing would have defeated the very purpose of censorship. Hence, from almost the very beginning, censorship directives were communicated orally.

D'Penha further stated that he personally received such oral orders from various authorities in the Ministry of Information and Broadcasting as well as other ministries. These orders were rarely documented in writing. Most instructions were instead recorded in a logbook (comprising four volumes) maintained by the Duty Room of the Censor Department. A few representative excerpts from the Indian Censorship logbook are reproduced below:

1. No story is to be cleared pertaining to Parliament business or Supreme Court appeal filed by Prime Minister. No reference to the case (12 July 1975).

2. As per instructions ... only the date fixed for hearing of PM's appeal is to be given. Lawyers' name may be given; no names of judges are to be given (14 July 1975).
3. Reports on proceedings in the Verghese vs. Birla case should be reduced to the minimum and should be very brief; the arguments need not be mentioned. If they are allowed, should not be more than a paragraph or two (22 July 1975).
4. There has been a "*bandh*" in Ahmedabad, organised by the ruling party (Janta Front). If the agencies' and the correspondent's copies say that the "*bandh* was a flop" it may be allowed, provided the description of the bandh does not go against Censor instructions.
5. Any statement made by the Chief Minister of Gujarat, criticising any action taken by the Centre should be spiked, but if his statement is innocuous it may be allowed. In case of any doubt, please ring up Additional Chief Censor, U.C. Tiwari (26 July 1975).
6. No reports, comments (including editorial), articles, statements or news on bonus to employees shall be allowed until further instructions from us (4 September 1975).
7. (i) No adverse criticism of the Ordinance on Bonus by Trade Unions in Public Sector Organisations is to be allowed;
   (ii) Editorial comments on bonus are permissible;
   (iii) These comments should be within the official explanation on the bonus issue and should not support an agitational approach;
   (iv) That these comments are subject to precensorship;
   (a) Teleprinter message to all State Censors have been sent on the above lines, with the following additions:

Words like "shock", "deplore" or "ill-advice" should be altered to "disappointed" or "surprise" (26 September 1975).

8. Please ensure that today's Allahabad High Court judgment upholding MISA detenus' right to move High Court under Article 226 is not published in the State. Instruct your Censor in Allahabad to kill the story (30 October 1975).
9. As required, the official version of JP's release with instructions not to give prominence to the news and not to use photographs was communicated to agencies and local papers … (13 November 1975).
10. KMLP (Gujarat) has been dissolved. There is likelihood of some members issuing statements withdrawing support to the Janta Front Government in Gujarat. Such statements should be allowed. Statements pledging support to the Janta Front government by some of the members should be spiked (Instruction CC) (11 February 1976).
11. All the statements made by the Janta Front Leaders alleging that Centre or the Congress was out to topple their ministry or that Janta Front would take to agitation, etc. should not be allowed. The statement of KMLP leaders dissolving their party, in support of the Janta Front, is also not to be allowed. Anything which is unhelpful to the present plan of the Centre should be killed (15 February 1976).
12. As desired by JCC(P), all the local dailies and news agencies were informed that Tulmohan Ram's case should be sent to us for pre-censorship. All references to L.N. Mishra, Chattopadhyaya and N.K. Singh are to be deleted (5 March 1976).
13. About mid-day today, the office of *Veekshanam* daily (Cochin) was searched by the police for reasons not known. This daily newspaper is run by the Kerala Pradesh Congress Committee.

Some of the newspapers which referred a story on this to me were advised not to carry anything for the time being.

NB: This development assumes more importance in view of the widening rift within the Congress Party in Kerala. The faction rallying behind the PCC President—who publishes the daily—is very sore about the police search. The police portfolio is held by Congress Minister Karunakaran, who is aligned with the rival faction in the party.

(This incident is likely to precipitate further) (22 April 1976)

14. State Censors have been advised not to permit any comments or references about the transfer of high court judges (1 June 1976).

In practice, censorship was utilised for suppressing news unfavourable to the government, to play up news favourable to the government and to suppress news unfavourable to the supporters of the Congress Party. In his statement before the Commission, D'Penha admitted that this was done under the instructions of the ministers/ministry. He also said that various items of news referring to factionalism in the Congress Party were also censored on instructions; but he has not said whose instructions they were.

Ramnath Goenka, founder of *The Indian Express*, was one of the few fearless media stalwarts who defied the proscriptions of the Emergency and devoted himself to defending the freedom of the press. It is characteristic of any authoritarian regime to seek the silencing of the free press. When the government issued an order banning articles critical of its policies and even cartoons with humorous content, many expected Bal Thackeray and his Shiv Sena to protest. Instead, the Shiv Sena surprised many by expressing solidarity with Indira Gandhi and adopting a position of compliance.

However, K. Sankara Pillai, eminent cartoonist and founder of *Shankar's Weekly*, chose a path of silent protest. He shut down his press and sent the key to Indira Gandhi along with a note declaring that his press had lost its relevance. In a powerful reminder, he noted that he had founded the press with the blessings of, and in the presence of, her father Jawaharlal Nehru. This announcement of Shankar—whom the nation had honoured by awarding the Padma Shri, Padma Bhushan, and Padma Vibhushan—shocked the Congress government and came as a morale booster to all those ranged against the Emergency.

The Emergency curbs on free press, however, could not choke the dissemination of information entirely. Anti-Emergency forces kept the public informed through a campaign aimed at raising awareness of the truth. The Lok Sangharsh Samiti, which spearheaded such efforts, used a language that touched the hearts of the oppressed. Through their persistent activism, ordinary people in the northern belt—often referred to as the "cow belt"—defeated despotism through a silent revolution and restored democracy and civil rights. The established media of today would do well to draw lessons from the experiences of the Emergency.

6

Total Revolution

One of India's most significant contributions to mankind is the realisation of the need for a perfect synthesis between the material and the spiritual aspects of life. Our forefathers understood that such a balance is essential for the sustenance and evolution of the human race. Great national leaders like Mahatma Gandhi sought to discover the real soul of India and, through it, to uncover universal truths. Loknayak Jayaprakash Narayan (JP) was another such visionary—a true embodiment of sacrifice and devotion to the nation. Millions of Indians regarded him not only as a national leader but also as a noble human being.

JP's journey from socialism to "Total Revolution", and from materialism to spiritualism, offers great lessons for all. For a long time, he was known as a socialist leader. In fact, Nehru himself described him in 1948 as the future Prime Minister of India. Over time, however, JP came to realise that a purely socialist model, devoid of Gandhian ideals, could not adequately address India's deep-rooted socio-economic issues. As the torchbearer of the Sarvodaya Movement, he was involved in several creative experiments aimed at building a brighter future for India. But the genes of active revolution were always within him, which became active on many occasions when the nation confronted crises.

Realising that 15 years of the Sarvodaya Movement had not brought the nation any closer to its goals, JP proposed the concept of "Total Revolution" (*Sampoorna Kranti*). This movement began taking shape in the 1970s, through youth and student organisations, and it emerged as one of the key catalysts that led to the declaration of the Emergency in 1975. Through Total Revolution, JP sought a transformative overhaul of existing governments and political parties. Between 1973 and 1975, he aimed to lead a non-violent mass movement against corruption, injustice and erosion of values.

The Quit India Movement stands as a glorious chapter in the history of India's freedom struggle. Raising the powerful slogan "Do or Die", the Quit India Resolution, passed on 8 August 1942, asked the British rulers to leave India immediately. In response, the British government banned the Congress Party and leaders including Gandhiji were imprisoned. The movement went on to become the biggest mass uprising during the independence struggle. Amidst this, JP operated underground and emerged as a hero of the movement. In 1943, he was arrested and subjected to brutal police atrocities.

A leader of rare humility, JP never aspired for any position. When the Janata Party came to power in 1977, he firmly declined any official post. During the pre-independence era, he championed the cause of the people as the spokesperson of the socialist faction within the Congress. Later, he led the Socialist Party in independent India and was also associated with Acharya J.B. Kripalani's Kisan Mazdoor Praja Party. Still, none of these roles satisfied him.

In 1972, he successfully persuaded the notorious Chambal bandits to surrender and reintegrate into the mainstream. However, his sincere efforts during the 1970s to reform the increasingly corrupt Congress government bore little fruit. It was against this backdrop that he supported the student-led agitations against corruption in Bihar and Gujarat between 1973 and 1975, and assumed the spiritual leadership of the Bihar protests.

JP plunged into the crucial battle with a firm conviction that true social-economic and political justice could be achieved only through a complete transformation of every sphere of public life—an ideal he called "Total Revolution". He believed this revolution could be brought about through Gandhian, non-violent methods without any violence or chaos.

On 6 March 1975, JP led a symbolic march to Parliament and submitted memorandums to the Speaker of the Lok Sabha and the Chairman of the Rajya Sabha. These documents outlined the just and reasonable demands of the people, urging the authorities to acknowledge and act upon them without delay.

JP was deeply pained by the ongoing misery and injustice faced by the common people, even several decades after the country's independence. The crux of Total Revolution was a vision articulated by Mahatma Gandhi himself: "Real Swaraj (independence) will come, not by the acquisition of authority by a few, but by the acquisition of the capacity by all to resist authority when it is abused".

Here are the opening lines of a poignant poem that JP unveiled while issuing the clarion call for Total Revolution against the ruling apparatus of 1974–75, which was immersed in corruption and had deviated from the right track:

> "Waves keep on calling me,
> How do I keep quiet on shore,
> Waves keep on calling me."

In the foreword for the book *Total Revolution*, JP wrote:

> Twenty eight years are over since independence; still people suffer. Starvation, poverty, corruption and inflation are shooting up. Nothing can be done without bribe whether in government offices, banks and even for purchasing a ticket. People are trampled by all sorts of injustices. Educational institutions have turned havens of corruption. The future of hundreds of thousands of youths is in dark. They get an education which ultimately spoils their lives; education of slavery, education to push the pen! They knock every door for jobs and they get no job! Unemployment keeps on rising. Despite the slogan of *Garibi Hatao* (eradicate poverty), poverty

> has increased during the recent past. Land of the small farmer is being encroached.
>
> Eighty two percent of the Indian population lives in villages whereas 18 per cent lives in towns. Village population has been divided into classes. Landlords do have commercial stakes. They are employed too. The landless do not have anything. Laws like Land Reforms Acts, etc. were introduced for their benefit. But, they are all futile; they brought no benefit. By God's grace, violence has not broken out. What should be the soul or *atma* of the villages is the big question India's national reconstruction faces. Divisions between the exploiters and the exploited, and the rich and the poor are already deep-rooted. Removing these inequalities is not enough; how to ensure the social and economic equality is the one million dollar question. (Courtesy: Publication of Kerala Gandhi Smaraka Nidhi, 1975)

JP firmly believed that absolute political power resides with the people. Through the call for Total Revolution, he reminded the rulers that it will be the autocracy of a party, not democracy, if the people are dissatisfied even after voting their representative to power. People do not elect representatives to the Assembly and Parliament to engage in corruption or deceit; they expect them to discharge their duties honestly and sincerely. They also have the right to recall their representatives when they fail in their duties. JP presented Total Revolution before the people as a constructive and progressive idea.

JP rose to challenge the establishment when he could no longer tolerate the moral and administrative decay brought on by the corrupt Congress regime. Between 1969 and 1975, over 2,700 elected representatives, including ministers, indulged in floor-crossing. Corruption became the order of the day. Starvation and poverty stalked the country. Elections were derailed.

It was in this deteriorating political climate that JP and his colleagues decided to lead a mass agitation. Power was never on his agenda. On the other hand, he believed in uniting the people to fight and defeat injustice. However, Indira Gandhi and her caucus viewed this rising movement as a threat. They attempted to suppress it using the full force of the state.

The overwhelming public support for JP's movement rattled the ruling establishment and became one of the reasons that prompted the declaration of the Emergency. The Total Revolution and the nationwide anti-corruption campaign rendered the Delhi rulers sleepless. Indira Gandhi and her coterie had never faced a challenge of that order.

7

People's Declaration of Rights

The following is the Declaration of Rights submitted to the Speaker of the Lok Sabha and the Chairman of the Rajya Sabha by JP, representing the people (This declaration was announced at the conclusion of the Parliament march, jointly organised by Sarvodaya leaders and organisations like the Bharatiya Jana Sangh, Congress (O), Socialist Party and Bharatiya Lok Dal.)

We, the people of India, have assembled here to express solidarity to the uprising of the people of Bihar, which represents the aspirations of all citizens of India. It is the duty of the citizens of a nation to react against the gross disrespect to the basic precepts of good governance and the welfare of the people. The march was aimed at the restoration of justice and the preservation of democracy.

We hereby pledge to work for a Gandhian model Total Revolution which can bring into existence socioeconomic equality, real democracy and moral values.

We draw your attention to the following needs which have to be granted for the realisation of the long cherished aspirations of the people.

Elections in Bihar and Gujarat

The people have lost faith in the Bihar Assembly. The assembly is afraid of getting in touch with the people. It has shut itself inside gun points and fences. It has long ceased to act according to the pulse of the people. The government has unleashed a rule of anarchy and trampled upon civilian rights.

It is disheartening to see the Bihar Assembly act as though it is a party to the rampant corruption by the government instead of protesting against it. It is long since the supreme authority of the people of the state started to demand the ouster of the corrupt government.

It has been a year since the corrupt government in Gujarat was ousted and its assembly dissolved. Yet, free and fair elections have not been held. So, our first demand is to remove the Bihar government from power and dissolve the assembly, followed by immediate assembly elections in both Bihar and Gujarat.

Protect the Socio-economic Rights of the People

The harmful policies of the government have led to economic depression on one hand, and have accelerated poverty, unemployment and rising price on the other. More than 60 per cent of the population is partially starving—and this number continues to grow. Communal inequality is also on the rise.

It is high time the socio-economic rights of the people were fulfilled. The following steps have to be initiated:

1. Ensure that all poor citizens, who constitute up to 60 per cent of the population, have access to essential commodities at affordable prices.
2. Prices of essential commodities must be linked to the expenditure, with parity maintained between the prices of industrial and agricultural products.
3. Need-based income and wage should be guaranteed for all.
4. Economic inequality should be reduced to a ratio of 1:10.
5. Land laws must be revised to ensure just and equitable land distribution.
6. Employment should be guaranteed to all. As a first step, appropriate technology should be applied to develop

agriculture and rural economic resources. Industrialisation should focus on large-scale employment through human power.

To make these goals a reality, there should be a government with a clear vision rooted in indigenous development. The import of luxury goods should be banned, and such commodities should be produced in our country.

Democratic Rights and Freedom of Citizens

Contrary to the essence of the Indian Constitution, the government continues to uphold the state of Emergency. Lawful governance has been replaced by Internal Security Act, DIR and Ordinance Rule. As a result, a vast majority of citizens are being denied their democratic rights. Lawful and peaceful mass protests are being suppressed by the government using police force.

To restore, strengthen, and safeguard democratic principles, we demand the implementation of the following measures:

1. The Emergency of 1971 and all other laws that curtail citizens' rights must be repealed.

2. Teachers and other employees in schools and colleges should be granted full political and organisational freedom.

3. Officials and employees in public sector, commercial and industrial organisations must also be given political and organisational freedom.

Free and Fair Elections

Parliament and the legislative assemblies should function according to the will of the people. Elections should not be influenced or manipulated by money, power or coercion. Therefore, we demand the following:

1. The fast implementation of electoral reforms as unanimously recommended by the Joint Parliamentary Council, which includes members from the ruling party as well.
2. The government should not be allowed to announce major policies, grant projects, lay foundations stones or adopt measures intended to sway voters.
3. A restructured Election Commission comprised of individuals of spotless credentials. The members should be elected by a council whose members should include the Chief Justice of the Supreme Court, the Prime Minister and the Leader of the Opposition.
4. Political parties should submit a detailed report of election expenditure, and candidates should disclose expenses, including the amount spent by the party for each candidate.
5. Opposition parties must be given equal access to All India Radio, television, department vehicles, aircraft and other government facilities during elections.
6. Complete prohibition of liquor sales on the day of election and the day preceding it.
7. Ban on vehicle movement on election day, except for emergency services.
8. The counting of votes should be on the basis of polling booths. The details of ballot papers should be disclosed after the polling. Each polling booth should be allowed only one extra (reserve) ballot box.
9. It should be ensured that the candidates and booth agents in each booth are provided details of the number of ballot papers used, along with the serial numbers of the first and the last ballots issued.
10. Lowering the voting age to 18 years.
11. The Constitution should be amended to include the right to recall a candidate.

8

Emergency: A Background

The period from 25 June 1975 to 21 March 1977—when a fear psychosis shook the very foundations of civil life in independent India—is known as the Emergency. The extended terror of those 21 months marked the darkest period in the history of independent India. The abuses of power during this time laid bare the dangerous consequences of undermining democratic values, showing how quickly such erosion can easily lead to despotism.

It was T.S. Eliot who spoke of "cunning passages and contrived corridors" in history. In India, these became starkly visible during the tyrannical regime of Indira Gandhi under the Emergency. History has not authentically recorded the cunningness of the crooked and the virtuous deeds of the brave who rose to confront that dark period. A study of the Emergency should have involved a vigilant search for truth; however, no sincere effort has been made to present the younger generation with an accurate picture of the Emergency and its horrors. Those who fought a life-and-death battle against the Emergency find themselves sidelined in the national narrative, while, ironically, self- proclaimed warriors of the Emergency turn up every year to seize the limelight—spreading untruth and concocting stories.

As per the Indian Constitution, the people of India are the sovereign occupants of the nation. Yet, during the Emergency, they were brutally stripped of their civil rights. Patriots and democrats were suppressed under the weight of authoritarian rule.

The 21 months proved to the world how despotism can disseminate fear, and also how the power of the masses can confront despotism.

It is difficult for students of history to digest the contention of former President Pranab Mukherjee that Indira Gandhi was unaware of the prerequisites of declaring the Emergency, and that it was Siddhartha Shankar Ray and others who persuaded her to take that step. Mukherjee's unabashed loyalty to Indira Gandhi may have led him to distort the truth. History will not absolve former President Fakhruddin Ali Ahmed for officially declaring the Emergency, nor will it forgive Indira Gandhi for unleashing a regime of terror. Mahatma Gandhi and other eminent leaders, who were at the forefront of India's freedom struggle, envisioned a nation founded on moral principles. But Indira Gandhi pursued power through unscrupulous means, ruling the nation according to the whims and fancies of her family and, at times, manipulating the judiciary to further her objectivities.

The political dominance of the Indian National Congress suffered a major blow in the 1967 general elections, when more than half of India's prominent states voted the party out of power. In response, Indira Gandhi and her close allies resorted to every possible tactic to regain control and consolidate authority around her. She deliberately began to design "cunning passages and contrived corridors" of power. She ruthlessly resorted to corruption and favouritism.

Many in political circles allege that Indira Gandhi was behind the mysterious deaths of Nagarwala and a few officials who were reportedly on the trail of some illegal financial dealings. The Congress Party, led by her, influenced the senior judges in order to form a "committed" judiciary. She also engineered a major split in the Congress.

N. Sanjiva Reddy was the unanimous choice of the Congress Working Committee for the post of President of India, and Indira Gandhi herself was among the first to endorse his nomination. However, behind the doors, she covertly advanced V.V. Giri as a rival candidate and ensured his victory—a move widely condemned as unethical. It is also believed that she enlisted the backing of the Russian lobby to achieve this outcome. During the Emergency, the atmosphere of blind allegiance reached its peak when the then Congress president, Dev Kanta Barooah, famously declared the disturbing slogan: "India is Indira – Indira is India."

The committee that drafted the Constitution clearly stipulated that an Emergency could be declared only under exceptional circumstances and with the explicit consent of the Cabinet. But on 25 June 1975, Indira Gandhi declared Emergency without convening a Cabinet meeting or informing senior ministers and the Cabinet Secretary. A formal Cabinet meeting was held only the following morning. Preparations to arrest prominent Opposition leaders had been made days in advance. In a coordinated move to suppress dissent, power supply to newspaper offices in Delhi was disconnected. Using MISA and DIR, the government effectively held the entire nation captive.

The Allahabad High Court had annulled Indira Gandhi's election to Parliament, citing electoral malpractices. At the same time, Indira Gandhi was also unsettled by the charged political atmosphere, particularly the nationwide anti-corruption movement led by Jayaprakash Narayan. She was also annoyed by the Congress Party's resounding defeat in the Gujarat Assembly elections. According to the Shah Commission, it was this turbulent political atmosphere that prompted Indira Gandhi to declare Emergency.

In the 1977 general elections, the people of North India exercised their voting rights judiciously to put an end to the despotic rule and dispel the darkness of the Emergency. But the results also revealed a stark contrast—voters in the southern states, including Kerala, largely supported the autocratic measures of Indira Gandhi. The end of the Emergency can also be seen as the victory of JP's mass movement, which rallied under the powerful slogan: "Abdicate the throne; the people are marching!"

9

Timeline of Emergency

Some political observers and historians have interpreted Indira Gandhi's imposition of the Emergency as a necessary response to a political crisis. They are of the view that she was compelled to take this drastic step due to the growing unrest allegedly initiated by JP and the Opposition. However, this interpretation stands in stark contrast to the actual sequence of events. It was the Allahabad High Court's verdict on 12 June 1975—invalidating Indira Gandhi's election due to electoral malpractices—that triggered a political upheaval. The fact that the Opposition gained the right ammunition just as the High Court ruled that the Prime Minister had engaged in serious electoral irregularities is, at best, a remarkable coincidence.

At the same time, it cannot be denied that JP had already launched the Total Revolution, a movement underpinned by widespread public support and backed by the entire Opposition. His call for sweeping systemic change had gained significant momentum across the country. Moreover, the Supreme Court's refusal to grant an unconditional stay to Indira Gandhi's appeal against the High Court verdict further weakened her political standing.

In the wake of the court ruling, the entire Opposition, except the CPI, demanded the Prime Minister's resignation on moral grounds. With growing public support, the Opposition announced a plan of action for continuous agitation beginning 29 June 1975. They outlined a course for a non-violent, peaceful protest. At no point was there any indication that the agitation would turn violent.

The Congress Party, lacking both ideological clarity and democratic resolve, found itself unable to counter the rising tide of dissent. By then, public sentiment had largely turned against the government.

Indira Gandhi and her cohorts grew increasingly anxious as the Opposition gained ground—most notably through its success in the Gujarat Legislative Assembly elections. She feared that her political dreams would be shattered by the rising stature of JP. While democracy thrives on dissent, criticism and the right to protest, the Prime Minister failed to show the political maturity necessary to recognise these movements as legitimate expressions within a democratic framework.

From the day she assumed power, Indira Gandhi had exhibited an unmistakable autocratic streak, abandoning ethical politics at both the personal and organisational levels. Intolerance was evident in every decision she made. She transgressed the basic decorum of democracy—respect for the Opposition. Her attempts to render the judiciary ineffective could never be justified. It was not mere coincidence—but rather with her tacit approval—that her close confidants began raising provocative questions in Parliament, such as, "Why can't we have a committed judiciary?" and "Why can't the media be nationalised?" Indira Gandhi stubbornly refused to consult with the Opposition and even stifled internal party debates on major policies and decisions. Over time, it became increasingly apparent that her administration was drifting towards authoritarianism, with troubling signs of a nascent fascist regime.

In an interview with the *New York Times,* Indira Gandhi remarked, "Many countries have given up democratic forms of governance for the speedy implementation of policies. It is necessary to lay the foundation for progress." This statement revealed her growing disillusionment with democratic processes. Around the same time, senior socialist leader Madhu Limaye publicly recounted a conversation with Leonid Ilyich Brezhnev, General Secretary of the Soviet Communist Party (and later the President of the Soviet Union), who had asked him, "Why does India need Opposition parties? Aren't Opposition parties a hindrance to an emotional connection between the people and the government?" Such remarks—whether made in India or elsewhere—showed a growing authoritarian mindset and a justification for silencing democratic dissent for the sake of efficiency and unity.

From the very beginning, there were numerous instances that revealed the despotic tendencies in Indira Gandhi's style of governance. It is clear that the Emergency was not a spontaneous political reaction, but rather the culmination of a calculated and deliberately harmful strategy.

A close analysis of the Emergency timeline reveals that it was a well-planned conspiracy, orchestrated by Indira Gandhi after she assumed the presidency of the Congress Party, and influenced in part by Soviet ideological leanings. The day after the Emergency was declared, veteran CPI(M) leader A.K. Gopalan dubbed Indira Gandhi "Lady Hitler"—a label that finds justification in the series of events that preceded and followed the imposition of authoritarian rule.

Emergency Timeline*

1971 March: Indira Gandhi returns to power as the Prime Minister with a two-thirds majority in the Lok Sabha.

1973 April: Justice A.N. Ray is appointed as Chief Justice of the Supreme Court, superseding three senior judges. This unprecedented move, in retaliation for an adverse judgment pronounced by these three judges, triggered protests and led to the resignations of the three slighted judges.

1974 January: Student agitation erupts under the banner of the *Navnirman Samiti* against the corrupt Congress Chief Minister of Gujarat, Chimanbhai Patel.

1974 April: Students launch an anti-corruption agitation under the banner of the *Bihar Chhatra Sangharsh Samiti*, demanding the resignation of the corrupt Congress government in Bihar, led by Chief Minister Abdul Ghafoor. They later invited Jayaprakash Narayan (JP) to lead the movement.

1974 May: George Fernandes asks the Indian Railways employees to launch a nationwide strike, demanding wage hikes in line with inflation. The government brutally cracks down on the three-week-long strike.

1974 September: The Opposition corners Indira Gandhi in Parliament over the Pondicherry Licence scandal.

1974 November: A bilateral meeting between Indira Gandhi and JP over the dissolution of the Bihar Assembly is abruptly cut short. The *Kshethr Samrakshan Samithi*'s agitation demanding the Assembly's dissolution is dealt with an iron-fisted response, with a vicious crackdown on the protesters.

1975 January: In the wake of the Pondicherry Licence scandal, Union Minister Lalit Narayan Mishra is shifted from the Ministry of External Affairs to the Railways Ministry. On 2 January, he is fatally injured in a bomb blast at Samastipur, Bihar, and succumbs to his injuries the following day. (Although convictions in the case came over four decades later, his family has long alleged that the true conspirators were shielded by the government, and innocent people were wrongfully punished.)

1975 January 8: Siddhartha Shankar Ray writes to Indira Gandhi, urging her to declare an internal Emergency and to arrest all those opposing the government.

1975 June 12: In the 1971 Lok Sabha elections, socialist leader Raj Narain was defeated by Indira Gandhi in the Raebareli Lok Sabha constituency. He subsequently filed an appeal challenging her victory. Justice Jagmohan Lal Sinha of the Allahabad High Court upheld the appeal and disqualified Indira Gandhi on the grounds of election malpractices. Meanwhile, the Janata Front, led by JP, swept the Gujarat Assembly elections.

1975 June 18: The Congress Parliamentary Party meeting reaffirms its trust in the leadership of Indira Gandhi.

1975 June 18: Vacation judge Justice V.R. Krishna Iyer issues a partial stay on the Allahabad High Court verdict delivered by Sinha.

1975 June 20: A huge rally is organised by the Congress at the Boat Club, New Delhi, to express support for Indira Gandhi.

1975 June 23: Preparations are underway for the arrest of Opposition leaders.

1975 June 25: At a massive rally in New Delhi's Ram Lila Maidan, JP asks Prime Minister Indira Gandhi to step down from her position as the Prime Minister. The Opposition parties announce weeklong nationwide *satyagraha* from 29 June. President Fakhruddin Ali Ahmed signs the declaration of the Emergency. Power supply to the offices of the print media in New Delhi is cut off. Several Opposition leaders, including JP, Morarji Desai, Atal Bihari Vajpayee and L.K. Advani, are arrested and detained past midnight. A few Congress leaders, such as S. Chandra Shekhar and Ram Dhan, are also taken into custody.

1975 June 26: A Cabinet meeting held at around 8 a.m. decides to approve the imposition of a state of Emergency. Press censorship is put into effect, and I.K. Gujral is replaced by V.C. Shukla as the Information and Broadcasting Minister.

1975 June 28: After a two-day hiatus, newspapers resume publication. While country-wide protests continue, the media largely refrains from carrying news that is critical of or against the government.

1975 June 29: Journalists gather at the Delhi Press Club to protest against the Emergency. In many places, bar associations hold protest meetings.

1975 June 30: MISA is amended to allow arrests without notice, at any time and in any place. RSS chief Balasaheb Deoras is arrested at the Nagpur Railway Station and detained under MISA.

1975 July 4: Several organisations, including the RSS, Ananda Marga, Jamaat-e-Islami and Naxalite groups, are banned.

1975 July 21: Parliament is convened to ratify the declaration of the Emergency.

1975 August 5: The Democracy Act of 1951 is amended with retrospective effect to facilitate the negation of the disqualification of Indira Gandhi's election. This amendment allows her to override the Allahabad High Court verdict and overcome the disqualification.

1975 August 15: Bangladesh President Sheikh Mujibur Rahman and his family are assassinated in Dhaka (some consider this a setback for the dictatorship).

1975 September: A Delhi High Court verdict declares the arrest of veteran journalist Kuldip Nayar under MISA to be illegal.

1975 November 7: The Supreme Court upholds Indira Gandhi's election from Raebareli, thanks to the constitutional amendment.

1975 November 12: JP is granted parole and is hospitalised due to kidney damage.

1975 December 30: The Youth Congress convenes in Chandigarh and elects Sanjay Gandhi as its leader.

1976 January: Parliament passes a resolution to postpone the Lok Sabha elections.

1976 January 31: The government dismisses the DMK-led government headed by M. Karunanidhi.

1976 March: The Janata government in Gujarat, led by Babubhai Patel, is toppled. Bharatiya Lok Dal leader Charan Singh is released from jail.

1976 April 19: Police opens fire on a gathering protesting against sterilisation camps at Turkman Gate in Delhi.

1976 April 28: The Supreme Court delivers an anti-people, anti-constitution verdict upholding the suspension of basic rights during the Emergency, with Justice H.R. Khanna writing a brave and historic dissent note.

1976 May 4: Kishore Kumar's songs are banned from broadcast on All India Radio and Doordarshan.

1976 June 10: George Fernandes is arrested in Calcutta.

1976 August 10: Dr Subramanian Swamy of the Jana Sangh, who had evaded arrest, makes a dramatic appearance in Parliament before slipping away from the police—a humiliating setback for the government.

1976 October: The 42nd Amendment of the Constitution is passed.

1976 November: An amendment to the Constitution is passed, granting Parliament unlimited power to amend the Constitution, with such amendments placed beyond judicial review.

1976 November: An amendment is introduced to extend the term of Parliament by one year.

1976 December: At the Guwahati AICC session, Sanjay Gandhi is informally projected as Indira Gandhi's heir apparent, while A.K. Antony voices partial criticism of the Emergency during the meeting.

1976 December 4: Opposition leaders Charan Singh and Biju Patnaik meet Home Minister Om Mehta to strike a deal with the government.

1977 January 1: Biju Patnaik sends a letter to Indira Gandhi, suggesting specific steps and stressing the need for reaching a compromise with the Opposition.

1977 January: Indira Gandhi responds positively to the Opposition leader's letter, stating that democracy can be restored if the Opposition agrees on certain fundamental issues.

1977 January 18: It is declared that the Lok Sabha elections will be held in March 1977, and a few Opposition leaders have been released from prison.

1977 January 20: The Janata Party is launched.

1977 February: Jagjivan Ram resigns from the Congress and forms the Congress for Democracy.

1977 March 16–20: General elections are held.

1977 March 20: Indira Gandhi is defeated in Raebareli, and Sanjay Gandhi in Amethi. The Janata Party wins a majority of the Lok Sabha seats.

1977 March 21: Emergency is lifted. The ban on the RSS and other organisations is revoked.

1977 March 24: Morarji Desai is sworn in as the fifth Prime Minister of India.

---

* Courtesy: Various books, including *The Emergency: A Personal History* by Coomi Kapoor

10

Constitutional Autocracy

Indira Gandhi and the Congress Party steered the nation towards an autocratic rule by misusing the Constitution and the parliamentary system. Articles 14, 19, 21 and 22 of the Constitution, which guarantee fundamental rights to citizens, were suspended during the Emergency. A bench of three judges in the Supreme Court decreed that no one could challenge the unlawful imprisonment of a citizen. This verdict came after rejecting a dissenting opinion from Justice H.R. Khanna, who was later hailed for standing up for justice and human rights. In the same case, Attorney General Niren De argued that a citizen could not approach the court if their right to life was violated

The Indian media largely acquiesced to media censorship, with a few notable exceptions such as *The Indian Express* and *The Statesman*. L.K. Advani, reflecting on the Emergency period, commented that the Indian media "crawled when it was asked to kneel".

The Emergency regime drew comparisons to Hitler's dictatorship. Like Hitler, Indira Gandhi manipulated the democratic constitution of India. Both leaders claimed that their nations were under threat. In 1930, Hitler staged the Reichstag fire to create the illusion of a national emergency and blamed the Opposition for the act. Indira Gandhi employed a similar tactic. While in Germany it was proclaimed, "Hitler is Germany as Germany is Hitler ", Indira Gandhi was portrayed in the same light by AICC president D.K. Barooah, who declared "India is Indira and Indira is India".

Though Indira Gandhi announced a 20-point programme during the Emergency, its execution was minimal. The Congress propaganda described the Emergency as a period of discipline and progress. Like Hitler, Indira Gandhi imposed press censorship to suppress dissenting voices and incarcerated national leaders. During the Emergency, much like Hitler's regime in Germany, Indira Gandhi ushered in a form of fascism in India.

Some political theorists argue that, according to the Indian constitution, the Prime Minister is essentially an elected autocrat. They suggest that the government is controlled by the legislative body. The government is a creation of the Cabinet, which is fully under the control of the Prime Minister. Since it is the prerogative of the Prime Minister to pick the Cabinet, some contend that the Prime Minister can be considered an elected dictator. Furthermore, when a Prime Minister resigns, the entire Cabinet ceases to exist. However, these specious arguments have no place in a genuine democracy.

When Indira Gandhi realised during the Emergency that she had lost popular support, she attempted to cling to power by positioning her younger son, Sanjay Gandhi, as her political heir. However, she did not realise that measures like evicting slum dwellers for urban beautification, muzzling of the media, and jailing political opponents only further alienated her from the public. While she had initially won peoples' support through actions such as the nationalisation of banks and slogans like "*garibi hatao*" (eradicate poverty), her increasingly autocratic style of governance distanced her from the common man, who had to bear the brunt of her oppressive rule. Her rout in the 1977 elections clearly underscored this shift, showing how the masses in North India—once her strongest supporters—completely rejected her.

A silent revolution, based on the Gandhian principle of non-violence and spearheaded by Lok Sangharsh Samiti, led to the restoration of human rights and democratic values in 1977. On 21 March 1977, the Emergency was lifted, and the ban on the RSS and other organisations was also removed. The fall of Indira Gandhi reminded the nation of the words of Abraham Lincoln: "No man is good enough to govern another man without that other's consent." This principle applies not only to individuals but also to nations.

No nation has the moral right to rule over another. True freedom exists when a nation rules itself; when one nation dominates another, it becomes an act of autocracy. A nation that denies another's freedom does not deserve freedom itself. On 21 March 1977, India cast off the darkness of autocracy.

JP entered the struggle with a resolve to ensure social, economic and political justice for the common people. He was confident that his Total Revolution movement could only succeed through Gandhian means of non-violence. In his book on Total Revolution, JP wrote:

> Almost three decades after independence, people at large are still in pain. Rampant corruption makes their life miserable. Even educational institutions have become corrupt. The education given to the children is futile. Unemployment is alarmingly on the rise. Despite slogans of eradicating poverty, it is also on the rise.
>
> The rural people are divided into classes. Even land reform rules have become ineffective. It is fortunate that the oppressed have not turned to violence. The only solution is to make our villages economically independent and to bring economic and social equality to the villagers.

JP sought to remind the ruling class that democracy is not just about power but also about the people. He believed, "When power neglects the people, the spirit of democracy is lost. When elected representatives forget their duty and misuse power, the people have the right to call them back." Frustrated with the corruption of the Congress government, JP chose the path of struggle. His concerns were not only about corruption and poverty but also about the failing electoral system. JP was not interested in seizing power but in ending corruption that made life difficult for the people. Indira Gandhi failed to recognise the broad popular support JP had and attempted to suppress his movement. In fact, her inability to put down JP's movement was an important factor in the eventual declaration of the Emergency.

11

Emergency Excesses

India is a unique nation, inherently opposed to despotism and fascism, with a deep-rooted aversion to such forms of rule. After the Emergency was imposed, it didn't take long for the people to realise the extent of its horrors. As reports of government excesses and police brutality spread, the public was filled with fear and alarm. The blatant violations of human rights, justified under the guise of slum clearance and family planning initiatives, amounted to a direct trampling of the very spirit of the Indian Constitution. These atrocities sparked murmurs of disapproval from the international community. However, the world also witnessed India's commitment to democracy on 21 March 1977.

The Justice Shah Commission was inundated with complaints regarding the destruction of slums and police violence, including the murders of innocent people. Below is a list of some of the complaints received by the Commission regarding the excesses during the slum evacuation process:

Name of State/Union Territories	Total No. of Complaints
I. States	
Andhra Pradesh	75
Assam	35
Bihar	226
Gujarat	18
Haryana	300

Name of State/Union Territories	Total No. of Complaints
Himachal Pradesh	18
Jammu & Kashmir	1
Karnataka	126
Kerala	63
Madhya Pradesh	628
Maharashtra	89
Manipur	18
Meghalaya	0
Nagaland	0
Odisha	251
Punjab	66
Rajasthan	193
Sikkim	0
Tamil Nadu	15
Tripura	4
Uttar Pradesh	425
West Bengal	204
II. Union Territories	
Andaman & Nicobar	0
Arunachal Pradesh	0
Chandigarh	4
Dadra & Nagar Haveli	0
Delhi	1248
Goa, Daman & Diu	3
Lakshadweep	0
Mizoram	0
Pondicherry	1
II. Ministries/Departments etc. of Central Government	28
Total	**4039**

The Shah Commission gathered substantial evidence establishing that Sanjay Gandhi and his associates were responsible for the atrocities committed in areas such as Turkman Gate in Delhi during the Emergency. Many were arrested under draconian laws such as MISA, DIR and COFEPOSA Act. Those arrested were denied justice and deprived of basic human rights. Below is a list of those held under these laws, as documented by the Shah Commission:

Name of State/Union Territories	MISA	COFEPOSA Act	DIR
I. States			
Andhra Pradesh	1,135	45	451
Assam	533	53	2,388
Bihar	2,360	240	7,747
Gujarat	1,762	307	2,643
Haryana	200	2	1,079
Himachal Pradesh	34	0	654
Jammu & Kashmir	466	57	311
Karnataka	487	119	4,015
Kerala	790	97	7,134
Madhya Pradesh	5,620	11	2,521
Maharashtra	5,473	400	9,799
Manipur	231	16	228
Meghalaya	39	6	20
Nagaland	95	0	4
Odisha	408	3	762
Punjab	440	73	2,423
Rajasthan	542	14	1,352
Sikkim	4	0	0
Tamil Nadu	1,027	285	1,644

Name of State/Union Territories	**MISA**	**COFEPOSA Act**	**DIR**
Tripura	77	25	99
Uttar Pradesh	6,956	126	24,781
West Bengal	4,992	80	2,547
II. Union Territories			
Andaman & Nicobar	41	0	88
Arunachal Pradesh	0	0	1
Chandigarh	27	1	74
Dadra & Nagar Haveli	0	2	3
Delhi	1,012	48	2,851
Goa, Daman & Diu	113	68	0
Lakshadweep	0	0	0
Mizoram	70	0	136
Pondicherry	54	6	63
Total	**34,988**	**2,084**	**75,818**

12

Inhuman Atrocities

India possesses a unique and enduring spirit —one that refuses to kneel before autocracy or fascism. It took time for the true colours of the dark Emergency period to be revealed to the public. Restlessness grew among the people as reports of massacres, police atrocities and unforgettable tragedies began to surface. Human rights were violated under the guise of family planning and slum clearance, actions that trampled upon the very soul and spirit of the Constitution.

Foreign nations began to question whether India still deserved to be called a "civilised community". But, on 21 March 1977, the people of India answered resoundingly—they declared themselves true democrats and a politically enlightened society.

The Justice Shah Commission received a multitude of complaints about the brutal eviction of slum dwellers and crimes, including murders, executed during the Emergency. Here is a list of the atrocities unleashed in the name of slum clearance:

Name of State/Union Territories	Total No. of Complaints
I. States	
Andhra Pradesh	75
Assam	35
Bihar	226
Gujarat	18
Haryana	300

Name of State/Union Territories	Total No. of Complaints
Himachal Pradesh	18
Jammu & Kashmir	1
Karnataka	126
Kerala	63
Madhya Pradesh	628
Maharashtra	89
Manipur	18
Meghalaya	0
Nagaland	0
Odisha	251
Punjab	66
Rajasthan	193
Sikkim	0
Tamil Nadu	15
Tripura	4
Uttar Pradesh	425
West Bengal	204
II. Union Territories	
Andaman & Nicobar	0
Arunachal Pradesh	0
Chandigarh	4
Dadra & Nagar Haveli	0
Delhi	1248
Goa, Daman & Diu	3
Lakshadweep	0
Mizoram	0
Pondicherry	1
II. Ministries/Departments etc. of Central Government	28
Total	**4039**

Hundreds of pieces of evidence were presented before the Justice Shah Commission, clearly implicating Sanjay Gandhi and his coterie in the brutal actions that occurred in Turkman Gate and several other areas across Delhi. During this period, the misuse of power and rampant police atrocities became the norm, with laws and individual rights routinely violated. Thousands were arrested under repressive laws such as MISA, DIR and COFEPOSA Act. Those detained under these harsh measures were stripped of even the most fundamental human rights, including the right to life. The following are details of the arrests made under these anti-democratic actions:

Name of State/Union Territories	MISA	COFEPOSA ACT	DIR
I. States			
Andhra Pradesh	1,135	45	451
Assam	533	53	2,388
Bihar	2,360	240	7,747
Gujarat	1,762	307	2,643
Haryana	200	2	1,079
Himachal Pradesh	34	0	654
Jammu & Kashmir	466	57	311
Karnataka	487	119	4,015
Kerala	790	97	7,134
Madhya Pradesh	5,620	11	2,521
Maharashtra	5,473	400	9,799
Manipur	231	16	228
Meghalaya	39	6	20
Nagaland	95	0	4
Odisha	408	3	762
Punjab	440	73	2,423
Rajasthan	542	14	1,352

Name of State/Union Territories	MISA	COFEPOSA ACT	DIR
Sikkim	4	0	0
Tamil Nadu	1,027	285	1,644
Tripura	77	25	99
Uttar Pradesh	6,956	126	24,781
West Bengal	4,992	80	2,547
II. Union Territories			
Andaman & Nicobar	41	0	88
Arunachal Pradesh	0	0	1
Chandigarh	27	1	74
Dadra & Nagar Haveli	0	2	3
Delhi	1,012	48	2,851
Goa, Daman & Diu	113	68	0
Lakshadweep	0	0	0
Mizoram	70	0	136
Pondicherry	54	6	63
Total	**34,988**	**2,084**	**75,818**

The workers and leaders of CPI (M), Bharatiya Jana Sangh, Socialist Party, RSS, Congress (O), Congress Reformists and Naxalites were among the MISA detenues in Kerala. The various methods of custodial police torture* in Kerala, documented by a subcommittee led by O. Rajagopal and appointed by the Kerala unit of the Janata Party during 1977–78 are as follows:

Uruttal

The infamous and brutal torture method known as *uruttal* (meaning "rolling") was implemented in most police stations and the torture chambers of the Crime Branch (of Police) in Kerala. It was something unheard of in civilised countries. The Congress-CPI regime did not need to invest much in this inhuman method of torture—only a wooden bench, a heavy rod (either wooden or metallic), a thread and nothing else! In most cases, the victims were stripped of their clothes before being brought to the *uruttal* chamber, with some being allowed to wear only underwear in rare instances. The victims were then laid on the bench for interrogation. The police called it the "bench of truth", and, the method of laying the victim on the bench was called "Rest on the bench of truth".

The victim's head would hang beyond the length of the bench, ensuring that he could not stretch his body during *uruttal*. His hands were tied together with his clothes, and his legs were also bound. His underwear or vest was stuffed into his mouth to prevent any sound. The rod was then placed across his waist.

Two policemen held either end of the rod and rolled it down to the victim's toes. As it moved along the body, it pressed against flesh and nerves. If the police felt that the pressure was not enough to inflict harm, they would sit on either side of the rod and roll it further. In some cases, the policemen would stand on either end of the rod, holding the hanging ropes, adding more pressure. The experience was akin to the proverbial "killing someone inch by inch".

Since the victim's mouth was stuffed with clothes, no one could hear his cries—not even his groans. After two or three rounds of *uruttal*, even the strongest man would be in unbearable agony, writhing in acute pain. At that point, the policeman would remove the gag from the victim's mouth and resume interrogation. If the desired information was not obtained, the victim's mouth would be stuffed again and the torture repeated. After two or three such cycles, the victim would often fall unconscious.

The policemen would then pull the clothes out of the victim's mouth, untie his hands and sprinkle water on his face until he regained consciousness. The victim was then taken to another room, where he will be chained. This was the post-*uruttal* chamber, where he would see several others like himself—broken, battered and immobile. None of them could stand or move; they passed urine and stool where they lay.

Their bodies were covered in infected ulcers oozing with pus. The rooms reeked of a foul stench—a nauseating mix of pus, blood, sweat, urine, and excreta. Between 20 and 40 detainees were crammed into spaces meant for only five or six. They wore nothing but underwear and did not even have a piece of cloth to spread on the floor. When they looked at the waist and lower body of a newly arrived post-*uruttal* victim, the swelling and pain intensified, leaving the victim unable to move.

The injuries caused by *uruttal* would lead to severe inflammation. By the following day, the victim would be in such a state of collapse that he might even pray for a quick death. Flies swarming over the open wounds would cause intense, unbearable pain. For the first four to five days after their arrest, the victims were denied even drinking water, let alone food.

After three or four days following the initial *uruttal*, the police would present the victim before their superior. He would prod the inflamed wounds on the victim's thighs with his swagger stick and ask the torture squad: "Ready?" The interrogation would then resume. If they still failed to squeeze the required information, they subjected the victim to *uruttal* again. This time, a single round would be enough to make him writhe in pain, tremble in fear and lose consciousness. He would beg for a drop of water. Then, he would be thrown back into the same filthy room.

In one instance, a man in such agony begged a fellow detainee to urinate into his mouth to quench his thirst. The arrested and tortured were crammed into an underground torture chamber at the Crime Branch's torture facility. The only ventilation and light came from two small windows high on the wall. Though the space could barely hold three or four people, about 15 to 20 men were stuffed inside. The stench of human waste, mixed with the odour of pus from festering wounds, drifted out through the windows. Passersby walking along the verandah would cover their noses with their hands to block the unbearable smell. At the Kakkayam torture camp, even the sentries resorted to burning incense sticks while on duty to mask the stench.

Heating

The victim was made to sit on the floor, leaning against the wall, with his legs stretched out in front of him. His toes were tied together. The police would then beat the soles of his feet with a cane soaked in oil. Cold water was poured over the feet, producing a bubbling sensation. The beating would pause briefly for interrogation. If the victim failed to give the desired information, the beating would continue—often until the cane broke. In most cases, the victim lost consciousness. But the policemen would then untie his toes and force him to jump up and down. This was reportedly done to reduce the risk of nerve and muscle damage caused by the torture.

Double Action

The victim is made to stand close to the wall, and then slapped forcefully across the face. The impact of the slap would cause his head to strike the wall behind him.

Clipping

The policemen would press the victim's throat forcefully with their fingers. His gullet and wind pipe would be constricted for a while, causing his eyes to protrude due to lack of breath. Nevertheless, they would continue pressing. Eventually, the throat would sustain injuries. For the following several days, the victim would be unable to eat or even drink.

Kavadiyattam

Both of the victim's hands are raised and tied together—at the wrists, elbows and upper arms. His legs are also bound. A *lathi* (a heavy baton) is tied horizontally behind his neck and inserted between his upper arms. He is then made to stand still in an attention posture. Within just five minutes, searing pain grips both sides of his body. The victim begins swaying from side to side, resembling a *Kavadiyattam* performer (a traditional Hindu ritual dance where devotees carry a decorated arch on their shoulders in devotion to Lord Subrahmanya). Soon after, he collapses, his face hitting the floor.

Flying the Plane

Both legs of the victim are tied together. His hands are bound behind his back with a long rope. One end of the rope runs through a pulley fixed to the ceiling, allowing the policeman to lift or lower the victim by tightening or loosening the rope.

Hook

Entrails are pressed and twisted by pressing the fingers into the lower belly. When this action is performed repeatedly, the entrails break.

Kicking in the Navel

The policemen kick the victim in the belly with their boots. Two or three kicks are sufficient to damage the kidneys, causing the victim to pass blood instead of urine. He will then be made to sit on the floor with his neck hanging forward, while a policeman sits in a chair behind him. The policeman then kicks the victim's backbone several times, drawing pleasure from the victim's agony.

Cut with the Hands

The victim is forced to raise his arms, after which the policeman cuts on the ribs with his hands. This act is extremely painful and can, in some cases, result in fractured ribs.

Dog Lock

Two victims are made to stand in a bent-over position, with their buttocks pressed together. Both are made to thread their arms beneath their thighs, clasp each other's hands and pull. While they pull against each other, policemen repeatedly beat, kick, and punch their backs.

Pulling the Penis

The nude victim's penis is pulled with a spanner. Then the penis is placed on a desk, where a policeman beats it with a stick. A metallic wire is subsequently inserted into the urethra.

Line Treatment

Policemen form two lines. The victim is made to stand at one end of this formation and is then ordered to walk through the middle. As the victim moves forward, each policeman from both sides assaults him with kicks, punches, and beatings.

Playing with the Human Ball

Policemen form a circle, with the victim forced to stand in the centre. They then kick him from one side to another, seemingly deriving pleasure from the victim's suffering. If the victim falls, the kicker is said to have committed a "foul".

Plucking the Hairs

This painful form of torture involves the plucking of pubic and facial hair, causing the hair follicles in the dermis to swell and result in intense, acute pain.

Fanning

Both of the victim's hands are tied to the blades of a fan, which is then turned on at its maximum speed. The victim rotates in the same speed.

Imaginary Chair

The victim is made to sit on a chair, which is then abruptly removed. The victim is forced to sit in the same manner, with bent knees raised in the air as if still sitting on the chair. After some time, intense pain develops in the victim's legs and hands, eventually causing him to fall down.

Etham

The victim is made to hold his own ears with his hands, the left ear with the right hand and vice versa. He then stoops, touches his elbows to the floor and stretches straight, repeating this action a thousand times or more.

Electric Shock

The victim endures cruel torture through electric shocks applied to his feet and temples.

Mental Torture

The nude victim is brought before the policemen and officers, who are fully clad in uniform, and is subjected to mental torture by them.

Hanging Torture

The victim's hands and legs are tied together, and then the torture squad hangs him upside down before beating him.

These atrocities were perpetrated daily in the custody chambers of the Crime Branch and in police stations across Kerala. The same group of officers trained other policemen in various torture methods and took leading roles in executing these brutal practices.

---

* Courtesy: *Adiyanthiravasthayude Anthardharakal* (The Undercurrents of Emergency) by K. Raman Pillai.

13

Heroes in the Shadows

The long list of patriots who tirelessly organised underground movements to resist the horrors of the Emergency, and those who made supreme sacrifices to protect Indian democracy, will forever be an invaluable part of India's contemporary history. This list includes unsung heroes—those who were martyred, who worked in the shadows, and who braved death, enduring unimaginable suffering and lasting misery due to the severe torture inflicted upon them by the police. Some spent their remaining days in despair, having lost everything they once held dear. Among these bravehearts, several stand out for the courage and brilliance they exhibited during the dark times. The following is an account of those heroes:

- As many as 1,10,806 people were arrested without having committed any offence during the Emergency and imprisoned without trial.
- Many detainees were tortured to death during incarceration.
- Media personnel were subjected to harassment professionally and personally.
- A total of 25,692 state and Central government employees were unjustly sacked from their jobs for not toeing the official line.
- Residents of Delhi were rendered homeless after their dwellings were demolished by bulldozers.

- Public sector and government employees were persecuted for refusing to carry out unjust government orders. Many individuals involved in the resistance risked their lives by providing shelter to victims of the Emergency.
- Citizens were forcibly subjected to mass vasectomies under Sanjay Gandhi's five-point programme. Judges and lawyers stood by those who were subjected to precautionary arrests and imprisonment under Emergency laws.
- Justice H.R. Khanna boldly upheld truth and human rights, fully aware that doing so would cost him the position of the Chief Justice of the Supreme Court.
- Leaders and followers of Opposition political parties—such as Congress (O), Bharatiya Jana Sangh, Bharatiya Lok Dal, Akali Dal, DMK, CPM, Muslim League (Opposition), Congress Reformists, and others—bravely fought against the atrocities of the Emergency.
- The RSS fought the Emergency through non-violent means. Their underground work inspired the public at large and played a pivotal role in the fall of Indira Gandhi and the restoration of democracy in India.
- Justice J. C. Shah undertook the arduous task of conducting a judicial inquiry into the atrocities committed during the Emergency, accepting only a token fee of Re. 1 for his service.
- The government headed by Morarji Desai, which came to power after the Emergency, was compelled to reverse the anti-people policies and programmes implemented during that period.
- The people of North India displayed remarkable political maturity by routing the Congress Party.
- Many people came forward to testify or submit evidence before the Shah Commission.

- It was Member of Parliament Era Sezhiyan who recovered and made public the Shah Commission Report, which was allegedly shredded by the government.
- Many journalists and writers raised their voices in protest against the Emergency.
- Scores of people risked their safety to circulate underground publications, spreading democratic values during a time when press freedom was severely curtailed.
- The Lok Sangharsha Samiti organised *satyagraha*s in which thousands of people participated, bravely facing police atrocities and imprisonment.
- Many Indians living abroad played a key role in spreading anti-Emergency awareness and propaganda in their countries of residence.
- Ultimately, it was the Indian voter who reaffirmed that sovereign power in India rests not with the rulers but with the people.
- JP's Movement united the masses in a widespread struggle against corruption, authoritarianism, and the erosion of democratic rights.

14

Diverse Ways of Agitation

Renowned French writer and Nobel laureate Romain Rolland was a scholar who conducted an in-depth study of the histories of various nations, including India. He once wrote of India: "If there is a land on earth that sheltered and fostered all dreams ever since human beings learned to dream, that is India."

Throughout human history, the struggle against injustice has often been marked by bloodshed and violence. However, India has largely followed a different path—one rooted in peace and justice. So, instances of violence in Indian societies have been relatively rare. India seldom pursued imperial or colonial expansion, even during times of great strength.

During the fight against the Emergency, the resistance movement adopted diverse and innovative strategies. Among the prominent leaders was George Fernandes, a charismatic figure who bravely opposed the authoritarian rule imposed during the Emergency. However, George Fernandes believed that violence was at times necessary to achieve the goal. Because of this conviction, he chose not to work with the Lok Sangharsha Samiti, a movement committed to non-violent resistance.

The core group organised by George Fernandes to resist the Emergency included renowned actress Snehalata Reddy, M. S. Appa Rao, C. G .K. Reddy, Viren J. Shah, journalist K. Vikram Rao, and lawyer Prabhudas Patwari. George Fernandes went underground to evade arrest and sought to inform the world that a strong anti-

Emergency sentiment prevailed in India. Although he was against homicide, he believed the government could be weakened by sabotaging infrastructure such as bridges and public enterprises using dynamites.

His brother, Lawrence Fernandes, was arrested in Karnataka and subjected to brutal torture. He was released after the intervention of Madhu Dandavate, who was also imprisoned under MISA. George Fernandes continued campaigning against the Emergency in disguise until he was arrested in connection with the Baroda Dynamite Case on 10 June 1976, in Calcutta (now Kolkata).

Snehalata Reddy was George Fernandes' most trusted associate. A nationally acclaimed actress, she won a national award for her sterling performance in the film *Samskara*. After her arrest, she was also subjected to brutal torture. Although she had been healthy and active, the continuous abuse took a severe toll on her health. She became a martyr for democracy on 20 January 1977, just five days after her release from prison.

Her final film, *Sone Kansari*, was released posthumously and became an instant hit, with millions flocking to theatres to see their beloved actress and courageous leader. In her prison diary, she noted that the police even intimidated her daughter in a bid to silence her resistance against the Emergency. When the Morarji Desai government came to power after the Emergency, George Fernandes, who became a Cabinet minister, declared that he could never forgive the previous government and its despotic leader.

It was the Lok Sangharsha Samiti that led the fight against the Emergency. A committee based on revolutionary ideas was formed under the leadership of Jayaprakash Narayan to resist the Emergency, and it later came to be known as the Lok Sangharsha Samiti. The first national committee of the Samiti was led by Morarji Desai, with Nanaji Deshmukh serving as general secretary and Ashok Mehta as treasurer. Morarji Desai was imprisoned on 25 June 1975, and Deshmukh was arrested two months later. The committee continued its activities under S. M. Joshi as the new president and Ravindra Verma as secretary.

The Kerala unit of the committee organised a historic resistance under the leadership of M. P. Manmadhan and K. Raman Pillai. The RSS, although banned during the Emergency, was the driving force behind much of the agitation. However, after the Emergency was lifted, the RSS adopted a policy of forgive and forget, choosing not to seek revenge against the former government.

Even before the Emergency was declared, the RSS had extended support to the Lok Sangharsh Samiti organised by JP, as it respected the committee's ideals of truth, commitment, and transparency. This support became one of the key reasons the government banned the RSS after the declaration of the Emergency and subjected its workers to widespread torture across the country.

Indira Gandhi's animosity towards the RSS was evident in her address to the nation through All India Radio after the Emergency's proclamation. In a letter to Indira Gandhi dated 21 June 1975, recommending the declaration of an Emergency, Siddhartha Shankar Ray explicitly advised action against the RSS and Ananda Marga.

Despite the ban, the RSS provided strong backing to the Lok Sangharsh Samiti and played a key role in leading non-violent agitations inspired by Gandhian principles.

There were several leaders who, like George Fernandes, believed that change could not be achieved through peaceful means. Under the circumstances then, such a perspective was understandable. However, the Lok Sangharsh Samiti successfully continued its nonviolent movement. Many brave fighters, who dedicated the best years of their lives to the agitation, continue to live among us.

George Fernandes fully understood the intensity of Indira Gandhi's despotic tendencies and was deeply sceptical of the general elections she declared during the Emergency. Initially unwilling to stand as a candidate in the 1977 elections, Fernandes eventually relented under pressure from JP. He became a candidate from Muzaffarpur in Bihar. Though he was in jail and unable to campaign for a single day, he romped home with a massive margin of over three lakh votes.

The Lok Sangharsh Samiti achieved a remarkable mandate against the Emergency through a completely peaceful agitation. In the 1977 general elections, Indira Gandhi's Congress Party could win only two seats out of 238 constituencies in North India, most of which had traditionally been Congress strongholds. Meanwhile, in South India, states like Andhra Pradesh and Kerala gave Indira Gandhi a face-saving victory. This historic political transition in India, brought about by the willpower of the Indian voter, can rightly be called a Gandhian model revolution.

15

The Days When the Constitution Collapsed

One of the reasons why the international community holds our parliamentary system of democracy in high esteem is that the fundamental rights of citizens are protected by the Constitution. However, all such rights were suspended during the Emergency. The right to life is ensured in Article 21 of the Constitution. No one, except through a court of law, has the authority to violate this right. This is one of the core principles of the Constitution. A citizen has the right to approach a court of law when their right to life is denied. During the Emergency, these rights were systematically trampled upon.

In the Supreme Court and in several High Courts, the government argued that a citizen has no right to file a habeas corpus petition, even in cases involving threats to another person's life. Nine High Courts ruled that, under such conditions, constitutional courts had limited jurisdiction. The appeal against this by the government was considered by a Constitutional Bench of the Supreme Court in what came to be known as the ADM Jabalpur Habeas Corpus case.

In this case, Chief Justice A. N. Ray and senior judges—including Justices M. H. Beg, Y. B. Chandrachud and P. N. Bhagwati—ruled that even if a person was arrested on the basis of personal vendetta, they had no right to challenge it in a court of law during the Emergency. This was the majority verdict.

However, Justice H. R. Khanna, the second-most senior judge on the bench, issued a powerful dissenting opinion. He argued against the majority, defending the fundamental right to life and liberty. Justice Khanna knew that his dissent would cost him the position of Chief Justice of India, to which he was next in line. Nevertheless, his courageous stand earned him a place in history as a fearless champion of justice who upheld the Constitution at great personal cost.

The public's resentment toward the judges who sided with the tyrannical government during the Emergency was later acknowledged by Chief Justice Ray in his autobiography. He eventually admitted that some of his rulings had been unjust. When legislations were later enacted to rectify the excesses of the Emergency, the verdict of these four judges was officially deemed unjust, while Justice Khanna's solitary dissent laid the groundwork for new legal principles. Justice Khanna proved that, even as a developing nation, India upheld a commendable sense of justice and a strong commitment to democracy—even during a period as dark as the Emergency.

During the trial in the Supreme Court on a habeas corpus petition, Justice Khanna posed a critical question to the then Attorney General of India, Niran De: "The 21st sub-section of the Constitution guarantees a citizen the right to life. If a police officer kills a man on the grounds of personal vendetta, can there be any legal protection?" Niran De responded that no judicial remedy was available while the Emergency was in force. He told the court: "You may be taken aback by my answer. I am also shocked. But in such situations, the court cannot take any legal actions against the violation of rights."[1] Though Niran De technically won the case for the government, he later congratulated Justice Khanna for his courageous dissenting opinion.

If someone were shot by the police out of personal vendetta, the law was helpless. Thamban Thomas, a socialist leader and High Court lawyer in Kerala, was arrested under MISA. When his arrest was challenged through a writ petition, T. C. N. Menon, former CPI

1. H. R. Khanna, *Neither Roses Nor Thorns* (Delhi: Eastern Book Company, 1985), p. 82.

MP and then Additional Advocate General, chillingly remarked that under the laws in force at the time, Thamban Thomas was "nonexistent"!

In the Bombay High Court, the government's lawyer argued that the court had no authority to ensure basic amenities for MISA detainees in prison. All these indicate the despotic nature of the Emergency, where political power was exercised with brutality and insensitivity. Opposition leaders were imprisoned and constitutional and other amendments were introduced arbitrarily. The 38th Constitutional Amendment (24 July 1975), the 39th Amendment (8 August 1975), the 40th Amendment (27 May 1976), and 42nd Amendment (11 November 1976) clearly demonstrate how the authorities bulldozed the legal system to suit their interests.

The notorious 39th Amendment was aimed at absolving Prime Minister Indira Gandhi of the charges in the election case that had cost her parliamentary seat. Later, based on this amendment, the Supreme Court quashed the Allahabad High Court verdict that had declared her election invalid. Justice Khanna remarked that the display of loyalty to the government by one of the judges during the trial was deeply troubling. The amendment, which effectively placed the Prime Minister's election conduct beyond judicial scrutiny, was later repealed by the Janata Party government. During the Emergency, the very foundations of parliamentary democracy decayed. The following is a list of some other laws amended during the Emergency:

The Amendment of the Internal Securities and Protection Law of 5 August 1975

Its objectives were:

a) If an order for preventive imprisonment was cancelled, a new order could still be issued against the same individual.

b) Those imprisoned under Article 16 were not eligible for release on bail or any other form of legal assurance.
c) A newly introduced Article 16 imposed significant restrictions on the right to seek judicial redress.

The Amendment of the Election Rules of 6 August 1975

a) All cases declared invalid under Article 8a were required to be submitted to the President, who, in consultation with the Election Commission, had the authority to overturn the court's decision.
b) As per the amended Article 77(1), the date of an election ordinance was to be treated as "the official date of nomination for the candidate". It also exempted government employees from executing ordinary procedures.
c) A Gazette notification related to the appointment, resignation, or similar actions of a government employee can be accepted as proof. This amendment gave retrospective validity to several ongoing election cases, including those pending before the Supreme Court.

The Amendment Law of 10 August 1975

a) The elections of the President and the Vice President cannot be challenged in any court of law.
b) Similarly, the elections of the Prime Minister and the Speaker of the Parliament were placed beyond the consideration of a court of law. Decisions regarding these elections were to be made by a committee constituted by the Parliament, and all pending election petitions were brought under this amendment.

MISA Amendment Law of 25 January 1976

a) One who is released as per an order cancelled could be re-imprisoned under a new order.
b) The Central government was granted the authority to demand information from state governments regarding individuals held under precautionary imprisonment.
c) All details concerning those under detention could be kept confidential, and the publication of such information was strictly prohibited.

Prevention of Publication of Objectionable Matter Act of 2 February 1976

a) The definition of "objects to be protested" was expanded to include words, expressions and visual symbols that were deemed defamatory towards the President, Vice President, Prime Minister, or State Governors.
b) Copies of any publications released in violation of imposed bans could be confiscated.
c) A bail amount could be obtained from those printers, publishers and editors who the authorities believe would publish objectionable content.
d) The Central government was empowered to declare specific publications as subject to confiscation.

When India became independent, the makers of the Constitution sought to uphold Baron de Montesquieu's principle of separating the executive, judiciary, and legislature into independent and distinct branches of government. Their intent was for these pillars of democracy to function autonomously, without encroaching upon one another's domains. Article 50 of the Directive Principles of State

Policy reinforces this by advocating for the separation of the judiciary from executive control.

The Constitution empowers the apex court not only to function independently of the executive but also to review and strike down laws enacted by the legislature if they are found to be unconstitutional. Dr B.R. Ambedkar emphasised that it is the duty of the courts to protect constitutional rights, and that such remedial measures constitute the very soul of the Constitution. However, during the Emergency, both the executive and the judiciary negated these very cardinal principles.

Although the Constitution guarantees the independence of the judiciary from executive control, between 1972 and 1976, several Union Ministers openly called for a judiciary "committed" to the government. Judges who resisted such pressures were often subjected to governmental retaliation, while others began delivering judgments that favoured the ruling establishment. The credibility of the Supreme Court suffered during this period, notably with its controversial decision to voluntarily reopen the landmark Kesavananda Bharati case—an act that drew widespread criticism and raised concerns about judicial overreach. The Supreme Court's conduct during the Emergency remains a troubling chapter in the history of independent India's judiciary.

16

The Shah Commission Report Vanishes

In 1977, the Janata Government appointed a commission, headed by Justice J. C. Shah, to investigate the atrocities committed during the Emergency. Justice Shah's credentials were beyond dispute, and there were no complaints about the Commission's work. The Commission conducted a thorough and impartial inquiry, and produced a detailed report on the Emergency excesses.

The Shah Commission Report served as a stark warning to the world about the dangers of democracy sliding into autocracy. And the international community was ready to recognise the relevance of its findings. However, in 1980, the Indian government, led by the Congress, sought to conceal the report. Though the findings of the Commission had merit, those in power ensured that not a single page of it see the daylight. Worse still, no protest was raised against this political chicanery. In a similar vein, the government also destroyed the copies of the Justice Kapoor Commission Report, which had investigated the assassination of Mahatma Gandhi. Such actions by rulers weaken the very foundations of our democracy.

The Shah Commission had travelled across the country, collecting evidence in the form of documents and tape-recorded testimonies. A public hearing was also held, allowing for broader participation. Relevant articles from national newspapers in both English and Hindi were gathered, and the entire body of evidence was submitted to the Central government.

The Shah Commission had worked diligently to submit its report on time, which was presented in three stages. According to the Commission's findings, those who were found guilty included Indira Gandhi, Sanjay Gandhi, Rajiv Gandhi, Pranab Kumar Mukherjee (who later became the President of India) and Navin Chawla (who in 2009 became the Chief Election Commissioner).

The report was submitted on 6 August 1978. Following this, the Morarji Desai government appointed a committee to take appropriate action on the Commission's findings. However, internal issues within the Janata Party hindered any further progress. On 15 June 1979, Morarji Desai resigned, and the opportunity to act on the report was lost. It is indeed a serious offence that political parties and national organisations failed to discuss the conclusions of the Commission or use its findings for constructive reform.

Indira Gandhi capitalised on the political unrest at the Centre, and returned to power in the general elections of January 1980, which effectively sealed the fate of the Shah Commission Report. To this day, there has been no serious discussion about the suppression of the report. According to information available in Wikipedia, Indira Gandhi's government destroyed all copies of the report, and it is no longer available, even in the Parliament library. The destruction of the report is considered a crime as grave as the atrocities committed during the Emergency.

However, the well-known parliamentarian and writer Era Sezhiyan published a book titled *Shah Commission Report: Lost, and Regained* in 2010. In his book, he managed to produce parts of the report collected from sources in London and Australia. The issue of destroying official documents, such as the Shah Commission Report and the Justice Kapoor Commission Report, must be seriously addressed. Acts like these, which involve the deliberate suppression of critical evidence, cause incalculable harm to democracy.

17

Relevance of a Missing Chapter

The absence of Chapter 15 from the Shah Commission Report was a clear indication of how the world's biggest democracy had been reduced to a mere façade. This missing chapter contained the essence of the entire report, highlighting more than 30 critical points. It is believed to have included guidelines on how to overcome the challenges faced by democracy. Had these suggestions been made public, they would undoubtedly have been accepted by all in the years that followed.

The Shah Commission deemed the declaration of the Emergency a clear abuse of power. It provided details of how innocent people were intimidated and falsely charged for selfish political motives. The Commission accused the government of suppressing the press, preventing newspapers from speaking the truth. As protests were brutally crushed, India became, in the Commission's view, the "graveyard of democracy". The values of morality were eroded, and the image of the bureaucracy was sullied.

The Commission emphasised that the manner in which the Emergency was declared—without consultation or proper discussion—should be seen as a warning to the nation. It pointed out that the Prime Minister's recommendation for the Emergency to the President was made without any prior deliberations. The Commission rejected Indira Gandhi's justification, that she could not consult the Cabinet because of the urgency, as not only unconvincing but also unlawful.

The Commission found that officials were instructed to initiate Emergency procedures at midnight on 25 June 1975, even before the official declaration of the Emergency. The arrests under MISA and disconnecting power to the press in Delhi were seen as preparatory steps for the Emergency. There was no critical economic crisis or breakdown of law and order that would have necessitated the Emergency, nor were there any recommendations or reports suggesting such a move. The nation faced no threat to its security from internal or external sources. The Commission concluded that the Emergency was declared solely to address political exigencies. It further emphasised that the Constitution was committed to ensuring that the government machinery was not misused to serve the interests of any single individual in power.

The Commission noted that media censorship was unnecessary and should never be repeated. It emphasised that the media has a vital duty to protect democracy. The Commission recommended that the government ensure that news regarding court proceedings and parliamentary affairs reach the public without any obstruction.

The Commission found that many appointments made during the Emergency were unlawful. It also expressed concern about the misuse of the Internal Security Act against individuals.

It was deeply troubling to see the secret collusion between the police and the judiciary to imprison citizens and deny them bail through the application of non-existent or fabricated laws. When aggrieved citizens sought redress in the courts, they were once again imprisoned for doing so. The Commission noted that this method of executing justice, where the police and judiciary acted in concert, violated the fundamental principles of the Indian Penal Code. The Commission issued a stern warning about the potential derailment of the judiciary.

The Commission pointed out the necessity of the bureaucracy working under moral principles. It called for the transformation of the bureaucracy into a real tool for serving the people and for the restoration of the vitality of democracy.

The Shah Commission Report can be seen as a crucial guideline for those who fight for human freedom and democratic rights. The Indian Police Commission, which was tasked with studying and recommending improvements to the Indian police system, drew heavily from the Shah Commission Report. A discussion of its recommendations could help ensure freedom and justice within the functioning of the police system.

18

The Role of Judiciary

The Emergency led to the collapse of the four pillars of India's constitutional system: the Legislature, Executive, Judiciary, and Media. The Indian Parliament and Assemblies followed the dictates of autocracy without discussion or protest. With Opposition leaders imprisoned, the government enacted wilful legislation without any checks. The people were left powerless under the despotic rule of the Executive, while the media became subservient. The Judiciary, which should have been the safeguard of democracy, failed to rise to the occasion. Within the Judiciary, some worked hand in glove with the authorities for personal gain, while others fought boldly for democratic and human rights.

The Judiciary faced a scathing attack after the Golaknath and Kesavananda Bharati cases. In the Golaknath case, the Supreme Court rejected the claim that the government had unlimited power to amend the Constitution. The verdict explicitly stated that Parliament has no right to effect amendments that would take away the fundamental rights of citizens. In the Kesavananda Bharati case, a majority of the 13-member Constitutional Bench declared that the government had no authority to alter the basic structure of the Constitution. Although the verdict validated the 24th Constitutional Amendment, it was still a setback for the government. The Supreme Court ruled that Parliament did not have the power to abrogate fundamental rights. In a clear act of retaliation, Indira Gandhi's government appointed Justice A. N. Ray—who was fourth in the seniority list—as Chief Justice of India, superseding three senior judges: Justices J. M. Shelat, K. S. Hegde, and A. N. Grover. The power to appoint judges was with the government in those days. Indira Gandhi's government refused to accept the Supreme Court's ruling that Parliament could not alter the basic structure of the Constitution, and argued that the Constitution had no such inherent structure.

However, in the landmark Kesavananda Bharati case, Justices K. S. Hegde and A. K. Mukherjea identified the following features as fundamental to the Constitution:

1. The sovereignty of the nation should not be destroyed and another nation should not be kept as a satellite nation.
2. Democratic government should not be substituted by racial or autocratic government.
3. Independent states should not be formed by destroying the unity of the nation.
4. The secular structure of the country should not be replaced by a religion-based structure.
5. The rights of the citizens and minorities should not be cancelled.
6. The mandate to build a welfare nation should not be negated.
7. The duration of the two houses of parliament should not be extended indefinitely.
8. The right to amend the Constitution should not be misused by amending some articles for selfish objectives.

The events that unfolded in the country during the Emergency validated the concerns expressed in the Kesavananda Bharati case by the three judges who subsequently resigned. In his judgment, Justice H. R. Khanna drew a chilling parallel to Adolf Hitler, who had used the sub-section 48 of the Weimar Constitution to declare an Emergency and ultimately establish a Nazi dictatorship. Justice Khanna warned that similar patterns were happening in India. As early as 1973, several ruling party members and ministers had argued in Parliament for a "committed judiciary"—one aligned with the government's agenda. During the Emergency, as the government amassed unchecked power, the judiciary lost its dignity and independence.

Dr Ambedkar had remarked that sub-sections 32 and 226 were the most powerful Articles in the Indian Constitution. However, during the Emergency, the government effectively nullified the spirit and function of these Articles. Justice Khanna, who had delivered a lone dissent in defence of civil liberties, was denied elevation to the position of Chief Justice—a move widely perceived as political retribution. In protest, he chose to resign. Governance suffered as a result of such wilful and authoritarian acts by the rulers.

Despite the repressive environment, segments of the legal community rose in protest. The Supreme Court Bar Association, along with similar bodies in various states, lodged strong opposition, defying the Emergency's restrictions. Eminent lawyer Nani Palkhivala refused to represent Indira Gandhi in court as an act of civil protest. Fali S. Nariman resigned from his position as Additional Solicitor General, and Ram Jethmalani, then president of the Indian Bar Council, stood firmly against the growing autocracy.

Justice Khanna's stand served as a powerful morale booster for all those who stood for justice and constitutional integrity. In stark contrast, however, some judges proved their petty-mindedness by becoming a part of the autocratic regime. Justice Ray lacked the courage to decline the post of Chief Justice—an appointment he did not merit by seniority or moral standing at the time. Justice M.H. Beg, too, succumbed to the lure of power by accepting a position he neither legally nor ethically deserved at the moment of crisis. Justice Ray's later attempt to review the Kesavananda Bharati verdict further exposed the subservience of the Chief Justice to the Prime Minister's office during the Emergency. That era in Indian history stands as a stark reminder of Abraham Lincoln's timeless words: "Nearly all men can stand adversity, but if you want to test a man's character, give him power."

19

The Dual Faces of Emergency

When the Emergency was declared at midnight on 25 June 1975, the people of India were stripped of their liberties and democratic rights. Press freedom and fundamental rights were suspended, silencing dissent across the country. Shortly thereafter, 26 organisations, including the RSS, were banned. The resistance put up by the RSS and the Jana Sangh can rightly be seen as a second freedom struggle, which was a defining moment in the history of the nation. The *satyagraha* organised by the Lok Sangharsh Samiti further galvanised this resistance. The dark period of the Emergency brought many challenges, but it also gave national organisations an opportunity to show their commitment to democracy.

The cowardice of the CPI came to the fore during this time. The party supported the Emergency that literally trampled on the fundamental rights of the proletariat. When Muslims were subjected to compulsory vasectomy and demolitions at Turkman Gate, the Muslim League, which posed as the protector of the minorities, the Kerala Congress and the "Indira" Congress backed the despotic regime in exchange for political gains. The then Kerala Chief Minister C. Achutha Menon saw the Emergency as a tool to suppress the JP Movement. He convened a meeting of the district collectors in Thiruvananthapuram and instructed them to take harsh action against anyone opposing the Emergency.

The Communists had clamoured for the resignation of Indira Gandhi when the Allahabad High Court annulled her election to Parliament on 12 June 1975. But the same Communists later played second fiddle to her autocratic policies. Achutha Menon, acting as an emissary of Indira Gandhi, travelled to the USSR in a bid to justify the Emergency to the world. It was only after the Emergency was withdrawn that the CPI admitted their mistake.

A. K. Gopalan's Call

In a statement issued after the declaration of the Emergency, Communist leader A.K. Gopalan (AKG) exhorted his party cadres and the people of Kerala to rise up against the tyranny of Mrs Indira Gandhi, whom he described as a "female Hitler". He warned that the people might lose even their freedom to breathe. *Deshabhimani,* the mouthpiece of the CPI(M), wrote: "Indira is haunted by the ghost of Hitler. She has ruthlessly established an autocratic regime in India." The CPI(M) and its allies organised a few customary resistance programmes, but many party cadres became inactive when they truly understood the horrors of the Emergency. About a hundred CPI(M) leaders were imprisoned under MISA. In some cases, leaders like Pinarayi Vijayan were subjected to brutal police torture. A few of these leaders refused to secure their release through an apology or by accepting the twenty-point economic package.

Plan of E. M. S. Namboodiripad

Professor M. P. Manmadhan, who shared a cell with E.M.S. Namboodiripad (EMS) as a fellow prisoner, recalls that EMS suggested a hunger strike in jail to get A-class facilities as he was not satisfied with the C-class conditions. While AKG called for a life-and-death struggle against the Emergency, EMS took a more "practical" approach and wrote: "The possibility of regaining individual and democratic rights is too remote; the majority in the Central Committee had the opinion that the popular leaders should go along the legal way of agitation." This may have led him to mistakenly believe that economic reasons were the primary cause of the Emergency.

The CPI(M)'s fear of the prevailing conditions of the Emergency is evident from the writings of BJP leader K. Raman Pillai. Pillai expressed his desire to meet EMS through veteran Marxist leader Krishna Das, who promised to arrange a meeting at the MLA hostel. However, when Pillai arrived, he could only meet V.S. Achuthanandan, who informed him that EMS was not willing to meet someone who was on the police's hit list *(Adiyanthiravasthayude Anthardhaarakal,* p.106).

While AKG was fighting boldly against the fascist policies of Indira Gandhi, EMS met her and endorsed some aspects of the Emergency. This was later disclosed by CPI leader M. N. Govindan Nair. Meanwhile, organisations like the Jana Sangh were denied access to the government to voice their grievances. JP and other popular leaders were depicted as communal fascists by Indira Gandhi. The CPI (M) leaders' meeting with the Prime Minister in such a politically charged atmosphere was severely criticised.

Socialist Party leader M. P. Veerendra Kumar was the convener of the Opposition front in Kerala when the Emergency was declared. The Socialist Party in Kerala strongly resisted the Emergency. Veerendra Kumar was arrested and his properties were confiscated. Leaders of Jamaat-e-Islami were also arrested, and the organisation was banned. Although the Naxalites did not launch any significant movements against the Emergency, they faced brutal police repression. The custodial death of engineering student P. Rajan during the Emergency became a widely discussed issue in the country.

A.K. Gopalan –A Martyr

AKG had taken a stance against EMS's misguided policies during the Emergency. It was his relentless struggle against the Emergency that ultimately cost him his life, a truth that the CPI (M) tried to conceal. In his book *Kaal Nootandu* (*Quarter of a Century*), Cherian Philip recounts the last days of AKG. He reminisces that, despite his failing health, AKG continued to organise protests against the Emergency. In December 1976, while addressing a gathering of party workers at his hometown of Peralassery in Kannur district, he defied a police ban on using microphones. This led to a heated confrontation with a police inspector who tried to stop his speech. Overcome with emotion, AKG collapsed. He was taken to the Thiruvananthapuram Medical College, where he breathed his last.

PART - II

THE SHAH COMMISSION REPORT

20

The Shah Commission's Findings on Circumstances Leading to Declaration of Emergency

In the 1971 Lok Sabha elections, Indira Gandhi was elected from the Raebareli constituency, defeating Raj Narain and others. Raj Narain subsequently filed a petition in the High Court of Allahabad, challenging Indira Gandhi's election on a number of grounds, inter alia, alleging misconduct by her. The Allahabad High Court pronounced its judgment on 12 June 1975. Justice Jagmohan Lal Sinha of the Allahabad High Court ordered:

> In view of my findings … this petition is allowed and the election of Indira Nehru Gandhi respondent No. 1 to the Lok Sabha is declared void.

The Court further ruled that:

> The respondent No. 1, accordingly, stands disqualified for a period of six years from the date of this order, as provided in Section 8A of the Representation of the People Act.

The Court further directed:

> The operation of the said order is accordingly stayed for a period of twenty days. On the expiry of the said period of 20 days or as soon as an appeal is filed in the Supreme Court, whichever takes place earlier, this order shall cease to carry effect.

Following the judgment of the Allahabad High Court, which set aside the election of Indira Gandhi, there was a spurt of political activity in Delhi in particular and in the rest of India in general.

Apparently, an effort was made by the followers of Indira Gandhi to create an atmosphere where she, notwithstanding that she was unseated and disqualified from standing for election, could continue to remain and function as Prime Minister of India. To support this, numerous demonstrations, rallies, and meetings were organised by her supporters in Delhi and elsewhere.

The post-judgment situation in Delhi and some of the neighbouring states was described by several witnesses. Bhawani Mai, the then Inspector General of Police, Delhi, stated that there was a noticeable increase in activity following Justice Sinha's verdict. Several demonstrations, rallies and public meetings were organised between 12 and 25 June. While many of these events supported the Prime Minister, a few were against her. And all this created a tense atmosphere, but fortunately, no untoward incident occurred.

Misuse of Public Utility Services

Krishan Chand, the then Lieutenant Governor of Delhi, stated that soon after the pronouncement of the Allahabad High Court judgment, he was called to the Prime Minister's residence. However, he sent his secretary Navin Chawla in his place. He learnt from Navin Chawla that in response to potential law and order issues arising from Opposition rallies, a decision had been made to organise pro-Prime Minister rallies. For this purpose, people had to be brought in from various places. Krishan Chand also stated that he was told that public utility services, such as the New Delhi Municipal Committee (NDMC), the Delhi Transport Corporation (DTC) and the Delhi Electric Supply Undertaking (DESU), would be mobilised to assist in organising these rallies. He further stated that rallies and bringing people to the Prime Minister's residence continued after 12 June to demonstrate support for the Prime Minister.

Records from the Delhi Transport Corporation reveal that between 12 and 25 June 1975, a total of 1,761 DTC buses were requisitioned by the All India Congress Committee or the Delhi Pradesh Congress Committee to organise rallies in support of Indira Gandhi. J. R. Anand, who was working as a Traffic Manager at that time, stated that buses were mostly booked on his own orders and that he did it in pursuance of the decision taken by the DTC Chairman, who was also the Lieutenant Governor. The decision to provide full cooperation in organising the rallies, including arranging buses for participants, was made during a meeting at Raj Niwas.

Anand stated that DTC's standard procedure for special hire by a private party required a formal application along with advance payment. However, these formalities were bypassed for the AICC bookings. The buses were instead booked based on telephonic instructions from Navin Chawla, the secretary to the Lieutenant Governor. For larger bookings, details about the number of buses and the parties and their destinations were given by Navin Chawla. For small bookings, Navin Chawla directed Anand to coordinate with specific Congress leaders for further instructions.

Anand further stated that on 12 and 20 June, a large number of buses were booked, requiring the withdrawal of buses from their regular operations and thereby disrupting normal DTC services. Between 12 and 25 June 1975, the number of buses hired for special use far exceeded the normal booking limit for private parties, which is five buses per depot, with daily bookings surpassing the maximum capacity of 95 buses. These excessive bookings by the AICC and individual Congress leaders severely impacted DTC's normal operations and caused widespread inconvenience to the public. Anand also stated that an amount of Rs 4 lakhs in special hire charges for the buses was still outstanding from the AICC and the DPCC for over two years.

On 13 June 1975, the entire fleet of 983 buses plying on Delhi routes was taken off the roads and diverted to converge near the Prime Minister's residence. Residents of Haryana, Punjab, Rajasthan and Uttar Pradesh—states either bordering or near Delhi—were transported in vehicles commandeered by state authorities for a rally in support of Indira Gandhi. A large number of these vehicles violated the Route Permits Rules under the Motor Vehicles Act, and in many cases, government vehicles were used without any payment being made.

The DTC records clearly corroborate witness testimonies indicating that government employees were compelled to assist in organizing these rallies. Jaswant Singh, Depot Manager at DTC, provided a statement listing the names and designations of such officials, the number of buses assigned to report to them and the relevant dates, which are given below:

Name of the Officer and Designation	Date of Report	No. of Buses Reported
SHO Police Station, Faridabad	12-06-1975	26
Smt. Meenaxi Dutta, SDM	–do–	2
K.D. Nayar, SP, New Delhi Parliament Street Police Station	–do–	2
	16-06-1975	2
	26-06-1975	4
SHO Police Station, Gurgaon	12-06-1975	99
SHO Police Station, Rai	–do–	95
Bakshish Singh Gill, DySP Enforcement	–do–	16
Director of Transport	–do–	34
B. L. Anand, SDM	–do–	1
Sareen, Dy. Director, Delhi Admin., Delhi	17-06-1975	2
PA to Chief Secretary, UP	19-06-1975	60
PA to Chief Minister, Bihar	20-06-1975	40

Rallies were held in New Delhi to demonstrate support for Indira Gandhi to continue as Prime Minister despite the order of the Allahabad High Court. The DTC, the NDMC, and the DESU participated in these rallies. K. D. Nayar, the then Superintendent of Police, New Delhi, admitted that he regularly visited and supervised the law and order arrangements in the vicinity of the Prime Minister's residence. According to him, participants in these rallies carried banners indicating the organisations and the unions to which they belonged, and they used transport provided by their respective organisations to attend the rallies.

Bringing in People from Neighbouring States

The participation in the rallies was not confined to Delhi alone. Lieutenant Governor Krishan Chand deposed that

> ... Some neighbouring States like Haryana, Rajasthan, and Western UP also sent contingents for the purpose. All these arrangements were made under instructions from the P.M.'s House conveyed through Mr. Dhawan and the P.M. was kept informed about the developments from time to time.

The DTC records also clearly show that a number of buses were deputed to make trips outside Delhi. Under the Motor Vehicles Rules, buses travelling outside the Union Territory of Delhi are required to obtain special permits from the State Transport Authority. However, the Secretary of the State Transport Authority informed the Commission in a letter dated 28 November 1977 that

> ... as per records maintained in this office no contract carriage permits were issued to the DTC for carrying contract parties outside the Union Territory of Delhi or to any private parties for use of the DTC vehicles outside the Union Territory of Delhi during the period from 12th June, 1975 to 25th June, 1975.

At a high-level meeting held at Raj Niwas, it was decided that the buses would be sent to neighbouring districts in Haryana and UP and instructions were issued to allow the buses to pass the barriers; that to ensure that the buses reached their destinations in these states, the officers of the DTC were deployed to accompany the buses. Anand further stated that he had been assured by Navin Chawla that the police authorities and state transport authorities had been instructed to allow the buses to cross state borders without the required route permits.

Raj Roop Singh, Inspector and SHO of the New Industrial Township, Faridabad, stated that after the announcement of the Allahabad High Court judgment, he received a telephonic message from the Police Headquarters in Gurgaon informing him that about 100 DTC buses would be arriving from Delhi to transport people in support of Indira Gandhi. He was instructed that the buses would report to the police station and, upon request from the Labour Inspectors, officers of the Industries Department and other government agencies, he should permit them to take the buses.

Raj Roop Singh further stated that the police station began receiving telephonic messages from various locations, and the buses were subsequently directed to the relevant officers. The majority of the buses were taken by officers of the Labour and Industries Departments, who used them to transport factory workers from Faridabad to Delhi. No records were maintained with regard to the number of buses received or dispatched.

The police was also instructed to arrange trucks or other vehicles, such as four-wheelers, to carry people to Delhi. For this purpose, the police approached the truck unions and transport companies to supply the required number of vehicles. This operation was conducted under the direction of the District Magistrate. The trucks were assembled at the SDM's court in Ballabgarh, where Block Development Officers (BDOs) or Tehsildars took charge of them. *Patwaris* and *Gramsewaks* were assigned to accompany the trucks to various villages, where they collected people and brought them to Delhi.

Sub-Inspector Khan Chand, SHO of Sadar Police Station, Gurgaon, stated that the SSP, Gurgaon, along with senior civil officers, had also arrived at the scene. Under the directions of these senior officers, some buses were sent to the city, while others were dispatched to various factories to transport people to Delhi.

Sub-Inspector Jagdish Lal, SHO of Police Station City, Gurgaon, stated that:

> ... The empty trucks passing the road were also sometime detained and asked to report at the Tehsil Headquarters for the purpose ... BDO and Tehsildars used to take charge of these vehicles and detailed the Patwaris, Gramsewaks etc. for taking these vehicles to villages and bringing people from there for taking them to Delhi.

Bansi Lal's Directive

N. K. Garg, District Magistrate, Rohtak stated that on 12 June 1975, Bansi Lal, the Chief Minister of Haryana, rang him from New Delhi at around 10.30 a.m. and informed him that the Prime Minister had been unseated by the Allahabad High Court judgment. Bansi Lal instructed that truckloads of people be sent to the Prime Minister's residence starting from 2.30 p.m., and directed Garg to contact MLA Lala Krishan Das, who would muster the Congress workers. He further indicated that the people should raise slogans in support.

Garg immediately got in touch with Krishan Das and conveyed the message to him. He also summoned Senior Superintendent of Police (SSP) S. H. Mohan and asked him to arrange as many trucks as possible to transport people to Delhi. Garg added that he received a similar message from Ch. Dalbir Singh, the then Deputy Minister for Shipping in the Central Cabinet. The statement of Garg was corroborated by SSP S. H. Mohan.

M. K. Miglani, who was then serving as District Magistrate, also confirmed the instructions given by Bansi Lal. According to Miglani, he learnt from local leaders that out of the 100 DTC buses that had come to the Faridabad factory area, only about 40 buses—filled with people—were able to proceed, whereas the remaining buses returned empty due to an insufficient number of factory workers being mobilised.

On 13 June 1975 and again on 18 June 1975, about 800 to 900 employees of the DESU participated in rallies outside the residence of Indira Gandhi, following a call by the Delhi State Electricity Workers Union. This was supported by the statements of S.N. Srivastava, Chief Labour Welfare Officer, DESU, and K.P. Saxena, Controller, Rajghat Power House.

Another major rally took place on 20 June 1975, for which as many as 497 DTC buses were requisitioned by the organisers—far exceeding the permissible limit of 95 buses. Efforts were also made in Haryana to mobilise more people for the rally.

The state of affairs in Punjab was no different. Chief Secretary R. S. Talwar admitted that:

> When it came to my knowledge that official machinery was being utilised for organising transport and mustering men and money for the purpose, I advised the then Chief Minister not to let Government and semi-Government agencies and their personnel being used in support of a political struggle with which they as such were not concerned. This advice was not liked, nor did it have much effect and official machinery continued to be utilized for mobilising men, money and transport to be sent to Delhi.

Special Trains Arranged

According to the records of the Northern Railway, three special trains were arranged—one each from Varanasi, Lucknow and Kanpur—on 19 June 1975, which arrived in New Delhi/Delhi on 20 June. Two of these trains were booked by known Congressmen. While the identity of the party requisitioning the special train from Varanasi was not recorded in the file, it is noted that the train was arranged for Congress delegates. For the return journey, two special trains were sent on 21 June 1975.

From Rajasthan, 58 trucks belonging to the State Electricity Board were ordered by the Chief Minister to be placed at the disposal of the workers' union. Although the Chairman of the Electricity Board, Mangal Behari, had directed that appropriate charges be levied, no payment for these hire charges was made either by the government or the workers' union.

On 22 June 1975, the Opposition parties organised a rally which was to be addressed by Jayaprakash Narayan. This raised considerable concern in the official circles, as reflected in the statement of Lieutenant Governor Krishan Chand, who stated that:

> Several meetings were also held in the Home Ministry to consider as to how best the situation developing from the speeches of Jayaprakash Narayan could be dealt with. At the official level, the view was that whatever might be done in respect of other leaders, Jayaprakash Narayan's arrest would make it more difficult to preserve public peace than if he was not arrested … This view eventually did not prevail. However, Jayaprakash Narayan could not come to Delhi to address the meeting at Ramlila Grounds on June 22, 1975.

Government Bodies Vie with Each Other

While government bodies competed to show their support or sympathy for the Prime Minister by misusing government resources, there were government employees, high-ranking and lowly placed, who refused to be a part of what they considered to be wrong and improper. They objected to the use of government resources for political purposes.

R. N. Bhatnagar of the NDMC opposed the diversion of NDMC trucks from their normal deployments to proceed to the Prime Minister's House, even going so far as to lay in front of one of the trucks that was being diverted. He argued that while employees and authorities were welcome to show their support for Indira Gandhi, it should not be at the expense of civic resources.

Certain employees of the DESU, who refused to participate in these rallies, were allegedly beaten up by the more enthusiastic amongst the supporters of the Prime Minister.

Mangal Behari, IAS, the Chairman of the Rajasthan Electricity Board, became a victim of the Rajasthan government's wrath after he refused to comply with the demand to send Electricity Board workers in official trucks to attend the rally in Delhi on 20 June 1975.

While the government resources in Delhi and elsewhere were being used to demonstrate support for the Prime Minister, the law was applied discriminatorily in favour of the Congress Party. The enforcement of Section 144 of the Criminal Procedure Code, which prohibited gatherings, had been a regular feature around the Prime Minister's House. However, this was relaxed for demonstrations and rallies organised by the Congress Party in support of Indira Gandhi.

This matter was reported to the President, who sent for the Lieutenant Governor of Delhi and enquired why the other political parties were not being afforded the same facilities. The Lieutenant Governor informed the Commission that he had explained to the President that if the Opposition parties were also granted the same facilities, it could lead to clashes, potentially creating a law and order situation. The Lieutenant Governor further stated that this relaxation regarding Section 144 of the Code of Criminal Procedure was granted in favour of the Congress Party at the instance of the Prime Minister.

Ministers' Movements Watched

While demonstrations of sympathy and support for the Prime Minister were being organised, the Intelligence Bureau (IB) was simultaneously deployed to monitor several prominent Congress leaders and ministers. The Shah Commission came across a "Top Secret" note dated 18 June 1975, sent by the then IB Director to the Prime Minister's Secretariat. It contained matters which among other things could have been compiled only on the basis of a physical surveillance and telephone tapping of the individuals involved. This discovery raised a critical concern about the violation of privacy of individuals, including that of government ministers, for reasons unrelated to national security. It underscored the misuse of intelligence resources for political purposes.

Jagjivan Ram, a minister in Indira Gandhi's Cabinet, informed the Shah Commission that his movements were being monitored and his telephone was being tapped even before the Emergency was formally declared. He based this assertion on information provided by officials who remained loyal to him. Jagjivan Ram was very critical of the IB, accusing it of supplying the Prime Minister with a mix of accurate, inaccurate and fabricated information. He further stated that the surveillance on him only intensified after the Emergency was imposed.

Jagjivan Ram strongly condemned the physical surveillance of ministers and citizens, as it was a blatant violation of civil rights and individual freedoms. He noted that this intrusive monitoring began even before the Emergency and only intensified during it. In his view, it had not ceased even after the Emergency was lifted. He was particularly critical of the misuse of the IB for political purposes, such as evaluating the Congress Party's electoral prospects and vetting the suitability of its candidates. According to him, IB officers were often misled by candidates with vested interests, resulting in distorted and unreliable feedback being passed on to the Prime Minister.

Drastic Steps Mooted

The decision to take certain drastic steps including the declaration of the Emergency was, apparently, in contemplation even as early as 22 June 1975. That day, R.K. Dhawan rang up Andhra Pradesh

Chief Minister J. Vengala Rao, and told him to be available in Delhi on 24 June 1975 when the judgment of the Supreme Court relating to the stay order applied for by Indira Gandhi was expected to be announced. Presumably, the order which the Supreme Court would make was to be the deciding factor to determine the drastic action contemplated to be taken. If the judgment had been in the nature of a categorical and an unconditional stay, probably no action of the nature, which was ultimately taken, would have followed. But the Supreme Court gave only a conditional order. On 24 June 1975, the vacation judge of the Supreme Court, Justice Krishna Iyer delivered his judgment on the appeal of Indira Gandhi. The operative portions of the judgment are as follows:

(i) Subject to paragraph (iii) below there will be a stay of the operation of the judgment and order of the High Court under appeal.

(ii) Consequently, the disqualification imposed upon the appellant as a statutory sequel under Section 8A of the Act and as forming part of the judgment and order impugned will also stand suspended. That is to say, the petitioner will remain a Member of the Lok Sabha for all purposes except to the extent restricted by para (iii) so long as the stay lasts.

(iii) The appellant petitioner, a Lok Sabha Member, will be entitled to sign the register kept in the House for the purpose and attend the session of the Lok Sabha. But she will neither take part in the proceedings in the Lok Sabha nor vote, nor draw a remuneration in her capacity as a Member of the Lok Sabha.

(iv) Independently of the restrictions under para (iii) on her Membership of the Lok Sabha, her right as Prime Minister or Minister so long as she fills that office to speak in and otherwise to take part in the proceedings of either House of Parliament or attend sitting of the Houses (without the right to vote) and to discharge other functions such as are laid down in the Article 74, 75, 78, 88 etc. or under any other law and to draw salary as Prime Minister shall not be affected or detracted from on account of the conditions contained in the stay order.

Since the judgment was conditional, it appears to have been decided that the plan of taking drastic action was to be gone through with expedition and despatch.

According to Krishan Chand, Lieutenant Governor of Delhi, a decision had been made as early as the evening of 23 June to take Opposition leaders into custody shortly after the Opposition rally scheduled for 24 June. Lists of the Opposition leaders to be arrested were already under preparation at that time.

According to a report dated 18 June 1975 by IB Director Atma Jayaram, considerable political activity took place between 15 and 18 June. A key aspect of this activity was that leaders such as Krishan Kant, Chandra Shekhar and Mohan Dharia were actively advocating the view that Indira Gandhi should step down and that the party should elect a new leader. Lakshmi Kantamma also supported this position. Krishan Kant explicitly stated that so long as Indira Gandhi remained in office, the Opposition would have "a one-line programme", which, he warned, could snowball into a revolution.

Mohan Dharia was advised by Y.B. Chavan on the afternoon of 17 June not to raise any dissent in the parliamentary party meeting on 18 June. Chandra Shekhar and Krishan Kant met H.N. Bahuguna on 17 June at UP Nivas. Substantial portions of this report have not been verified to be correct and some of them have been denied by Jagjivan Ram, who made a statement before the Commission.

Some Important Events between 23 and 25 June 1975

It was expected that a rally would take place, headed by Jayaprakash Narayan, on 24 June 1975. On the evening of 23 June, an indication was given to Lieutenant Governor Krishan Chand by R.K. Dhawan that the Opposition leaders may have to be taken into custody after the rally. Lists of prominent political leaders to be arrested were prepared by the Superintendent of Police (CID) at the Prime Minister's House. Krishan Chand stated that he was shown the lists and that changes were made in the lists and continued to be made from time to time as a result of discussions at the Prime Minister's House. But he did not see the final list. He also stated that the Opposition rally did not take place on 24 June as announced and so the action proposed to be taken that day was stayed.

On 24 June, Justice Krishna Iyer announced the judgment. The initial Hindi broadcast on All India Radio conveyed the full content of the verdict, which provoked strong public reactions. In response, the Information and Broadcasting Minister spoke to the Director of News. Shortly thereafter, a revised Hindi version was aired, which was crafted to present the judgment in a manner favourable to Indira Gandhi, mirroring the tone of the English bulletin broadcast at 4 p.m.

In the meantime, authentic copies of the judgment were obtained. According to Krishan Chand, once the full implications of the verdict were grasped, it was decided that drastic action would be taken against Opposition leaders at the first sign of any attempt to unseat the Prime Minister. Indira Gandhi resolved that this action would be initiated on 25 June after the Opposition rally.

On 24 June, J. Vengala Rao received a telephonic message from R.K. Dhawan, requesting him to meet the Prime Minister the following day. According to Vengala Rao, Indira Gandhi informed him on 25 June that, given the prevailing conditions, a decision had been made to take strong and deterrent measures. Anticipating public resentment and the possibility of violent reactions, she emphasised the need for comprehensive preventive action, including the arrest of persons deemed likely to incite unrest.

He was also instructed to convey the message to the Chief Minister of Karnataka. Both the Chief Ministers of Karnataka and

Andhra Pradesh were asked to remain available by telephone on 25 June, when the final decision of the Government of India would be communicated to them by R.K. Dhawan. An IAF aircraft was arranged for Vengala Rao to travel to Bangalore, where he met with the Chief Minister of Karnataka and relayed the Prime Minister's message. That evening, he returned to Hyderabad using the same aircraft.

On the morning of 25 June, P.C. Sethi, Chief Minister of Madhya Pradesh, was briefed at the Prime Minister's residence by Om Mehta, Minister of State for Home Affairs, regarding the guidelines to be observed in detaining certain persons deemed capable of inciting disturbances. According to P.C. Sethi, the meeting took place in the presence of the Prime Minister.

The Prime Minister had attempted to contact Harideo Joshi, Chief Minister of Rajasthan, but was unable to reach him. She then instructed Sethi to convey the message to Joshi on his way back to Bhopal. Sethi travelled via Banswara on an IAF aircraft to deliver the message before returning to Bhopal.

Misuse of IAF Aircraft

The records maintained at the Air Headquarters of the IAF confirm the flights of Vengala Rao, P.C. Sethi and Harideo Joshi by the IAF aircraft on 25 June. No payments were apparently made by anyone for their use.

S.K. Misra, who was the Principal Secretary to the Chief Minister, Haryana, told the Commission that between 12 noon and 2 p.m. on 25 June, he received from Delhi a telephonic information from Bansi Lal, the Chief Minister of Haryana, asking him to alert the Deputy Commissioners to remain at their headquarters and to be available on telephones and to reserve huts at Sohna Tourist Complex for two VIPs who were to reach there on the night of 25/26 June. Lists of persons to be taken into custody were to be prepared by ADIG, CID.

Misra met Bansi Lal at about 10 p.m. on his return from Delhi. At that time, the latter told him that an Emergency was expected to be declared that night. This statement of S. K. Misra is corroborated by the statement of N. K. Garg, the then Deputy Commissioner, Rohtak, who had also met Bansi Lal at Rohtak at about 4.30 p.m. M. K. Miglani, who was the Deputy Commissioner at Gurgaon, took steps to reserve two huts in the Sohna Tourist Complex on 25 June.

The District Magistrate of Darbhanga (Bihar) had conveyed to the then Chief Minister of Bihar a message that the Chief Minister of Bihar was to contact the Prime Minister's House at about 9 p.m. on the night of 25 June. The Chief Minister is reported to have told the District Magistrate that he wanted to rush back to Patna the same night by road and he wanted to know the provisions under the Defence of India Rules with regard to the Press. The Chief Minister told the District Magistrate to convey to the Home Secretary and IGP to meet him at his residence at about 2.30 a.m. on the intervening night of 25/26 June.

According to Krishan Chand, all arrangements for the impending arrests were discussed during a meeting held on the afternoon of 25 June in R.K. Dhawan's office. Present at the meeting were Om Mehta, Bansi Lal and Bajwa, the Superintendent of Police (CID), Delhi Administration. Later that evening, around 7.30 p.m., Krishan Chand convened a meeting at Raj Niwas, attended by the Chief Secretary, IG Police, Deputy Commissioner, DIG (Range) and others.

J.K. Kohli, the Chief Secretary of Delhi, was directed to visit the Tihar Jail to ensure that adequate arrangements were made to accommodate those expected to be detained during the night of 25–26 June. Kohli visited the jail around 8.15 p.m., assessed the availability of space, and informed the Superintendent of the Jail to be prepared to receive approximately 200 "Naga Political Prisoners" by the following morning.

No Morning Edition of Certain Newspapers

Efforts were made to ensure that some important newspapers would be unable to publish their morning editions on 26 June. B.N. Mehrotra, former General Manager of the Delhi Electric Supply Undertaking, stated that he was summoned to Raj Niwas by the Lieutenant Governor around 10 p.m. and instructed to disconnect the electricity supply to the press establishments from 2 a.m. that night. According to Krishan Chand, these orders had come directly from the Prime Minister's House and were to be strictly implemented. Mehrotra confirmed that the instructions had been carried out and reported compliance to Navin Chawla, Secretary to the Lieutenant Governor, at around 2 a.m.

Efforts were also made to suppress newspaper publication in cities like Chandigarh and Bhopal. In Chandigarh, N.P. Mathur, the Chief Commissioner, had not received any formal instructions from the Home Secretary or other senior officials in Delhi. On 25 June, Mathur contacted Home Secretary S.L. Khurana by phone to verify the instructions allegedly issued by the Chief Minister of Punjab. Khurana denied any knowledge of such directives. As a result, Mathur chose not to act on the verbal orders he had received from Punjab Chief Minister Zail Singh, which included locking up The Tribune and its editor Madhavan Nair.

News Gagged

Initial instructions were issued by the Chief Minister of Madhya Pradesh around 9 or 10 p.m. on 25 June, directing that news of the arrests should not be published in newspapers in Bhopal and other key locations.

It appears, therefore, that the Chief Ministers of several states were taken into confidence as early as the morning of 25 June and were clearly instructed to act upon receiving directives from the Prime Minister's office. Those who were informed included the

Chief Ministers of Andhra Pradesh, Karnataka, Madhya Pradesh, Rajasthan, Haryana, Punjab, Bihar and West Bengal. The Lieutenant Governor of Delhi was fully apprised of the situation even before 25 June.

Imposition of Emergency Suggested by Ray

Siddhartha Shankar Ray, the Chief Minister of West Bengal, received a message from the Prime Minister's Secretariat on the morning of 25 June and subsequently went to her house. When Indira Gandhi entered the room where he was waiting, she was holding several reports. She expressed concern that the country was facing a grave crisis and, in light of widespread indiscipline and lawlessness, she felt that decisive action was necessary. According to Ray, she had mentioned on two or three earlier occasions that India needed "shock treatment" to restore order.

Ray recalled that one such conversation took place shortly before the Allahabad High Court judgment was announced on 12 June. At that time, he had advised her that existing laws were sufficient to manage the situation. He also cited the success his government had achieved in addressing law and order issues in West Bengal within the framework of the prevailing legal system. According to Ray, the reports she read aloud suggested that there was unrest—or threats of unrest—in many parts of Northern India.

While they were in discussion, a bearer entered with a slip of paper, which Indira Gandhi read aloud. It was a report containing advance information about what JP was expected to say at a public meeting scheduled for later that day in Delhi. According to the report, JP would be calling for a nationwide mass movement within the next two or three days. His proposed actions included setting up parallel administrations and courts, instructing students to boycott universities, schools, and colleges, and urging police and armed forces personnel to disobey illegal orders. Ray noted that he did not know the source of this report.

According to Ray, Indira Gandhi was firm that India was drifting towards chaos and anarchy. Ray told her that he would like to consider the steps that had to be taken after consulting the relevant literature on the subject; that the Prime Minister gave him the impression that she was seriously disturbed with the conditions prevailing in the country. Ray left the Prime Minister's house but came back at about 4.30 or 5 p.m. and told her that she could consider Article 352 of the Constitution for the purpose of imposing Internal Emergency. Thereupon, Indira Gandhi asked Ray to go along with her to the President immediately.

She briefed the President with a summary of what she had shared with Ray regarding the prevailing situation. The President listened to her for about 20 to 30 minutes before turning to Ray and asking what the exact wording in the Constitution was. He then advised the Prime Minister to proceed with making her formal recommendation.

As they were leaving Rashtrapati Bhavan, Ray suggested that Indira Gandhi involve other senior leaders in the decision-making process. Although he did not name anyone specifically apart from Congress president D.K. Barooah, it was clear he believed broader consultation was necessary.

Following this, Indira Gandhi sought answers to three key questions:

1. Could a decision be made without referring the matter to the Cabinet—was that constitutionally permissible?
2. What should be the precise language of the letter to be addressed to the President?
3. What should be the exact text of the Proclamation?

Ray then consulted the Business Rules and a notification related to the 1971 Emergency proclamation. According to Ray, the rules outlined three categories of matters: the first included those that must be referred to the Cabinet; the second, those that need not go to the Cabinet at all; and the third, those that the Prime Minister could decide independently but which required subsequent Cabinet ratification. Indira Gandhi expressed her intention to make the decision herself and said she would convene a Cabinet meeting early the next morning. Ray advised her that if she wished to proceed independently, she should personally draft the recommendation to the President for the proclamation of an Internal Emergency and ensure she was fully informed about the relevant constitutional procedures and rules.

Ray prepared two drafts for the recommendation to the President. However, according to him, the letter that Indira Gandhi ultimately sent recommending the proclamation of the Emergency was not based on the draft he had provided. Later that evening, Barooah was called in, and his input was sought regarding the speech Indira Gandhi would deliver on the radio to announce the Emergency. Indira Gandhi, Barooah and Ray collaborated on drafting the speech—an exercise that took nearly three hours. The delays were largely due to repeated interruptions by Sanjay Gandhi, who kept entering the room and asking his mother to step outside. Each time, she would leave and not return for five to ten minutes.

Locking up of High Courts

After completing the speechwriting, as he was leaving the room, Ray was surprised to hear from Om Mehta that orders had been issued to lock up the High Courts the following day and to cut off electricity to all newspaper offices. Ray was taken aback, as he had previously advised Indira Gandhi that, even under the Emergency, no action could be taken without first framing the necessary rules. Ray said to those present that such drastic measures could not just happen. Disturbed by what he had heard, Ray decided to stay on and insisted on seeing Indira Gandhi again to express his concerns. He made it clear that he would not leave until he had spoken with the Prime Minister.

In the meantime, a visibly agitated Sanjay Gandhi told Ray he didn't know how to govern the country. Ray remained calm and firmly replied that Sanjay Gandhi should mind his own business and not interfere in matters beyond his domain. Later, when Ray informed Indira Gandhi about the planned closure of High Courts and the cutting of electricity to newspaper offices, she immediately said these actions should be stopped.

Om Mehta in his deposition before the Commission stated that he had given information to Ray in the Prime Minister's House regarding the intended closure of the courts and cutting off of the electricity connection.

Brahmananda Reddy, the then Home Minister, stated that he was called to the Prime Minister's residence around 10.30 p.m. and was informed about the need to impose an Internal Emergency. He told Indira Gandhi that there was already an Emergency in force, and that the powers available under the existing Emergency could be utilised to deal with the situation. He then left but was summoned again shortly thereafter. On his return, Indira Gandhi informed him that his earlier suggestion had been examined, but it was concluded that declaring an Internal Emergency was necessary. Brahmananda Reddy responded by telling her to proceed as she thought best.

He stated that he also signed a letter to the President making a reference to the telephonic conversation which the Prime Minister had with the President and appended the draft proclamation of Emergency for the President's assent along with his letter. The letter signed by Brahmananda Reddy was on a plain sheet of paper.

Akhtar Alam, who functioned as the Special Assistant to the President of India, stated that an important letter from the Prime Minister's House was delivered to him at about 10.30 p.m. on 25 June, and he delivered it to the President. The President who sent for his Secretary, K. Balachandran, and Neelkanthan, Deputy Secretary, who dealt with such letters. Some discussion ensued between the President and the Secretary about the wording of the letter, about which Balachandran raised certain doubts.

Around 11.20 p.m. Dhawan brought with him some papers. Akhtar Alam said that he did not know what the papers were, and he did not know whether the President signed them. The next morning at about 10.30 or 11, Akhtar Alam was given by the President the letter from the Prime Minister. He kept it in his custody till he handed it over to Balachandran when Akhtar Alam left the post in February 1977.

K. Balachandran in his deposition referred to a top secret letter received from the Prime Minister to the President. This letter referred to the discussion which the Prime Minister had with the President earlier in the day. She had stated that the President was satisfied on the imminent danger to the security of India due to internal disturbances. She also stated that if the President was satisfied on this score, a proclamation under Article 352(1) of the Constitution had become necessary; and that she was enclosing a copy of the draft proclamation for the President's consideration.

Balachandran stated that there was no draft proclamation enclosed with the letter. According to him, the Prime Minister had also stated that she was not consulting the Cabinet due to shortage of time and the matter was urgent; and that she was, therefore, permitting a departure from the Transaction of Business Rules in exercise of her powers under Rule 12.

According to Balachandran, he advised the President that it would be constitutionally impermissible for him (the President) to act in the manner suggested in the letter; he had to act on the advice of his Council of Ministers and, therefore, his personal satisfaction in this matter would not arise. The letter from the Prime Minister indicated that the Cabinet had not considered the matter. Moreover, it was worded in such a manner as would make it appear that the decision to declare the Emergency was that of the President based on his personal satisfaction.

The President, apparently, saw the force of this argument and contacted the Prime Minister on the telephone immediately. Afterwards, he left the President's room, and came back after about

10 minutes. In the intervening period, Dhawan visited the President and had delivered the draft of the proclamation of the Emergency for his signature. The President told Balachandran that he had signed the proclamation and given the same to Dhawan, who had taken it back with him along with the Prime Minister's letter. The next day, Alam told Balachandran over the telephone that a revised letter had been received from the Prime Minister, which was subsequently passed on to Balachandran by Alam in February 1977.

PM's Letter to President

The Prime Minister's letter and the proclamation of Emergency which are available in the President's office file are reproduced below:

> "TOP SECRET"
> PRIME MINISTER
> INDIA
> NEW DELHI June 25, 1975
>
> Dear Rashtrapatiji,
>
> As already explained to you, a little while ago, information has reached us which indicates that there is an imminent danger to the security of India being threatened by internal disturbance. The matter is extremely urgent.
>
> I would have liked to have taken this to Cabinet but unfortunately this is not possible tonight. I am, therefore, condoning or permitting a departure from the Government of India (Transaction of Business) Rules 1961, as amended up-to-date by virtue of my powers under Rule 12 thereof. I shall mention the matter to the Cabinet first thing tomorrow morning.
>
> In the circumstances and in case you are so satisfied, a requisite Proclamation under Article 352(1) has become necessary. I am enclosing a copy of the draft Proclamation for your consideration. As you are aware, under Article 352(3)

even when there is an imminent danger of such a threat, as mentioned by me, the necessary Proclamation under Article 352(1) can be issued.

I recommend that such a Proclamation should be issued tonight, however late it may be, and ail arrangements will be made to make it public as early as possible thereafter.

With kind regards,
Yours sincerely,
Sd/-Indira Gandhi

PROCLAMATION OF EMERGENCY

In exercise of the powers conferred by Clause I of Article 352 of the Constitution, I, Fakhruddin Ali Ahmed, President of India, by this Proclamation declare that a grave emergency exists whereby the security of India is threatened by internal disturbance.

New Delhi-25th June, 1975 PRESIDENT

On the basis of the evidence, it is clear that some of the important functionaries in the Home Ministry, the Cabinet Secretariat and the Prime Minister's Secretariat, who should have been consulted before such an important decision was taken, did not know anything about the proclamation of Emergency till very late. Some of them learnt about it only on the morning of 26 June.

P. N. Dhar, Secretary to the Prime Minister, said that he knew about it only when he was called to the Prime Minister's House around 11.30 p.m. on 25 June when he was given for perusal the draft of the speech that Indira Gandhi was going to make on the All India Radio.

B.D. Pande, the Cabinet Secretary, received a phone call from the Prime Minister's House around 4.30 a.m. on 26 June, informing him that a Cabinet meeting was scheduled for 6 a.m. He was already aware that the Emergency proclamation was to be announced that morning. However, he was surprised by the large number of arrests that had occurred between 25 and 26 June. Normally, instructions for such swift actions were communicated through the Ministry of Home Affairs via established official channels.

Emergency Not Discussed by Cabinet

According to B.D. Pande, the need for declaring an Emergency, or any situation justifying such a declaration, had not been discussed in any Cabinet meetings prior to 26 June.

IB Director Atma Jayaram stated that he learnt about the Emergency proclamation only after arriving at his office on 26 June.

Similarly, Home Secretary S.L. Khurana was informed of the Emergency only upon receiving notice of the Cabinet meeting on the morning of 26 June, sometime after 6 a.m. Consequently, he arrived at the meeting venue around 6:30 a.m., by which time the meeting had already concluded.

H. R. Gokhale, the Minister of Law and Justice, came to know about the proclamation of Emergency only during the Cabinet meeting held on the morning of 26 June. Neither he or his Ministry was consulted at any stage regarding the decision, nor was the document vetted by him or his Ministry.

Some notable aspects of the Emergency proclamation, as gathered from official records, include:

a) On the economic front, there was no alarming situation. On the contrary, the wholesale price index had declined by 7.4 per cent between 3 December 1974 and the last week of March 1975, according to the Economic Survey 1975–76, a Government of India publication.
b) On the law and order front, fortnightly reports sent by State Governors to the President of India and by Chief Secretaries

to the Union Home Secretary consistently indicated that the law and order situation was under complete control all over the country.

c) The Ministry of Home Affairs had received no reports from state governments indicating any significant deterioration in law and order in the period immediately preceding the proclamation of the Emergency.

d) The Home Ministry had not prepared any contingency plans before 25 June 1975 regarding the imposition of an Internal Emergency.

e) The Intelligence Bureau had not submitted any reports to the Home Ministry between 12 and 25 June 1975 suggesting that the internal situation warranted an Emergency.

f) The Home Ministry did not submit any report to the Prime Minister expressing its concern over the internal situation in the country. Even after the Emergency was lifted, the ministry did not possess a copy of the communication sent by the Prime Minister to the President recommending its imposition.

g) While the Director of the Intelligence Bureau, the Home Secretary, the Cabinet Secretary and the Secretary to the Prime Minister were not taken into confidence, R.K. Dhawan, then Additional Private Secretary to the Prime Minister, was involved in the preparation and promulgation of the Emergency from an early stage.

h) Om Mehta, then Minister of State in the Ministry of Home Affairs, appears to have been taken into confidence earlier than the Home Minister, K. Brahmananda Reddy, was brought into the loop only when the draft proclamation was sent to the President.

i) The Lieutenant Governor of Delhi and the Chief Ministers of Haryana, Punjab, Madhya Pradesh, Rajasthan, Karnataka, Andhra Pradesh, Bihar and West Bengal were given prior intimation by the Prime Minister. However, no such information was provided to the governments of Uttar Pradesh, Maharashtra, Gujarat, Tamil Nadu, Jammu and Kashmir, Tripura, Orissa, Kerala, Meghalaya and other Union Territories. In fact, H.N. Bahuguna, then Chief Minister of Uttar Pradesh, stated in his affidavit that he learnt of the Emergency on the morning of 26 June while having breakfast with Union Ministers Uma Shankar Dikshit and Keshav Dev Malaviya—both of whom were equally surprised by the development.

Indira Gandhi Summoned to File Statement

As stated earlier, a notice under Rule 5(2)(a) of the Commissions of Inquiry Rules was issued to Indira Gandhi requesting her to file her statement in terms of Rule 5(3). No such statement was filed by her. Indira Gandhi was also issued a summons under Section 8B of the Commissions of Inquiry Act. Though she responded to the summons, she declined to take oath and give evidence on oath when the Commission desired to examine her under Section 5(2) and according to the procedure analogous to the provisions of the Civil Procedure Code. But in one of the letters addressed by her to the Commission, dated 21 November 1977, in response to the invitation which was initially extended to her to assist the Commission, Indira Gandhi had submitted a detailed reply regarding certain matters and, inter alia, raising certain objections to the procedure adopted by the Commission. In the course of her reply, she touched on the subject of the declaration of Emergency and stated:

> I should further like to point out that the terms of reference of this Hon'ble Commission are one-sided and politically motivated, while they empower the Hon'ble Commission to enquire into the excesses committed during the Emergency, they are silent about the circumstances which led to its declaration. This country is vast and beset with deep-rooted and wide ranging problems.

The administrative machinery is fragmented. Urgent measures have to be taken. Programmes are implemented at various levels and by different individuals and agencies. Some excesses in their implementation cannot always be avoided nor do they always come to notice at that time, I have publicly expressed regret for any unjust hardship caused to any individual. But if the professed purpose of the inquiry is to check abuse of power in the future, it is equally imperative that the circumstances which created chaotic conditions in the nation before the emergency should also be enquired into and not allowed to be repeated. For two years preceding the emergency the country was in the grip of grave crisis. The economic situation had deteriorated due mainly to internal and international causes beyond our control. Interested parties and groups wished deliberately to aggravate the situation for their own gain. Freedom of speech and expression were used to spread hatred and parochial regional sentiments. Noble institutions of learning were turned into hotbeds of political intrigue. Public property was destroyed at the slightest excuse. A Minister in the present cabinet is reported to have proudly claimed, 'In November last (1975) in the Union State of Karnataka alone, we caused derailment of 52 trains'. The attempt was to paralyse national life. The dissolution of the Gujarat Assembly was forced by undemocratic means. Duly .elected legislators were beaten and intimidated into resigning from their seats in the Assembly. Relying upon the judgment of the Allahabad High Court, the demand for my resignation was made in the name of democracy and morality. But what was that morality and how did democracy come in? If at all, moral considerations were on my side as nothing had been found by the High Court against me which smacked of moral turpitude. I had lost on a legal technicality but law also gave me the right to reconsideration of the judgment by the highest court. And the act of seeking to remove a duly elected leader of the majority party through threats to gherao me and with a call to the Army and the Police to revolt could not be justified in the name of any known democratic principles. A chaotic state of affairs similar to that in India before July 1975 prevailed in France when de Gaulle came to power in 1958. His major response was constitutional reform and the introduction of Article 16 in the new constitution which goes a long way to show how necessary it became for my government to resort to the emergency provisions in the Constitution if India were to pull herself out of the impending disaster. The new Article provided Inter alia, that 'when the regular functioning of the constitutional governmental authorities is interrupted, the President of the Republic shall take the measures commanded by the circumstances' to restore order.

It must also be born in mind that it would be impossible for a democratically elected government to function effectively if it is to live under the fear of politically inspired inquisitorial proceedings against its policies and decisions by a subsequent government.

Indira Gandhi sent yet another reply dated 2 December 1977 in response to another invitation, which was extended to her by the Commission when the case dealing with the circumstances leading to the declaration of Emergency was coming up for hearing. The relevant portions of her reply are reproduced below:

In fact, that the declaration of Emergency, according to this Hon'ble Commission, might be an excess and, therefore, calls for an inquiry, is a matter which does not fall within the purview of this Hon'ble Commission. The proclamation of Emergency by the President was a Constitutional step. It was approved by the Cabinet and duly ratified by both Houses of Parliament in terms of Article 352(2) of the Constitution. After the ratification, the proclamation which was political in character, became an Act of Parliament. In the United States the exercise of political power by the President has been held to be beyond challenge. Chief Justice Marshall observed in Marbury V. Madison:

"By the Constitution of the United States the President is invested with certain important political powers in the exercise of which he is to use his own discretion, and is accountable only to his country in his political character and to his own conscience - The

Subjects are political. They respect the nation, not individual rights, and being entrusted to the executive the decision of the Executive is conclusive."

Under the Indian Constitution, on the other hand, the proclamation of Emergency has been made subject to ratification by Parliament.

No authority in this country, not excluding any commission appointed under the Commissions of Inquiry Act, can sit in judgment over such an Act of Parliament. For any political decision, the Government under our Constitution is answerable only to Parliament. If this Hon'ble Commission arrogates to itself the power to determine that the declaration of Emergency was an excess, this Hon'ble Commission will not only be stultifying the Constitutional Scheme, but also establishing a precedent which will make serious inroad into Parliamentary supremacy with disastrous consequences to Parliamentary freedom.

Even the terms of reference of this Hon'ble Commission do not warrant such an inquiry. They are strictly confined to the determination of alleged excesses during the Emergency or in the days immediately preceding it.

But apart from this, I should like to bring to the notice of the Hon'ble Commission that while making its pronouncement on my submission that the terms of reference were onesided and politically motivated and that it was equally imperative that this Hon'ble Commission should go into the circumstances which led to the declaration of Emergency, this Hon'ble Commission observed as follows:

But one thing I propose to bring to the notice, I am only concerned with the declaration of Emergency, if it amounts to an excess and not otherwise. If on consideration of the material before me, I am prima facie of the view that declaration of Emergency could be regarded as an excess, an inquiry in open will be made. If, however, there is no such view formed by me, no such inquiry will be made.

This observation of the Hon'ble Commission, I most

respectfully submit, is not sustainable. In the first place it is tantamount to saying: There shall be an inquiry into the declaration of Emergency if I can be damned in the process, but there shall be no inquiry if others whose actions justified the declaration of Emergency, are likely to be damned. Secondly, is difficult to imagine how this Hon'ble Commission can take any decision regarding the declaration of Emergency without full consideration of the range of circumstances and incidents which had accumulated, for a long time preceding the proclamation, into an imminent threat to paralyze duly elected Governments at the Centre and in the States.

Emergency Defended

During that period, ostensibly the attacks were concentrated upon me. In reality the political opposition had been using this strategy to weaken the Central Government and subvert its socialist and progressive programmes for quite some years. It was a question of change versus the status quo. Secular, democratic socialism on the one hand and retrograde, communal and capitalistic forces on the other had been struggling against each other to gain the upper hand. The split in the Congress in 1969 gave an edge to this confrontation. The nationalisation of banks and other measures which disturbed entrenched privileges and vested interests, and offered opportunity and help to the poor and weaker sections of our society, created such tremendous popular upsurge that communal and capitalistic elements probably lost all hope of being able to successfully fight on an ideological plane. Hence they changed their methods. Similar such political phenomenon was not peculiar to India. Recent history is replete with such instances.

This vicious campaign of character assassination and denigration waged by political opponents denuded Indian politics of all ideological debates. Even in the 1971 Lok Sabha elections, the opposition did not put forth any alternative economic or social programme. I was the focus of attack as the first target. Ordinary human decency was lost in the process. Their decisive defeat at the polls frustrated their faith in the democratic process. There was then a short interlude during which India faced one of the gravest challenges with which any nation has been confronted. The influx of ten million refugees from Bangladesh, aggression and the subsequent war, unprecedented country-wide drought and the global inflationary spiral aggravated by the oil crisis, and the other factors would have upset the economic balance of any rich and developed country. India was fighting for her economic survival. It was during this period that the then Opposition resorted to extra-constitutional means to paralyse our democratic institutions. As I have explained in my previous statement, there was hardly any sphere of national life which was not sought to be disrupted.

The inevitable distress of many sections of our people was exploited to mount attacks on duly elected Governments and Assemblies of the day. We cannot forget the tragic circumstances leading to the dissolution of the Gujarat Assembly only a few months after its constitution.

It was in this political atmosphere prevailing in the country that the judgment of the Allahabad High Court was delivered and was sized upon by the opposition to whip up political frenzy against me. Although I was in the immediate target, the real design was to dislodge the Congress Government and to capture power through extra-constitutional means. If a duly elected Government can be allowed to be pulled down by threats of violence and demonstrations in the streets and by incitement of the army and the police to revolt, the democratic structure of the nation would collapse. In 1958, while putting the case for constitutional reform the French Prime Minister, M. Gallard said, "Democracy is only in consequence an anarchy if those who hold power by the will of the majority do not also enjoy an authority corresponding to the responsibilities which they assume."

As Prime Minister of the country I could not abdicate my responsibility to stem the impending disaster merely for fear that my motive in proclaiming the emergency could be suspected.

When the democratic institutions of a nation are held to ransom, and the Government of the day rises to the occasion to meet the challenge, certain freedoms of some individuals might be affected. That in fact is the rationale behind Article 352 of the Constitution which authorises the declaration of Emergency. Emergency was not intended to cause suffering and I have expressed deep sorrow for any hardship caused.

It may not be out of place to draw the attention of this Hon'ble Commission to the present Prime Minister, Morarji Desai's recent observations in the Rajya Sabha that there was "nothing like absolute right to anybody". "Every right is subject to the right of the whole society. If the rights of the whole society are in danger, the Government is bound to take action to prevent that danger." In these circumstances, the Hon'ble Commission's predetermination of certain dates while circumscribing the scope of its inquiry, belies reality. It has been repeatedly proclaimed by members of the present Union Government that it was allegedly because of the Allahabad High Court Judgment of the 12th June, 1975, and the qualified stay given by the Supreme Court on 22nd of June, that the Emergency was declared for personal reasons, namely, to stultify the judgment by extra-legal means and to maintain my position as Prime Minister by extra-constitutional methods. I have to point out, with utmost respect, that the Commission appears to have projected the theory propagated by my political opponents.

By putting the inquiry before hand into a predetermined chronological matrix the evidence would naturally proceed under the conditioning of this predetermined matrix, and this untested material will be systematically publicised to make it appear as proof, This, in my humble opinion, directly defeats the ends of justice.

In response to the Commission's inquiry, the Cabinet Secretariat has brought to the notice of the Commission the relevant portions of the Government of India (Transaction of Business) Rules, 1961. Rule 7 of these Rules reads as follows:

All cases specified in the Second Schedule to these Rules shall be brought to the Cabinet.
Clause e (ii) of the Second Schedule of the Government of India (Transaction of Business) Rules, 1961, reads as follows: "Cases relating to a proclamation of emergency under Articles 352 to 360 of the Constitution and other matters related thereto."

In the light of the foregoing Rule, it is not understood how this provision could have been circumvented by the application of Rule 12 of the same Transaction of Business Rules. Rule 12 of the Government of India (Transaction of Business) Rules reads as follows: "12. Departure from Rules: The Prime Minister may, in any case or classes of cases, permit or condone a departure from these rules to the extent he deems necessary."

In this context, the following information furnished by the Cabinet Secretariat regarding the Transaction of Business is relevant to the issue:

The Business of the Government is transacted in accordance with the Transaction of Business Rules and the Allocation of Business Rules, both of which have been promulgated under Article 77 of the Constitution. The Allocation of Business Rules provides that the business of the Government shall be transacted in the Ministries, Departments, Secretariats and Offices specified in the First Schedule to these rules. The distribution of subjects among the departments is specified in the Second Schedule to these rules. While the President can, on the advice of the Prime Minister, change the allocation of business between departments, nothing in the rules seems to provide for the Prime Minister's Secretariat transacting any business allotted to a particular Ministry.

By virtue of entry 27 under the Home Ministry, matters relating to the emergency provisions of the Constitution (other than financial emergency) are to be dealt in the Home Ministry. This, read with Rule 3 of the Transaction of Business Rules, therefore, requires that all business pertaining to the emergency provisions shall be transacted in the Home Ministry, with cases relating to the proclamation of Emergency belng brought before the Cabinet.

The normal procedure for submission of cases to the Cabinet for the Ministry concerned to send a Note for the Cabinet to the Cabinet Secretariat. This note contains the proposal needing Cabinet approval and should have the approval of the Minister concerned. Thereafter the item is placed before the Cabinet and approval, if accorded is conveyed to the Ministry by the Cabinet Secretariat. If time is short, the Cabinet Secretariat obtains the approval of the Prime Minister under Rule 12 of the Transaction of Business Rules, and thereafter authorises the Ministry concerned to proceed further in the matter.

Since the Home Ministry has allotted the work relating to the Emergency provisions of the Constitution, proposals relating to the proclamation of Emergency should normally originate from that Ministry. This would be particularly so when the Emergency is to be declared on grounds of internal disturbances, as the Home Ministry deals with the intelligence Bureau, Preventive detention and National Integration. It is the Home Ministry which is in touch with the State Governments on matters relating to law and order. The Cabinet Secretariat did not however, receive any proposals from the Home Ministry in respect of the Proclamation issue on the 25th of June.

It may be pointed out that even in 1971, when a war was being waged with Pakistan, a proclamation of Emergency was issued without invoking Rule 12 of the Transaction of Business Rules. A regular meeting of the Council of Ministers was convened, and the Proclamation was issued thereafter, after obtaining clearance from the Home Ministry. The Cabinet Secretariat conveyed the authorisation to issue the proclamation to the Home Ministry. Thereafter, the Presidential proclamation was formally issued.

Emergency Declaration – PM's Exclusive Decision

The circumstances leading to the declaration of Emergency pursuant to the advice of the Prime Minister leave little room for doubt that the decision to impose Emergency, when there was already in existence an Emergency proclaimed as early as 1971, was exclusively the decision of Indira Gandhi. None of her Cabinet Ministers, except Brahmananda Reddy was even aware of the proposal to advise the President, pursuant to which a declaration of Emergency was to be made. Even Brahmananda Reddy, the Home Minister, was not consulted; but he was merely informed shortly before the advice was tendered, and his assistance was taken only for obtaining a letter from him intimating the decision of Indira Gandhi and for forwarding the draft Proclamation to the President, pursuant to which the declaration of Emergency was issued. This assistance of Brahmananda Reddy appears to have been taken only as a matter of form and merely because his assistance was perhaps required to formally forward the draft Proclamation to the President.

It is necessary, however, to say something about the internal Emergency, which was declared. Under Article 352, as is stood on the relevant date, "(1) lf the President is satisfied that a grave emergency exists whereby the security of India or of any part of the territory thereof is threatened, whether by war of external aggression or internal disturbance, he, may, by Proclamation, make a declaration to that effect." The condition on which an Emergency may be proclaimed is: the satisfaction of the President that Emergency exists whereby the security of India or any part of the territory of India is threatened, whether (a) by war, or (b) by external aggression, or (c) by internal disturbances. The satisfaction may be based on any one or more of the three grounds. The declaration of Emergency by the President has no different effect as the satisfaction of the President depends upon the existence of the state of war or of external aggression or of internal disturbance. Once a declaration of Emergency is made on satisfaction of one or more of the grounds, the consequences described by Articles 353 and 355 come into operation. It is open to the President to declare that the right to move the court for enforcement of any of the rights conferred by Part III of the Constitution as may be mentioned in the order shall remain suspended for the period during which thc proclamation is in force, or for such shorter period that may be specified in the order. The Constitution contemplates declaration of only one Emergency, whether the satisfaction of the President depends upon the existence of Emergency arising out of war or out of external aggression or internal disturbance. The Emergency, once declared, does not differ in its nature or implications based on whether the President's satisfaction is derived from the existence of war, external aggression, or internal disturbances.

It may be recalled that an Emergency had already been in effect since December 1971, and it had never been withdrawn. During this period, the Defence of India Rules promulgated under the Defence of India Act as a consequence of that Emergency, remained in force. Additionally, the provisions of Article 358, by which the fundamental rights under Article 19 were suspended, were also in operation.

In the opinion of the Commission, the Constitution does not contemplate a second Emergency being declared while an existing Emergency is still in effect, nor does it prevent the courts from entertaining challenges to the declaration of an additional Emergency. However, the provisions of the Constitution were amended by the 39th Amendment of the Constitution Act, which barred any legal challenge to such a declaration. Despite the existing Emergency and the powers it conferred, a second Emergency was proclaimed, and the original Rules, i.e. Defence of India Rules, were modified as the Defence and Internal Security of India Rules, 1975.

Shock Treatment

The 1975 Emergency was more in the nature of a shock treatment than a legally permissible Emergency.

If, however, an Internal Emergency could be declared separately from an External Emergency, the powers that were exercised before any Rules were framed—such as disconnecting the electricity supply to newspaper offices—were wholly unauthorised as no law conferred such power on any authority. Furthermore, the action taken by the authorities, under the directions of the Prime Minister, to arrest a number of political leaders was not supported by any law. As will be pointed out hereafter, no orders were issued under the Maintenance of Internal Security Act or any other statutory provision by any competent authority. Prima facie, therefore, the disconnection of electricity to newspaper offices and the arrests of a number of political leaders and others without complying with the requirements of law were unauthorised and amounted to wrongful arrests and detentions; and the disconnection of electricity was against the provisions of the Indian Electricity Act, 1910.

Assault on Individual Liberty

It may also be necessary to mention that the conclusions drawn by the Intelligence Bureau after placing political leaders and others under surveillance, including tapping of their telephones, raised a grave issue of public interest. This directly concerns the assault on individual liberty, which holds profound importance and significance in a democratic society.

Even government ministers were not spared by the Intelligence Bureau's actions; they were subjected to the indignity of being shadowed, and their telephones were tapped. The exercise of such powers, if at all necessary, must be explicitly authorised by statutory provisions and limited to circumstances strictly required to safeguard the security of the State—such as during grave internal disturbances, external aggression, or war—and not under normal or routine conditions.

Based on the materials placed before the Commission, there appears to be no statutory authority under which the Intelligence

Bureau acted. In his statement to the Commission, Atma Jayaram, the then Director of the Intelligence Bureau, stated that, "it was the normal or usual practice to give such intelligence orally or in writing". However, such action does not appear to be justified by any circumstances warranting the protection of the State against external aggression, war or internal Emergency.

It is for the government to decide whether or not the Intelligence Bureau may be used for collecting information for purposes other than those strictly necessary for the security of the State. It would certainly be a travesty of the democratic institutions if the government constituted by a political party is entitled to watch the activities of other political parties and even members of its own party. If, however, such power is to be conferred on this institution, it must be by a statute or statutory rules authorising it. It is also to be ensured that this watch or surveillance does not degenerate into abuse and/or misuse of authority. A provision should, therefore, be made to guarantee that it is resorted to only in extreme emergencies. In any event, this watch of the intelligence agency on individuals and the materials collected thereby should be open to scrutiny by a board or a panel composed of officers or of public men before authorising the continuance of the watch. It should be possible to harmonise the demands of the security of the State with democratic liberties.

The challenges faced by the Intelligence Bureau are becoming increasingly complex—too complex to be left solely to the judgment of one individual or even a limited hierarchy of officials directly involved in its operations. It must be recognised that the Intelligence Bureau, as an institution, plays a crucial and indispensable role in the nation's governance and security. Its ability to function efficiently, effectively and with impartiality and objectivity is directly tied to both the security of the State and the liberty of its citizens. Given the high stakes involved in ensuring the Intelligence Bureau's proper and purposeful functioning, it is imperative that it benefits from the advice, guidance and wisdom from a body composed of eminent, experienced and patriotic individuals drawn from diverse disciplines and whose loyalty and personal integrity are beyond reproach. Such a structure would, in turn, foster the necessary trust and confidence of the citizens in this vital institution.

This is only to emphasise that the Intelligence Bureau should not be entitled to act as a super-watchman over the activities of politicians to whatever party they belong. Its activities should be subject to regulation and control insofar as these activities concern some clandestine parts which have come to the notice of the Commission to ensure that this does not degenerate into misuse or abuse of authority. In a strict theoretical sense, in a democratic country, any secret operation conducted by the Intelligence Bureau which has come to the notice of the Commission would be contrary to the democratic norms. The Intelligence Bureau should not be its own judge of its operations with regard to its necessity or propriety, nor should it be allowed to act as an agency or an instrument of politicians or to degenerate into an institution of controlling opponents of the political party in power or elements within the party in power.

In the present case, the watch on a senior Minister of a Cabinet rank and tapping of the telephone of Jagjivan Ram could not be justified. It is somewhat mysterious that such surveillance should have been maintained and allowed to continue. There is no evidence as to who ordered it, what steps were taken to ensure that the reports emanating from the Bureau were tested and found to be correct; and what were the safeguards the government took to prevent and protect itself from acting on incorrect and incomplete information.

Watergate Affair

The Watergate Affair and its aftermath in the United States led to some very useful improvements of built-in safeguards for overseeing the activities of America's intelligence agencies.

The Commission recommends that appropriate safeguards are necessary and should be devised by the government to prevent the activities of the Intelligence Bureau from being used as an instrument of political spying either by the government or by someone in the government. This issue has been raised to generate public debate on the question.

It is also necessary to draw attention to the misuse of Air Force aircraft. It appears that Indian Air Force aircraft were used surreptitiously for the benefit of individuals travelling on State duty or for State work, contrary to proper protocol. According to the existing rules, those persons were not entitled to use these aircraft. The Commission recommends that the government frame appropriate rules regarding the use of such aircraft and carefully scrutinize whether their use on 25 June 1975 was justified. Additionally, the government should ensure that bills for the aircraft usage were duly tendered; if not, those responsible should be identified and held accountable.

MISA Misused to Harass Political Opponents

There were also gross irregularities in the way the provisions of the Maintenance of Internal Security Act (MISA) and the Defence of India Rules (DIR) were misused to the detriment of political opponents. This question will be dealt with at some length later. It may be sufficient at this stage to observe that the minimum requirements of the provisions of the MISA and the DIR were not complied with, either at the behest of Indira Gandhi or her aides and orders were made without any grounds, without any satisfaction or maintenance of any record to the satisfaction of competent authorities. The personal liberty of many citizens was taken away and they remained deprived of that liberty for substantial periods even in the face of the safeguards which were incorporated against misuse of section 16A of MISA. This was disregarded with impunity.

In Delhi and in other states, which had advance information about the promulgation of the Emergency, a large number of arrests and detentions followed under MISA. The safeguards guaranteed against the misuse of the Act were ignored and grounds of detentions were not furnished in a large number of cases. In many cases, grounds of detentions were prepared and even predated and sent days after the persons had been arrested and detained in jails. In a number of cases, the grounds of detention had no relevance to the factual position.

In a few cases grounds were fabricated by the police, yet the Magistrates did not hesitate to sign them. An era of collusion between the police and the Magistracy ensued.

Oral instructions were also issued from the State Headquarters for the arrests of persons under MISA. In quite a few cases, the persons were initially taken into custody under the preventive sections of law and thereafter detained under MISA. This was the device which appears to have been resorted to in Delhi shortly after the promulgation of the Emergency.

A number of persons were arrested on false charges under sections 108 or 151 of the Code of Criminal Procedure or under both these sections. Such persons were produced before the Magistrates, and the Magistrates in a number of cases either declined to grant bail or there was delay in effecting the orders of bail. In the meanwhile, orders of detentions were procured from the Magistrates, which were passed not infrequently on non-existent or fabricated grounds. The manner in which the provisions of MISA were used was nothing short of a perversion and mockery of its provisions, and all the safeguards that were promised in Parliament when the MISA Bill was enacted. Many apprehensions, which were expressed by the Members of Parliament, who spoke against the conferment of such wide powers when the Bill was enacted, came true. The safeguards enshrined in the enactment were rendered meaningless by the callous misapplication of this Act by the police and the Magistracy, in many cases with the full knowledge and concurrence of some of the state governments.

The use and/or misuse of this Act raises issues, which requires examination in the larger context. At no time, either normal or abnormal, should there be any possibility of misuse of the powers of arrest. It needs to be made clear to all those responsible for overseeing the correct application of the powers of arrest/detention by the junior officers that the senior functionaries at the bureaucratic and political levels would be held directly accountable for any misuse or abuse of the powers of arrest and detention.

The Government of India accepted the findings, observations and recommendations made by the Shah Commission of Inquiry in two Interim Reports. This was officially announced in the Lok Sabha on 15 May 1978 by Prime Minister Morarji Desai. The reports pertain to the excesses committed during the Emergency.

PART - III

PROMINENT LEADERS ON EMERGENCY

M. Venkaiah Naidu

Pinarayi Vijayan

K. Karunakaran

Cherian Philip on A.K. Antony

P.K. Vasudevan Nair

Arangil Sreedharan

P. Parameswaran

Prof. T.V. Eachara Warrier

U. Dattatreya Rao

M. P. Veerendra Kumar

21

Why We Must Record Emergency Narratives

M. VENKAIAH NAIDU

More than four decades have passed since Indira Gandhi unjustly imposed a state of Emergency in India on 25 June 1975. The 21-month ordeal ended on 21 March 1977, a day after her crushing defeat in the elections. A huge portion of India's population is under 35 years and has no recollection of that event at all. Nonetheless, Emergency narratives continue to grip the people's attention in the 21st century.

Some books on the Emergency, like *The Judgement: Inside Story of the Emergency in India* by Kuldip Nayar, *Two Faces of Indira Gandhi* by Uma Vasudev and *All The Prime Minister's Men* by Janardhan Thakur, came out during the short-lived Janata Party years. Then there was a long hiatus in Emergency literature after the Congress re-established its grip on power in 1980. The new custom of recalling the Emergency began only on its 20th anniversary in 1995.

We now look back on the Emergency to draw lessons. In this age of social media, the Right to Information and public interest litigation, citizens will not tolerate any abridgement of their fundamental rights and usurpation of institutions. Even the Supreme Court can no longer shut its door on citizens as it did during the Emergency, seeking remedy against illegal detentions, unauthorised demolitions, torture and mayhem.

The teeming millions cannot be taken for granted. The masses, even if poor and uneducated, can unseat an arrogant ruler. That is the power of parliamentary democracy.

In January 1974, a Nav Nirman Andolan arose in Gujarat against the corrupt regime of Chief Minister Chimanbhai Patel. It was an apolitical movement. It was so popular that Indira Gandhi forced Patel to resign, and subsequently, the Assembly was dissolved. This was the beginning. A student movement was simultaneously brewing in Bihar. The students agitating against the Congress government led by Abdul Ghafoor invited Jayaprakash Narayan (JP) to lead them. Under JP, who formulated the concept of *Sampoorna Kranti*, the movement soon turned against Indira Gandhi's rule. Talks between JP and Indira Gandhi on the dissolution of the Bihar Assembly broke down.

Corruption took root in Indira Gandhi's government. George Fernandes, who organised the railway strike in May 1974, described her as *Bhrastachar ki Gangotri*. In September 1974, the Pondicherry Licence Scam broke. Tulmohan Ram, a Bihar MP, who forged the signatures of 21 MPs to recommend import licences for a Pondicherry businessman, was ousted. But L. N. Mishra, the concerned minister and Indira Gandhi's fundraiser, was left untouched. Railway minister Mishra had become an embarrassment for the government when he died on January 3, 1975, in a bomb blast at the Samastipur Railway Station. The case remains unsolved after 42 years.

Meanwhile, JP's movement was gathering momentum. He described it as the second freedom movement. Siddhartha Shankar Ray, the Congress Chief Minister of West Bengal, advised Indira Gandhi to impose the Emergency and put her opponents in jail.

The Emergency came within a fortnight of the June 12 judgment by the Allahabad High Court holding Indira Gandhi guilty of election malpractices. Her appeal before the Supreme Court was admitted, but with an interim order that she could attend the House but not vote as an MP. The June 25 Ram Lila Maidan rally of constituents opposed to Indira was the last straw that broke the camel's back.

The Indira Gandhi government had already become unpopular when the Emergency was declared, although it commanded a nearly two-thirds majority in the Lok Sabha. Her victorious image after the 1971 war was completely sullied by her Emergency excesses. Imprisoning the Opposition leadership, amending the Constitution, censoring the press, supersession of judges, arbitrary transfer of judges, forcible sterilisation, and unauthorised demolitions completely stigmatised the Emergency. Her imprisonment of scores of leaders, including JP, Morarji Desai, Atal Bihari Vajpayee, Madhu Dandavate, L. K. Advani and Prof. Samar Guha, RSS functionaries and student leaders including this author under the Maintenance of Internal Security Act (MISA) turned the mood of the nation against her. When finally Indira Gandhi lifted Emergency and called an election, the Congress was trounced.

Four decades on, Emergency narratives continue to pour in. One of them is the case of Emergency Victims of Kerala who have converged on a single platform to fight for compensation and pension. But there has been, to the best of my knowledge, no official documentation of Emergency narratives. Possibly the Indian Council of Historical Research can plan a project over it.

Reproducing a relevant article written by Shri Venkaiah Naidu on 25 June 2017, with his consent.

22

Custodial Torture Will Not Silence Us

PINARAYI VIJAYAN

Chief Minister of Kerala

(Full text of the speech delivered by Pinarayi Vijayan, MLA, in the Kerala Assembly on 30 March 1977)

Sir,

At the very outset, I oppose this Vote on Account. An expenditure of (rupees) 101 crores and 23 lakhs has been given in it now. I have heard claims being made as though a huge amount of money is going to be spent. However, out of this, an amount of (rupees) 69 crores and 78 lakhs has been earmarked for public debt repayment. So, the balance will be around (rupees) 31 crores.

I do not intend at this moment to speak on other issues. As someone who is addressing this Assembly for the first time since 28 September 1975, I would like to present a few matters before this House.

After 28 September 1975, my name may have come up in this House on many occasions. The Honourable Chief Minister even mentioned in yesterday's reply that it had come up many times. I was arrested on 28 September 1975—the night on which all Communist Marxists in the state were arrested under the MISA—from my home.

My home falls under the jurisdiction of the Dharmadam Police Station and the Thalassery Police Circle. It was Circle Inspector Balaraman from the Koothuparamba Circle who came to arrest me.

He knocked on my door, and when I opened it, I asked, "What's the matter?" He replied, "I've come to arrest you." I asked, "Why have you come? On whose instructions?" He said, "There are special instructions—from the SP. I've been directed to arrest you right now."

The Koothuparamba Sub-Inspector (SI) and a posse of policemen accompanied him. I had just woken up from sleep. I changed my clothes and went with them to the police station. Until we reached the police station, their behaviour was courteous.

At the station, I was asked, "Is there anything in your pocket?" I handed over whatever I had. Then they said I would be put in the lock-up. "Is that necessary?" I asked. "Yes, that is our rule," they replied. While being taken to the lock-up, a policeman said, "Remove your shirt." "Should I be treated like an ordinary criminal?" I asked. "We cannot say anything. You better talk to the inspector," the policeman said.

I then told the inspector, "We are political workers! Should we be asked to remove our shirts?" The inspector then instructed the policemen, "Let him remain in his shirt. Let him be in the lock-up wearing it."

On my way to the lock-up, I was given a mat. I entered the lock-up room with it, spread the mat on the floor and sat on it. Within two minutes, the lock-up was closed. The light outside the room was switched off. Only a dim light remained inside.

Two young men (whom I later came to know were not from that police station but had been specially brought in for the purpose) opened the lock-up and entered. I was sitting there. I stood up. One of them came forward and asked me abrasively, "What is your name?" "Vijayan," I replied. "What Vijayan?" he asked. "Pinarayi Vijayan," I replied.

The two men then stood on either side of me. When I said "Pinarayi Vijayan", one of them repeated, "Oh! Pinarayi Vijayan!" By the time he repeated my name the second time, I received the first blow.

Perhaps they thought being beaten by just two men wasn't enough. A posse of police officers was standing outside the lock-up, and then three more persons, including the CI, entered. Now they were five of them.

There is no need for me to describe in detail the nature of the assault I was subjected to—those familiar with the conditions in Kerala can very well imagine it. All five of them beat me in the worst possible manner, in several stages and repeatedly. As they assaulted me, they kept shouting, "So, you rascal, you speak against officers? Against ministers?"—and each accusation was accompanied by more blows. I fell many times and tried to get up each time, standing as long as I could. Eventually I reached a point where I could no longer rise.

Seeing that I could not get up, they began stamping on me with their feet and continued until they were exhausted. The beating lasted for nearly 15 to 20 minutes. Finally, they left. I remained on the floor until the next day. My shirt was torn, my *baniyan* (vest) was torn and even my dhoti was torn; I was left only in my underwear. That was what happened to me in the lock-up.

The next morning, the entire team of policemen who had carried out the first round of torture was replaced. Then came the policemen from the Koothuparamba Police Station. They were known to me and were very courteous. Some of them, perhaps out of sympathy, even asked me, "Would you like to have some tea?" Such was their courtesy.

At 10 a.m., I was taken from there to Kannur. While entering the Kannur Police Station, another infamous SI—Pulikkodan Narayanan—was there. Anyone who saw me at that time would know the truth because I was unable to walk. In fact, I was physically shoved into the police jeep by others. Even while entering and leaving the police station, I was held up by somebody.

"Vijayan, your face has completely changed!" said Pulikkodan Narayanan. I was expecting a second round of thrashing. But somehow, there was no second round.

From there, by 12 p.m., I reached the Kannur Central Jail. It was up to the Deputy Jailor to complete the admission formalities. "There are marks of beating on my body, which you can also see. Please record it," I told him. He said, "I can record it only if there are wounds or injuries." I then removed my shirt and showed him. The marks were clearly visible. But he said there were no wounds. He was not even willing to record the marks of police torture. The lower portion of my left leg was fractured—I knew it was broken. But the Deputy Jailor refused to record it, claiming it was not a wound. Then I felt they were all part of an understanding.

From there, the comrades who were with me carried me to Block 8. Chandrasekharan and Sankarankutty were there, and they took me to their block. The next day, a doctor came and admitted me to the hospital. My leg was plastered, and it remained in a cast for six weeks. For months, I could not do anything without the support of others. I even needed help to take a bath.

I wrote about the incident to the Chief Minister. At that time, the Speaker was unavailable, so I also wrote to the Deputy Speaker. But I did not receive a reply from anyone. No one even bothered to respond or enquire about how all this had happened. Eventually, I filed a writ petition. When the petition came up for hearing before the High Court, the Court directed the Deputy Jailor to file an affidavit. In his affidavit, he averred that I had not been beaten at the police station. How he could say that, I do not know. The Deputy Jailor stated, "He had no injuries when he was brought to the jail."

However, there is a High Court finding on the matter. The High Court asked: "If that is the case, why are these injuries present?" The Court also questioned how the Deputy Jailor could state that there was no beating at the police station. The High Court remarked: "Not only that, the Deputy Jailor has filed such an affidavit under pressure. This is very serious. We hope the government will take necessary steps in the matter. At this juncture, which is something peculiar, we are unable to do anything more. Anyhow, we expect that the government will take appropriate action."

Later, I came to know that an inquiry was conducted regarding the incident. But no one ever asked me anything about it. While I was in the hospital, the Kozhikode DIG visited me once. When I asked him whether he had come as part of the inquiry, he said, "No, nothing like that. I just came to meet you when I heard you were here."

To this day, no one has questioned me. I heard that a Member of the Revenue Board was deputed to conduct the inquiry, and I also came to know that the inquiry had been completed. But not even once has anyone approached me or asked me anything. This is my experience!

Let me tell the entire members of this Assembly: we are all politicians, and as part of different groups, we often argue over various issues. But is there any political morality in ordering someone to be taken into a police station and tortured in lock-up? Is that politics? Should I believe that only a single Circle Inspector of Police—or just the Kannur DSP Thomas—had the courage to carry out such an assault? Never! If that had truly been the case, some action would have been taken against them. But no action was taken. Today, Balaraman is the Circle Inspector of Thalassery. On that day, while searching my home, he was not even the Circle Inspector of that area. After beating me up, Balaraman was told: "You go and take over as the Circle Inspector of Thalassery." Is it right?

Therefore, I want to say to the members of this Assembly is this: yes, we are all politicians, and we often argue with each other as part of different blocs. But we should not allow such things to become political weapons. This brings no credit to anyone. I don't believe any of you would truly support this kind of behaviour.

I have just one thing to say to Mr Karunakaran (the Chief Minister at that time). We have argued fiercely on many issues in the past, and we will continue to do so in the future. I had already mentioned this in a letter I sent to C. Achutha Menon. No one can stop us from raising our voices. But is this kind of police brutality what you call politics?

How many workers in the Communist Party have endured such torture? How many have died in lock-ups? How many were shot dead in police firing while leading agitations? How many were stabbed or gunned down by political goons? We know all of this. And yet, we continue working for our cause. We know that anything can happen to us at any moment.

But if someone thinks that torture in custody will silence us forever, they are completely mistaken. Yes, we may be suppressed for a time. But we will return, stronger. We will bounce back with renewed energy. That is all I have to say to Mr Karunakaran.

This is not credible; this is not politics. It is beneath your dignity. Today, you are the Chief Minister. Do you intend to carry this forward? Do you plan to continue in the same manner—letting the police loose on your opponents?

This Circle Inspector ordered multiple lathi-charges in Thalassery on the day votes were being counted—not once, but six or seven times! The votes of our four constituencies—Thalassery, Peringalam, Koothuparamba and Peravoor were being counted there, and thousands of people had gathered. These thousands were lathi-charged again and again, under the orders of this same Circle Inspector.

This is the same "hero" who, just two days before, had made the workers of Opposition parties stand in lock-ups without clothes. The same "hero" who created a horrific scene in the police station—tying nooses around the necks of certain people, and suspending them in the air—only because they were witnesses in a murder case.

At that time, there was a Home Minister to support and protect this Circle Inspector. And today, that same Home Minister is the Chief Minister! You must not carry forward this legacy. You must not follow this tradition. You had been governing by blindly trusting whatever the police tell you. The police claimed I was arrested from the Sivapuram party office. When? At 5.15 a.m.! But I had not visited Sivapuram at any time during that period. Still, the police said it, Mr Karunakaran said it, and the government records state it. But it is not true.

If Opposition party workers cannot engage in political activities with dignity and self-respect in this state, that is a very serious and unfortunate situation.

You must remember the fate of those who once ruled as autocrats. You must learn from their experiences. Not only have they all faded into irrelevance but even those who once guarded and supported them have turned against them.

Did we ever imagine a situation where Vayalar Ravi and Unnikrishnan would demand Sanjay Gandhi's expulsion from the Congress? Yet it happened. Haven't 50 Members of Parliament submitted written demands for his removal? That's the phase our politics has reached. So, you must read the writing on the wall and act accordingly.

Now, what is happening with the Cabinet here in Kerala? In the past, such decisions were made in Delhi—whether the Kerala Congress should be inducted, who should be its chairman, and so on. But what about now? Today, it has become a mono-act. Karunakaran and C. H. Mohammed Koya have taken over the roles of all the ministers. That is the current state of affairs.

Now, careful thought must be given to how long those currently aligned with you will remain loyal. Today, there is no one in Delhi to make decisions for you. So I say to Mr Karunakaran: govern with these realities in mind. This is politics. And when something needs to be said, it will be said—firmly and openly.

Trying to silence the Opposition through police repression will not succeed. It simply won't work. The people's movement in Kerala has always resisted such tactics. Karunakaran should remember the fate of such former police ministers and those who misused the police and sanctioned excesses. Their political careers did not end well. He hould keep that in mind while governing.

That is all I have to say.

I strongly oppose this Vote on Account.

Courtesy: M.P. Veerendra Kumar | *Mathrubhumi*

23

I have no Remorse

K. KARUNAKARAN

(Senior Congress leader, Home Minister of Kerala during the Emergency and Chief Minister four times)

When I look back, I don't feel any remorse. The Emergency was, in my view, a necessity of the time. That was the situation. The anti-government agitation led by Jayaprakash Narayan had created widespread uncertainty and unrest. There were even calls for the bureaucracy and the armed forces to disregard the instructions of the elected government. With no viable alternative to restore order, the declaration of Emergency became inevitable. And it brought a sense of discipline—government offices began functioning punctually, and trains ran on time. The measures taken by the government were intended to restore stability and instil a sense of security among the people.

Fundamental rights do not grant a licence to do anything. Freedom does not mean the liberty to behave whimsically. At that time, the violent tactics of Naxal politics—including public executions—were also prevalent. One of the greatest achievements of the Emergency, in my view, was the complete eradication of Naxal influence from Kerala.

However, there was one aspect of the Emergency I could not agree with: the censorship imposed on newspapers. By restricting the press, the government cut itself off from accurate and timely information. Suppressing freedom of opinion and a free press was a serious mistake.

Rajan's murder was an unfortunate incident that occurred during the Emergency. The police concealed the truth from the public, and the incident continues to cause me great sorrow and regret. In fact, the people had largely accepted the Emergency, in spite of all the criticism surrounding it. This is evidenced by the electoral results that followed, where we secured 20 Parliamentary and 117 Assembly seats—clear indicators of public support at the time.

Today, some people are portraying the events of the Emergency as part of a so-called "second freedom struggle" and are demanding pension and other benefits. In my view, such claims are exaggerated and unwarranted.

Courtesy: M.P. Veerendra Kumar | *Mathrubhumi*

24

A Humble Warning

CHERIAN PHILIP

(On Congress leader A. K. Antony's speech at Guwahati AICC)

The 1976 AICC session held in Guwahati, at the height of the Emergency, was nothing short of a political "Kumbh Mela". A vast stretch of open plains was transformed into a temporary city. Barren hillocks were levelled, and in their place, helipads and palaces were constructed. At the heart of this spectacle stood Jawaharlal Nagar and Yuvak Nagar.

As Indira Gandhi and Sanjay Gandhi were escorted to the venue of the session, thousands of girls with rosy complexion danced along both sides of the road, while choruses in praise of the mother and son echoed through the air. The national convention of the Youth Congress was held at the same location just prior to the AICC session, with Sanjay Gandhi's presence and vision taking centre stage.

The event was extensively covered by television cameras. The whole place was flooded with light. Cameras were constantly clicking. Addressing the gathering at Yuvak Nagar, Indira Gandhi remarked: "The youth have outdone all." She expressed confidence that Sanjay Gandhi's Five-Point Programme would complement her own Twenty-Point Programme, and together, they would bring about a transformative change in the country.

When the session began at Jawaharlal Nagar on 21 November, there was not much enthusiasm among the delegates. Many of the leaders appeared visibly worried. A feeling of foreboding seemed to pervade the atmosphere. The dominant topic of discussion was the possibility that elections might be postponed indefinitely and that the Emergency could continue for several more years. After the flag-hoisting and the inaugural session, a lunch break was announced at noon. The afternoon was scheduled for discussions on the economic resolution. However, a number of delegates from Kerala chose to skip the session and instead departed for a tourist centre in the scenic Shillong valley.

After lunch, A. K. Antony was sitting pensively in his room adjacent to the venue when T. V. R. Shenoy (*Malayala Manorama*), V. K. Madhavan Kutty *(Mathrubhumi)* and N. Raghunathan *(Kerala Kaumudi)* came there. They gave Antony a detailed account of the atrocities being committed, including the Turkman Gate incident. One of them then asked him: "Who will bell the cat?" Antony simply smiled. I was also in the room, listening to their conversation. (I had reached Guwahati as a special correspondent of the *Veekshanam* daily. At that time, I was a 22-year-old student with no formal training in journalism. My only strength was the encouragement I received from C. P. Sreedharan, the editor of *Veekshanam*. I was really flabbergasted by the sight of the session's venue. I would simply jot down whatever came to mind and send it to Kerala. Whenever I had doubts, I would seek help from T.V.R. Shenoy.)

By 3 p.m., Antony reached the venue, accompanied by Oommen Chandy and Sudheeran. A delegate from Mizoram moved the economic resolution, and Congress president D. K. Barooah invited Antony to second it. Antony began his speech in simple English, opening with a foreboding remark: "Something is amiss somewhere." The press contingent was all ears. There was pin-drop silence in the venue. Barooah and Indira Gandhi exchanged uneasy glances. On the dais, a shadow of discomfort passed across Sanjay Gandhi's face.

Antony proceeded to caution against the unhealthy tendencies that had taken root within the Congress organisation. "No one from outside can weaken or defeat the Congress. Only Congressmen can do that," he warned. "Since the declaration of the Emergency, a section of Congressmen has come to believe that they wield special powers. They are acting unilaterally and in an autocratic manner. In many places, the official leadership is misusing its authority. Even certain government officials have begun to think and behave in similar ways.

"I am personally unhappy about the postponement of the elections," Antony declared. "I cannot agree with the view that the elections were deferred to implement the Twenty-Point Programme or to consolidate the gains of the Emergency. It is a wrong and dangerous trend for Congressmen to call for postponing elections for five or ten years. Such propaganda and interpretation are harmful to the fundamental principles of democracy. The Congress must not deviate from the democratic tradition envisaged by Mahatma Gandhi and Jawaharlal Nehru," he added.

Shortly after concluding his address, Antony left the venue. Oommen Chandy, Sudheeran and I followed him. The immediate reaction came from H.N. Bahuguna, who had recently resigned as Chief Minister of Uttar Pradesh: "There is a danger!" he exclaimed. "I adore Antony," he added, without mincing his words.

Tulasidas Dasappa from Karnataka brought a shawl and draped it over Antony's shoulders. Priya Ranjan Dasmunsi hugged Antony warmly. Witnessing all of this, I felt a shiver run down my spine and was swept up in an exuberant mood until Oommen Chandy tapped me on the shoulder and gently reminded me, "Brother, news?"

Soon after, Oommen Chandy came to the press room. According to the Censor's directive, Antony's speech was not to be reported. However, with a quiet resolve to face whatever consequences might come, T.V.R Shenoy, V.K. Madhavan Kutty and N. Raghunathan sent the full text of Antony's speech to their respective offices in Kerala. I also sent it verbatim to *Veekshanam.*

Fearing that the news might not reach Kerala in time, Oommen Chandy made a lightning phone call to P.C. Chacko and informed him about Antony's speech. I went to the residence of Prabhakar

Barooah, a Malayalee in Guwahati town, and called the *Veekshanam* office.

Veekshanam published the full text under the headline "Antony's Warning". *Malayala Manorama, Mathrubhumi* and *Kerala Kaumudi* omitted some portions but conveyed the essence of his speech. *Amrita Bazar Patrika, The Indian Express* and *Deccan Herald* also carried shorter versions.

Courtesy: Cherian Philip, "*Kaalnuttandu*" and *Veekshanam*, and Shri A.K. Antony: Former Defence Minister, former Chief Minister of Kerala, former KPCC President, etc.

25

The Right of That Time

P.K. VASUDEVAN NAIR

(Former Chief Minister of Kerala and CPI leader)

When the Emergency was imposed, our party (the CPI) supported the move. However, the Party Congress held in Bathinda later termed it a mistake. The Emergency was imposed as a way out when Indira Gandhi's government—and more specifically, her prime ministership—faced a serious threat. When the liberation movement was launched under the leadership of Jayaprakash Narayan, it attracted support from communal and reactionary forces such as the Bharatiya Jana Sangh and the Swatantra Party. As adherents of Leftist ideology, we felt it was justified to counter an agitation backed by the very forces we were politically committed to resisting.

However, the Emergency ultimately served to strengthen the autocratic tendencies of Indira Gandhi. The CPI had vehemently opposed the anti-people programmes initiated by Sanjay Gandhi, who rose to prominence during that period.

Later, we came to realise that the Emergency was not imposed to protect democracy or the parliamentary system as enshrined in the Constitution. In my opinion, such a measure should never be repeated. In North India—Sanjay Gandhi's main area of operation—the memories of that period remain a lingering nightmare. But in Kerala, the Emergency failed to create much of an electoral impact. In the 1977 elections, the United Democratic Front (UDF) won all the parliamentary seats in the state, along with 117 out of 140 Assembly seats.

The CPI(M) had supported the anti-Congress front during the Emergency. The CPI later acknowledged supporting the Emergency as a mistake at the Bathinda Party Congress held in 1978. Our party eventually realised that forming an alliance with the Congress was a losing proposition. While it cannot be said with absolute certainty, that policy may well have contributed to a gradual erosion of public support for the CPI.

Courtesy: M.P. Veerendra Kumar | *Mathrubhumi*

26

The Second Freedom Struggle

ARANGIL SREEDHARAN

(Senior Socialist leader and former Union Minister of State for Commerce who was arrested during the initial period of the Emergency)

The Emergency proved the founding fathers of our Constitution wrong in their belief that the democratic structure they envisioned in the Constitution could never be distorted.

While drafting the Constitution, Ambedkar and Nehru never imagined that such a situation could arise. They believed the Indian Constitution would remain secure under all circumstances. But with the declaration of the Emergency, that confidence was shown to be misplaced. During that time, all Opposition leaders were either imprisoned or forced to go underground. I was arrested on 13 July and spent 18 months in Viyyur Central Jail. With leaders from various political parties imprisoned together, there was ample opportunity for exchanging views and ideas.

Before my arrest, people were already considering ways to resist the Emergency. The reaction of Marxist leader A.K. Gopalan (AKG) was particularly inspiring. AKG said that the Emergency was like a venomous serpent that must be killed with whatever stick was available.

I believe the government deliberately chose not to imprison certain CPI(M) leaders. Although many of their leaders, including

EMS, were initially arrested, they were all released after just two days. I could never fully understand the reasoning behind this. Perhaps the government feared that their continued detention might strain relations with the Soviet Union.

The Janata Party was eventually formed following a secret letter sent by Jayaprakash Narayan (JP), urging all Opposition parties to unite and form a common front. That movement played a pivotal role in defeating the Emergency. JP referred to that struggle as the "Second Freedom Movement".

Ironically, it was the largely illiterate population of the northern states that led the charge toward victory. In contrast, Kerala—the most literate state—responded weakly to this blatant violation of human rights and democratic principles. And there is no question of denying the fact that Kerala, in the subsequent elections, ended up supporting the dark forces behind the Emergency.

There could be several reasons for this. One likely factor was that Kerala had a Communist chief minister during the Emergency. The CPI even argued that the discipline imposed by the Emergency was more important than paying employees their bonus! Although Achutha Menon was the official chief minister, K. Karunakaran acted as the *de facto* ruler. There is hardly any possibility of another Emergency in India. But if it ever happens again, I fear many states might choose to separate from the Indian Union.

Courtesy: M.P. Veerendra Kumar | *Mathrubhumi*

27

Unfading Memories

P. PARAMESWARAN

(Director, Bharatheeya Vichara Kendram and former national vice-president, Bharatiya Jana Sangh)

I can hardly believe that 25 years have passed since the Emergency was declared. It's not just the swift passage of time that makes it feel unreal—the memories of that dark chapter remain vivid and haunting. Despite repeated efforts to suppress them, images of painful experiences, acts of inhumanity and cruel faces continue to resurface with unsettling clarity.

However, at this moment, I do not wish to revisit all of those memories—they reflect the demonic side of human nature. But just as there is darkness, there is also light. Amidst those shadows, I also witnessed strong divine qualities that stood out like a silver lining in the storm! Remembering the families and persons who embodied these virtues is a sweet experience.

Kerala was one of the states that bore the brunt of the cruel and naked atrocities during the Emergency. On the very day the Emergency was declared, a notification was issued declaring me a fugitive from the law, and the police began actively searching for me. At the time, I was in poor health, and the organisation decided that I should not surrender. As I required ongoing and consistent medical treatment, the Jana Sangh leadership and workers advised me to move to Tamil Nadu within a few days.

The Emergency was not enforced as harshly in Tamil Nadu. Compared to the rigid approach of Achutha Menon and Karunakaran in Kerala, the Karunanidhi government had taken a relatively softer stance. While public meetings and gatherings were completely banned in Kerala during that period, I distinctly remember attending a massive anti-Emergency rally at Marina Beach in Chennai—as a member of the crowd, quietly listening.

Among the many memories I carry from that time, I have to specifically mention about two families, who took me in and treated me as one of their own. One was a Malayalee family running a small-scale industry in Madras (now Chennai). The other was the family of K. Jana Krishnamurthi who is now the national vice-president of the Bharatiya Janata Party. He lived with his elderly mother, wife, and school-going children. Jana's financial condition was quite modest at the time.

Many persons engaged in underground work during the Emergency would pass through Madras, and I had the opportunity to meet them and gather information, often along with Jana. I also took part in several secret meetings. As my health gradually improved, the leadership decided it was time for me to join the Satyagraha movement in Kerala and surrender to the authorities. Accordingly, I returned to Palakkad and courted arrest.

My prison life, which lasted exactly one year, was spent in Viyyur Central Jail. I was allotted one of the best rooms in the facility. Given the uncertainty surrounding the end of the Emergency and the lingering fear that it might never end, that one year felt unusually long. I shared the room with O. Rajagopal, who is now a Union Minister. Although I had known him for a long time, it was during our imprisonment that I truly came to know him in and out.

Two things about Rajagopal remain vivid in my memory. First, he followed a meticulous daily routine without deviation. His day was structured around physical exercises, prayer, reading, an afternoon nap, and a game of badminton in the evening, more prayer and reading and then retiring to bed. The second was his remarkable equanimity. The difficult financial situation at home, the uncertain future of his two young children and the unpredictability surrounding his release from prison were more than enough to trouble any ordinary person. Yet, to truly appreciate the greatness of the example he set through his equipoise and exceptional presence of mind under such pressure, one only needs to contrast it with the anxious and erratic behaviour displayed by many other political leaders who were imprisoned alongside us.

Another rare and unforgettable experience was the time spent with the late M.P. Manmathan, who was lodged with us for a few days. Those moments offered a glimpse into an eventful life! As he recounted, for hours on end, stories of individuals and events in his own inimitable, humorous style, it felt as though we were journeying through the very history of an era. The fall of the "veils" that once concealed the true nature of many so-called great personalities—and the rise of "ordinary" people to prominence—was a fascinating spectacle to witness.

Another remarkable personality who transformed the otherwise intolerable prison life into something enjoyable and propitious was Swami Mridanandaji of the Thrissur Ramakrishna Ashram. He visited the prison every Wednesday to conduct religious classes, as permitted by the Prison Manual. We eagerly awaited his visits, welcoming him as a true messenger of God. He taught us the 18 chapters of Srimad Bhagavat Gita in great detail. For those of us plagued by restlessness and inner turmoil, his *Gitopadesha* was like a shower of nectar. Later, Swamiji confided that he had never missed a single session, undertaking it entirely of his own volition as a personal mission and a form of penance.

On a personal note, the greatest blessing I received during my imprisonment was the opportunity to write the biography of Mahayogi Aurobindo. That book was later released by K.P. Kesava Menon, editor of *Mathrubhumi,* at a function in Kozhikode—an event that remains vividly etched in my memory.

This article was written in 2000. Courtesy: M.P. Veerendra Kumar | *Mathrubhumi*

28

Quarter of a Century with the Memories of Rajan

PROF. T.V. EACHARA WARRIER

(The father of P. Rajan, the engineering student who died due to police torture during the Emergency)

The declaration of the Emergency was not in the interest of the nation. The country did not require it. It was imposed by Prime Minister Indira Gandhi solely to safeguard her hold on power. Haunted by the fear of losing prime ministership and unnerved by the growing momentum of the Jayaprakash Narayan movement, she resorted to this drastic measure. Thus, on the night of 25 June 1975, the Emergency was declared.

No one had any inkling of such a huge threat. The India that awoke the next morning was no longer the same country that had gone to sleep the night before. The changes that took place overnight were horrible. With censorship clamping down on newspapers, the public had no way of knowing what was truly happening around them.

During the Emergency, two fundamental rights of citizens were outrightly denied: the right to live and the right to know. My son Rajan is the perfect example of the denial of the right to live, while I am a prime example of the denial of the right to know.

It was on 28 February 1976 that the Kayanna Police Station was attacked. The very next day, a camp was set up at Kakkayam, under the command of Jayaram Padikkal. During the attack, a rifle was lost from the police station. In the aftermath, hundreds of youths were interrogated in a desperate search for information about the missing weapon.

When Rajan, who had participated in the Youth Festival held at Farook College, alighted from the bus in front of the college, he was immediately apprehended by the police. Soon after, I came to know that that he had been taken to Kakkayam. But, all my efforts to reach the place failed and I could not get anywhere near it.

The most striking aspect of this, to me, is that even the people in Kozhikode were unaware of the camp at Kakkayam and the events that transpired there until I filed a habeas corpus petition a year later. Meanwhile, the news had reached New York and London. I petitioned repeatedly for information about Rajan, but to no avail. It wasn't until after the Emergency was lifted that I filed a habeas corpus petition in the Supreme Court. Only then did the police finally admit that Rajan had been tortured to death at the Kakkayam Camp. In reality, Rajan had died at 4 a.m. on 2 March 1976, but his death was only officially acknowledged on 22 May 1977. To what extent the right to know was denied, one can imagine.

The only way to safeguard against the recurrence of an Emergency is for the people to remain eternally vigilant. It is true that the Morarji Desai government, which came to power after the Emergency, made it more difficult to impose such a regime by amending certain clauses of the Constitution. However, loopholes still remain. Therefore, it is only through constant public vigilance that we can prevent the return of those dark and repressive days.

Courtesy: M.P. Veerendra Kumar | *Mathrubhumi*

29

The First Arrest

U. DATTATREYA RAO

(BJP leader and former state vice president, Bharatiya Jana Sangh)

Even after 25 years, U. Dattatreya Rao continues to live with the haunting memories of the dreaded atrocities of the Emergency. He was arrested at 2 a.m. on 3 July 1975—making his the first arrest in Kozhikode after the Emergency was declared on 25 June.

Rao had led the protest marches and agitations against the Emergency in Kozhikode during the first week of its declaration. At that time, he was the state committee member of the Bharatiya Jana Sangh, the printer and publisher of the evening daily *Janmabhumi*, and managing director of the publishing company Matruka Pracharanalayam.

Rao was then residing near the Third Railway Gate. In the early hours of 3 July, a police team led by the Superintendent of Police (SP) Lakshmana surrounded his house. When the policemen knocked on the window with the baton, Rao awoke and opened the door, dressed in only a vest and a single dhoti. The police tied his hands behind his back and blindfolded him.

As bitumen for roadwork was heaped in front of his gate, the police van was parked some distance away. Rao was then literally dragged over the heap of bitumen to the vehicle. He was taken to the SP's office near Mananchira grounds and forced to sit on the floor of a room. There, he was interrogated about the whereabouts of K. G. Marar and O. Rajagopal. When he refused to respond, he was subjected to brutal torture—the soles of his feet were continuously beaten with a police baton until the policeman grew exhausted.

Then they laid him on the floor and began rolling a baton along his legs, from his ankles up to his knees. When he screamed at the top of his voice that the police were killing him, they tore off his vest and stuffed it into his mouth. One of the policemen then sat on his chest and sealed his mouth with his hands. By that point, Rao had passed out.

When he regained his consciousness, he found himself in a police lock-up. The station—what is now the Medical College Police Station—was still under construction. The cement floor of the room where he had been left was damp with water. The soles of his feet had turned blue from internal bleeding, and he was unable to walk. Senior officers came and interrogated him further. For the next two days, Rao survived on nothing but water from a tap.

At one point, Rao heard Nalarajan, the office secretary of the Bharatiya Jana Sangh, and Rajasekharan of the *Kesari* weekly talking in the adjacent room. Then they too were shifted elsewhere. On the evening of 5 July, he was taken blindfolded to the SP office. "SP Lakshmana got my detention order signed. Then, an SI carrying a pistol, along with three rifle-armed constables, escorted me in a police van to Thiruvananthapuram," he recalled.

It was only upon reaching Thiruvananthapuram that he had his first meal in three days. The prison doctor examined him and prescribed medication. Rao was unable to walk for nearly three months due to the severity of his injuries.

Rao spent six months in Thiruvananthapuram prison before being shifted to Thrissur prison, where he remained for 13 more months. Finally, in late January 1977, he was released, and thus ended a harrowing chapter in his life.

Courtesy: M.P. Veerendra Kumar | *Mathrubhumi*

30

Emergency Experience

M.P. VEERENDRA KUMAR

[Former Union Minister, managing director of *Mathrubhumi* and state president JD(U)]

Advocate P.S. Sreedharan Pillai is a blessed and talented personality. Though professionally a lawyer, he also possesses the soul of a sincere poet and the mind of a serious intellectual. His latest work, *Dark Days of Democracy*, reflects his inquisitiveness and analytical acumen. Pillai, who is also a senior leader of the BJP, offers the following reflections on the Emergency period (25 June 1975 to 21 March 1977):

"Fascism and autocracy were unified and imposed upon the people through the Emergency, causing serious damage to the nation's constitutional machineries. The bedrock of democracy and freedom was shattered using draconian laws and widespread oppression. Press freedom, an essential lifeline for any democracy, was destroyed through blatant censorship. Around 3,000 media houses were forced to shut down due to brutal repression. This speaks volumes about the horrifying atmosphere that was prevalent during the Emergency."

Indira Gandhi, the then Prime Minister of India, declared the Emergency on 25 June1975, against the backdrop of complex challenges faced by her government. Quoting a spokesperson of the Union Government, the media reported that "internal disturbances affecting the national security" led the President to declare

Emergency under Article 352 of the Constitution. Fakhruddin Ali Ahmed was the President of India during that period.

The Constitution permits the declaration of an Emergency not only in the event of war, external aggression, or armed rebellion, but also when the President is satisfied that such a threat is imminent. Unfortunately, none of these conditions existed or prevailed in our country at that time. The Emergency was declared simply because Indira Gandhi's supremacy and authority were being questioned.

Indira Gandhi, in her speech on 26 June 1975 while addressing the nation, stated: "When rebellious forces come to the forefront inciting communal hatred, posing a threat to the unity of the nation, and thereby adversely affecting the internal security of the country, a constitutional machinery such as the government can 'not' sit back and watch the proceedings." Without any delay, around 700 people, including Opposition leaders, were arrested. This was just the beginning, as arrests continued and jails were soon flooded with detenues.

The actual reason behind the declaration of the Emergency was the judgment of the Allahabad High Court in a case challenging Indira Gandhi's election from Raebareli constituency in the 1971 general elections. Raj Narain, who had lost to Indira Gandhi in Raebareli, filed an election petition alleging corruption and other malpractices. The said petition was allowed with cost, and Indira Gandhi was barred from contesting in any State Assembly or Lok Sabha elections for a period of six years.

When Indira Gandhi approached the Supreme Court to challenge the High Court judgment, the matter was considered by Justice V.R. Krishna Iyer, who was presiding over the vacation bench. Although the court stayed the impugned judgment, it clarified that Indira Gandhi could only participate in parliamentary proceedings and did not have any voting rights.

Pursuant to this, Jayaprakash Narayan and other Opposition leaders demanded her resignation on moral and ethical grounds. They also threatened to organise *satyagraha*s and *dharna*s across the country if she refused to step down. Even the "Young Turks" of the Congress, such as Chandra Shekhar and Mohan Dharia, took a tough stand against the Prime Minister. In this context, Indira Gandhi realised that it would be nearly impossible to conduct the upcoming Parliament session scheduled for July. Consequently, she initiated the declaration of the Emergency.

Pillai observed that during the Emergency, citizens could not even approach the courts to protect their right to life, freedom of speech and expression, or basic human rights. According to Justice Shah Commission, which was appointed after the Emergency to investigate the atrocities committed during that period, 1,12,890 people were imprisoned under laws such as MISA, DIR and COFEPOSA Act. The author cited several other instances to highlight the horrors of the Emergency and the resulting infringement of personal liberty.

It is also noteworthy that Pillai, who was a student during the Emergency, was at the forefront of the protests against it. He has also conducted a detailed study of the comprehensive movement led by Jayaprakash Narayan during that time.

Many of our national leaders, including Mahatma Gandhi, had recognised the soul of this beautiful country, India. Through their actions, they sought to embody the virtues of truth and honesty. Jayaprakash Narayan belonged to that extraordinary lineage. Pillai has portrayed Lok Nayak Jayaprakash Narayan as the very embodiment of dedication and sacrifice for the nation.

Jayaprakash Narayan, fondly known as JP—and once hailed by Jawaharlal Nehru as the "Future Prime Minister of India"— worked relentlessly for the upliftment of millions of poor people across the country. Initially, he pursued his vision through initiatives like the "Sarvodaya Movement". However, realising the limitations of these efforts, he laid the groundwork for the "Total Revolution" in the 1970s, mobilising students and youth organisations to support this larger cause.

Another reason for the declaration of the Emergency was the realisation that JP's "Total Revolution", which began as a movement against corruption, exploitation, injustice, violence, favouritism and autocracy in Bihar, had struck the nation like a tornado. JP launched this movement to ensure the comprehensive upliftment of all sections of society, thereby delivering social, economic and political justice to the public at large. Pillai further notes that JP believed that this "Total Revolution" could be achieved without resorting to violence or anarchy.

JP sought to remind the nation that democracy includes the people, not just those in power. "Democracy," he said, "contains two elements – one of the people and the other of power. But if power alone survives without the people, can it still be called a democracy? What would you call it then? It would simply be the supremacy of a single party – never a democracy. We have sent you to the Assembly or Parliament not to loot us or betray us, but to work honestly and serve the public responsibly. Have you gone there just to feed yourselves? The people also have the right to recall their representatives." JP's words were fuming on moral grounds.

Pillai has also highlighted the revolutionary work of socialist leader George Fernandes during the Emergency. "If we are dying, then we will die with pride" were the words of my close friend and colleague George Fernandes. He believed that even violence could be resorted to in order to achieve one's ultimate goals. Pillai observed the following about him:

"George Fernandes' fight was against autocracy. The core group he formed for this purpose included film actress Snehalatha Reddy, M. S. Appa Rao, C. G. K. Reddy, Viren Shah, journalist Vikram Rao, Prabhudas Patwari among others. George Fernandes also had significant influence in the socialist parties of Kerala. Socialist leaders like Arangil Sreedharan and M.P. Veerendra Kumar were booked under MISA. Veerendra Kumar, who went underground, was eventually arrested after his assets were attached and a non-bailable warrant was issued against him. George Fernandes remained in hiding for nearly a year, continuing his fight against the Emergency without being arrested.

"Snehalatha Reddy, the trusted aide of George Fernandes, sacrificed her life in the struggle against the Emergency. She had earned national acclaim for her performance in the Kannada film *Samskara.* She was a very beautiful and healthy woman, but the continuous torture had taken a toll on her health. She passed away on the fifth day after her release."

Pillai also discusses in detail the atrocities committed in Kerala during the Emergency. Engineering student Rajan had to sacrifice his life during this time. Rajan's father, Prof. Eachara Warrier, tirelessly searched for his son, who had gone missing during the Emergency. Finally, Prof. Warrier discovered that his son had died due to continued torture. Pillai also references Eachara Warrier's words from his book, *Memories of a Father*, in which he states, "The greatest atrocity committed during Emergency is the infringement of two facets of human right, i.e., right to live and right to information." The tragedy that befell his son serves as a prime example of the violation of the right to live. However, Warrier further emphasised that this tragedy also occurred due to the denial of the right to information.

Pillai also shares a personal experience related to the Rajan case. "In the suit filed by Shri Eachara Warrier at the Sub Court, Kozhikode, claiming damages from state for the death of his son, Pillai was among one of the lawyers who appeared for the claimant. Though tired and grief-stricken, Warrier finally won the case. A substantial portion of the damages awarded to him was used by him to construct a new ward in the General Hospital, Ernakulam, and to help the needy. Eachara Warrier, who fought the menace of the Emergency through self-sacrifice, has engraved his name as a humanitarian whose name cannot be erased from the history."

Let me share a few of my personal experiences as someone who directly faced the consequences of the Emergency. On the day the Emergency was declared, I was in Ernakulam along with my Socialist Party colleagues—Arangil Sreedharan, K.K. Abu Sahib, K. Chandrasekharan, and Viswambaran. At that time, Arangil Sreedharan was the state president of the party, I was one of the national general secretaries, and George Fernandes was the all India chairman. We were in Ernakulam for two days to attend the party's state conference. A joint meeting of the Opposition parties in the state was also convened, for which I was the convener of the committee.

The Opposition at the time consisted of the Socialist Party, CPI(M), Kerala Congress led by K.M. George, Congress (S) and All India Muslim League. Prominent leaders from these parties had also arrived in Ernakulam for the meeting. Socialist party leader Madhu Dandavate, MP, who was en route to attend the Parliamentary Committee meeting in Bangalore, had also reached Ernakulam that evening. It was late at night on 25 June that we learnt about the declaration of the Emergency from the *Deshabhimani* office. It was unbelievable! People from various parts of the country were already arrested. We were certain that more arrests would follow soon.

We understood that the constitutionally guaranteed rights had been taken away by the Central government. As a result, media censorship was imposed and people were being imprisoned. The MISA law, which empowered the Union government to detain anyone even without a trial, had been in existence well before the declaration of the Emergency. At the time, the government had claimed that the law would be used only against smugglers, black money holders, hoarders, and other economic offenders. However, quite conspicuously, after the Emergency was declared, many leaders—including JP—were arrested and jailed under MISA.

The Socialist Party decided to protest against the Emergency, regardless of the consequences. Arangil Sreedharan, Abu Sahib and Chandrasekharan issued a joint statement ridiculing the declaration of the Emergency and the violations of constitutional provisions. We then proceeded to Thrissur, where the party district committee had convened a meeting. Congress (O) leader Shankara Narayanan also accompanied us. During the journey, we noticed a police jeep following us. It became clear that we were under surveillance and could be arrested at any moment. However, we were not arrested that day. We reached Thrissur and, in the meeting, resolved to oppose the Emergency with full vigour. Afterwards, we proceeded to Kozhikode.

JP was arrested immediately. Socialist leaders like Raj Narain, Madhu Dandavate, Ramakrishna Hegde, J.H. Patel and Congress leaders like Chandra Shekhar, Mohan Dharia and other Young Turks were already arrested. Condemning the arrest, JP described the declaration of the Emergency as "*Vinasha Kaale Vipareetha Budhi*" (when destruction approaches, wisdom fails).

We noticed that people were slowly developing a sense of insecurity. Many fell silent. Even harmless comments were not uttered, fearing dire consequences. We witnessed how an entire society was becoming clouded and eclipsed by fear. The most frightening aspect of life during the Emergency was that a person could be restrained and detained without any particular reason.

P.K. Sankarankutty, V. Kuttikrishnan Nair, Abu Sahib and I had gathered at Arangil Sreeedharan's house. Party workers were deeply disturbed and infuriated. We decided that some of us would court arrest while others would go underground.

On 3 July, a joint Opposition meeting was convened, attended by leaders like A.K. Gopalan (AKG), EMS, K. Shankara Narayanan and Arangil Sreedharan. It was also decided to organise a protest march and picketing in front of the collectorates on 9 July. By then, various Opposition leaders had already been arrested. We later came to know that Arangil Sreedharan was arrested and taken to Viyyur Central Jail. Abu Sahib and I then went underground.

CPI(M) Parliamentary Party leader AKG personally advised me to go underground and continue protesting against the Emergency. I had met AKG on two or three occasions during those dark days. He extended great support to me during that time, and I have even written about those experiences.

During the course of my forced secret activities, the government decided to seize and attach my assets. Leaders from the Socialist Party, CPI(M), Jana Sangh, IUML, Congress (O) and Kerala Congress were arrested. Eventually, I was arrested and detained at

Kannur Central Jail. Leaders such as Pinarayi Vijayan, Kodiyeri Balakrishnan, Syed Ummer Bafakhi Thangal, M.V. Raghavan, and Cheriya Mammukkey were imprisoned along with me. V.S. Achuthananthan was in Poojappura Jail, while P. Parameshwarji and Arangil Sreedharan were held in Viyyur Jail. Jana Sangh leaders like K.G. Marar, O. Rajagopal, U. Dattatreya Rao and P.P. Mukundan were also imprisoned. Dattatreya Rao had sustained serious injuries due to police torture.

Setting aside all differences, the Opposition parties of India, along with progressive thinkers of the ruling party, stood united for the common cause of resisting the Emergency. This resistance was often described as India's second freedom struggle. If the government had declared the Emergency to keep its powers intact, the people rejected it through a silent rebellion.

When elections were declared in 1977, parties that protested against the Emergency such as the Socialist Party, the Jana Sangh, Bharatiya Kranti Dal, Swatantra Party and Congress (O) joined hands. Senior Congress leader Jagjivan Ram also allied with these parties. The Congress Party could win only a single seat in the whole of North India. Indira Gandhi received a befitting blow from the people of our country for dismantling our democracy. Ironically, she was defeated by Raj Narain! It is now part of history that Morarji Desai became the Prime Minister of India, and the five parties that fought together against the Emergency had jointly formed the Janata Party.

Pillai has included various analytical articles in this book. He has independently and in an unbiased manner analysed and recollected the history of the gruesome horrors of the Emergency and the historic protests by the people against it. It is a warning against autocratic and fascist tendencies and also a reminder of those bitter memories.

This is a true translated copy of the foreword written by Shri M.P. Veerendra Kumar for the author's Malayalam book on the Emergency, published by *Mathrubhumi*

PART- IV

ANNEXURES

Annexure - I

The Shah Commission Final Report: Summary of Findings, Observations and Recommendations

Chapter i

It outlines the terms of reference, details about the Commission's staff, the methodology followed by the Commission for categorising complaints and the approach adopted to initiate its work.

Chapter ii

This chapter includes the text of the Emergency proclamation along with important statutory provisions enacted thereafter.

Chapter iii

This chapter outlines the procedure followed by the Commission and its decision on objections raised concerning that procedure. The important findings are:

i. The proceedings of the Commission are neither of the nature of a civil suit nor of the nature of a criminal proceeding.

ii. The functions of the Commission under the Commissions of Inquiry Act are of an entirely different nature. The Commission is not concerned with the establishment of any civil rights or the infraction of those rights. The Commission is also not concerned to determine the infraction of any laws involving the imposition of any penalty upon a person charged with the commission of an infraction of a law. The proceedings are not of an adversary character. The Commission's duty is to conduct an inquiry into the subject matter of the enquiry when the subject matter is of definite public importance.

iii. The proceedings before the Commission will be "inquisitorial" in nature, meaning that the presiding officer takes upon himself the duty to ascertain the facts through witnesses, while also providing opportunity to persons concerned who may be affected by the determination of those facts.

iv. There is no warrant for the view that, once a notice under Section 8B is issued, the Commission is no longer obligated to issue a notice under Rule 5(2) (a), or that the issuance of a summons under Section 8B dispenses with the requirement of a notice under Rule 5(2) (a).

v. The proceedings before the Commission are aimed at determining the truth through a procedure devised by the Commission, based on the nature of the inquiry and essentially inquisitorial in character, as prescribed by the Act.

vi. The Commission rejected the contention that the appropriate procedure required it to issue a summons under Section 8B immediately after a witness, during the preliminary hearing, made a statement implicating a person in the commission of some impropriety, and that it had no option to act otherwise.

vii. Under Rule 5(2) (a), the Commission is under a statutory obligation to call upon persons who, in its opinion, should be given an opportunity to be heard, to furnish a statement relating to such matters as may be specified in the notice. This obviously does not mean that merely because a person is given an opportunity to be heard in an inquiry, they should not also be required to furnish to the Commission a statement relating to the matters as may be specified in the notice.

viii. Section 8B confers basic protection to any person by ensuring that they shall not be condemned without being heard by the Commission—that is, their conduct shall not be adversely commented upon, nor their version disbelieved, without first being given an opportunity to be heard.

ix. The proceedings of the Commission are not analogous to proceedings in a civil trial or enforcement of a civil right or obtaining relief for infringement of a civil right, nor of a criminal trial in which the conduct of a person or persons for the commission or infraction of the law is sought to be investigated. The function of the Commission is to determine facts relating to matters of public importance and by adoption of a procedure, which is not adversary in character, but inquisitorial in character.

x. The oath of secrecy taken by a Union Minister does not prohibit a minister from disclosing information before a Commission of Inquiry, particularly when the Central government has instituted the inquiry for the purpose of ascertaining facts relating to matters of public interest.

xi. The disclosure of information before a Commission of Inquiry, held in pursuance of a direction of the Central government, does not amount to a breach of the oath of secrecy of a minister, even after they have ceased to hold office.

Chapter iv

In this chapter, the Commission outlines the structure of the report and briefly describes the types of instances and activities examined. The general principle guiding the Commission has been that the excess complained of must be of such a nature that it could create a crisis of confidence or be of national importance.

Chapter v

Circumstances leading to the declaration of the Emergency on 25 June 1975:

i. Following the Allahabad High Court's judgment setting aside the election of Indira Gandhi, there was a surge of political activity, particularly in Delhi and across the rest of India.
ii. Apparently, Indira Gandhi's supporters made an effort to create an atmosphere in which she could continue to remain and function as Prime Minister. With that objective in mind, they organised numerous demonstrations, rallies and meetings in Delhi and other parts of India.
iii. Instructions were given at a meeting held at Raj Niwas, Delhi, that the DTC should provide full cooperation by arranging buses to transport people participating in rallies organised to express solidarity with the then Prime Minister.
iv. The standard procedure for private bookings, such as submitting an application in the prescribed form and making advance payment, was not observed by the DTC in the case of the bookings made by the AICC.
v. The number of buses booked between 12 and 25 June 1975 on hire was much above the normal booking allowed for private purposes.

vi. On 13 June 1975, the entire fleet of 983 buses plying on Delhi routes was taken off the roads and redirected to converge on the Prime Minister's house. In addition, residents of Haryana, Punjab, Rajasthan and Uttar Pradesh were sent in vehicles commandeered by the state authorities for this purpose. A large majority of these vehicles from neighbouring states failed to comply with the Route Permit Rules under the Motor Vehicles Act, and in many cases, government vehicles were used without payment.

vii. The DTC records clearly corroborate the testimony of witnesses that government employees were pressed into service to organise these rallies.

viii. Government organisations such as the DTC, the New Delhi Municipal Committee, and the Delhi Electric Supply Undertaking (DESU) also participated in these rallies.

ix. Under the Motor Vehicles Act, route permits were required for sending vehicles outside the Union Territory of Delhi, which was not done. Police authorities and the state transport officials had been specifically briefed and instructed to ensure that the buses crossed the border without the necessary route permits.

x. The state of affairs was not different in Punjab.

xi. In Rajasthan, according to records of the Rajasthan State Electricity Board, 58 trucks belonging to the Board were ordered by the Chief Minister to be placed at the disposal of the Workers' Union.

xii. Some employees of the DESU who refused to participate in the rallies were allegedly assaulted by overzealous supporters of the Prime Minister.

xiii. ... the law was also applied discriminatorily in favour of the Congress Party. The enforcement of prohibitory orders under Section 144 of the Criminal Procedure Code, which had become routine in the vicinity of the Prime Minister's residence, was selectively relaxed to allow demonstrations and rallies organised by the Congress Party in support of the Prime Minister.

xiv. The Intelligence Bureau (IB) was reportedly used to maintain surveillance on the activities of certain Congress leaders and ministers. This raises a very important issue regarding the infringement of individual privacy—even that of government ministers—for purposes not strictly related to national security.

xv. The decision to take certain drastic steps, including the declaration of the Emergency, was apparently contemplated as early as 22 June 1975.

xvi. Efforts were also made to prevent some newspapers from publishing their morning editions on 26 June 1975.

xvii. To varying degrees, the Chief Ministers of several states were taken into confidence as early as the morning of 25 June. They were instructed to take action upon receiving advice from the Prime Minister's residence that night.

xviii. Some of the special features, as gathered from official records, which may have a bearing on the proclamation of the Emergency are as follows:

  a. On the economic front, there was nothing alarming.
  b. Fortnightly reports on law and order indicated that the situation was under complete control across the country.
  c. No reports were received by the Home Ministry from state governments indicating any deterioration in the law and order situation in the period immediately preceding the proclamation of the Emergency.
  d. The Home Ministry had not prepared any plans regarding the imposition of Internal Emergency prior to 25 June 1975.

e. The IB had not submitted any report suggesting that the internal situation in the country warranted the imposition of an Internal Emergency.

f. The Home Ministry did not submit any report to the Prime Minister expressing concern or anxiety about the internal security situation.

g. Senior officers such as the Home Secretary, the Cabinet Secretary and the Secretary to the Prime Minister had not been taken into confidence about the intended proclamation of Emergency. However, R.K. Dhawan, the then Additional Private Secretary to the Prime Minister, was involved in the preparations for its promulgation from an early stage.

h. Om Mehta, Minister of State for Home Affairs, was taken into confidence much earlier than Home Minister Brahmananda Reddy. Only some Chief Ministers and the Lt. Governor of Delhi were informed in advance about the imposition of the Emergency.

xix. It is not clear how provision (clause e (ii)) of the Second Schedule of the Government of India (Transaction of Business) Rules, 1961, read with Rule 7 of these rules, could have been circumvented through the application of Rule 12 of the same rules (Para 5.65).

xx. The responsibility for matters relating to the Emergency provisions of the Constitution lies with the Home Ministry. Therefore, any proposal concerning the proclamation of an Emergency should ordinarily have originated from that ministry. However, the Cabinet Secretariat did not receive any such proposal from the Home Ministry in connection with the proclamation issued on 25 June 1975.

xxi. Even in 1971, when a war was being waged with Pakistan, a proclamation of the Emergency was issued without invoking Rule 12 of the Transaction of Business Rules. In that instance, a regular meeting of the Council of Ministers was convened, and the proclamation was issued only after obtaining the approval of the Home Minister.

xxii. The circumstances leading to the declaration of the Emergency, pursuant to the advice of Prime Minister Indira Gandhi, leave little room for doubt that the decision to impose Emergency … was exclusively hers. None of her Cabinet Ministers, except for Brahmananda Reddy, was even aware of the proposal … Even he, the Home Minister, was not consulted in the true sense; he was merely informed shortly before the advice was tendered and was involved only to the extent of providing a formal letter.

xxiii. In the Commission's view, the Constitution neither contemplates the proclamation of a fresh Emergency while one is already in effect, nor does it prevent the courts from entertaining any challenge to the declaration of such an additional Emergency. However, the provisions of the Constitution were amended by the 39th Amendment of the Constitution Act which prevented a challenge being raised. This was more in the nature of a shock treatment than a legally permissible Emergency, which could be declared according to the law then in force.

xxiv. If, however, an internal Emergency could be declared apart from the external Emergency, the powers which were exercised before any Rules were framed, i.e., disconnecting the electricity connections of newspaper offices, was wholly unauthorised, since there was no law which conferred upon any authority such power. Again, the action taken by the authorities under the directions of the Prime Minister to arrest a number of political leaders was not supported by any law.

xxv. Surveillance of political leaders and others—including the tapping of their telephones—raises a serious issue of public importance. Such powers, if they are to exist at all, must be exercised only when authorised by statutory provisions and strictly limited to circumstances necessary to safeguard the State in grave situations such as internal disturbance, external aggression or war, and not at other times.

xxvi. It would certainly be a travesty of the democratic institutions if the government were constituted by a political party who are entitled to watch the activities of other political parties and even other members of its own party. If, however, such power is to be conferred on this institution (Intelligence Bureau), it must be by a statute or statutory rules authorising it in that behalf. This watch of the Intelligence agency on individuals and the materials collected thereby should be open to scrutiny to a Board or a Panel composed of officers or of public men before authorising the continuance of the watch. It should be possible to harmonise the demands of the security of the State with the democratic liberties.

xxvii. Considering the stakes that are involved in the proper and purposeful functioning of the IB, it is imperative that it gets the benefit of advice, guidance and wisdom of a body of eminent, experienced and patriotic group of individuals drawn from different disciplines and whose loyalty and personal integrity can never be called into question. This in turn will generate the requisite faith and confidence of the citizens of the country in this very important institution on the fair, correct and proper functioning of which alone would eventually depend the safety, the security and the liberty of the people of this country.

xxviii. The Intelligence Bureau should not be entitled to act as a super-watchman over the activities of politicians. The activities of the Intelligence Bureau should be subject to regulation and control insofar as these activities concern some of the clandestine parts which have come to the notice of the Commission, to ensure that this does not degenerate into misuse or abuse of authority.

xxix. The Commission recommends that appropriate safeguards are necessary and should be devised by the government so as to protect the activities in the Intelligence Bureau being used as an instrument of political spying either by the government or by someone in the government. This issue has been raised to concentrate attention and, if considered appropriate, to generate public debate on the question.

xxx. It is also necessary to invite attention to the misuse of Air Force aircraft. It appears that for the benefit of individuals for travelling on State duty or for State work, Indian Air Force aircraft have been used surreptitiously and, according to the existing Rules, those persons were not entitled to the use of the Aircraft. The Commission recommends to the Government the framing of appropriate Rules in this behalf and also to scrutinise whether the use of the aircraft on 25 June 1975 in the circumstances was warranted and, if not, whether bills for charges appropriate were duly tendered and, if not tendered, to identify those responsible for breach of the Rules.

xxxi. Attention may also be invited to the gross irregularities to which the provisions of the Maintenance of Internal Security Act and provisions of the Defence of India Rules were misused to the detriment of political opponents.

xxxii. The manner in which the provisions of MISA were used was nothing short of perversion and mockery of its provisions, and all the safeguards and guarantees that had been promised in the Parliament when the MISA Bill was enacted were totally disregarded. Many apprehensions, which were expressed by the Members of Parliament, who spoke against the conferment of such wide powers when the Bill was enacted, came true.

xxxiii. The safeguards enshrined in the enactment were rendered meaningless by the callous misapplication of this Act by the police and the Magistracy. It needs to be made clear to all those responsible for overseeing the correct application of the powers of arrest/detention by the junior officers that the senior functionaries at the bureaucratic and political levels would be held directly accountable for any misuse or abuse of the powers of arrest and detention.

Chapter vi

The working of the Media of Information under the Information and Broadcasting Ministry during the Emergency

I. *Censorship*

i. During the two or three days when the censorship apparatus was being set up, power supply to the newspaper offices in Delhi remained disrupted.

ii. The guidelines issued by the Chief Censor exceeded the scope of the Rule 48 of the Defence and Internal Security of India Rules insofar as they prevented editors leaving editorial columns blank or filling them with quotations from great works of literature or from national leaders like Mahatma Gandhi, or Rabindranath Tagore. The Information and Broadcasting Ministry did not attempt to find out whether these guidelines were within the scope of Defence and Internal Security of India Rules or not.

iii. Parliament and court proceedings were also subject to censorship.

iv. Not merely was the publication of court judgments censored, but directions were also given as to how judgments should be published.

v. The actual work of censorship on a day-to-day basis went even beyond the scope of the guidelines. Orders were arbitrary in nature, capricious and were usually issued orally without any relation to the provisions of Rule 48.

vi. In practice, censorship was utilised for suppressing news unfavourable to the government, to play up news favourable to the government and to suppress news unfavourable to the supporters of the Congress Party.

vii. In *one* instance at least, for the magazine *Mainstream*, pre-censorship orders were issued particularly because of its critical attitude towards Sanjay Gandhi.

viii. Even after the elections were announced and censorship was relaxed, the government tried to pressurise the press by giving informally "off the record" warnings by veiled threats of what would happen to them after the elections if they did not comply with the directions of the government.

ix. During the Emergency, legislation was enacted to make censorship a part of the ordinary law of the land. Thus, the Prevention of Publication of Objectionable Matter Act was passed, the Press Council of India was abolished by an Ordinance and a Bill repealing the Parliamentary Proceedings (Protection of Publication) Act, 1956 was passed.

II. *Other pressures on the Press*

i. V. C. Shukla, at a Coordination Committee meeting held on 29 June 1976, asked the Principal Information Officer to prepare a list of newspapers which were to be categorised as friendly, neutral and hostile.

ii. The grading of friendly, neutral and hostile given to a particular newspaper was related to its views on a particular political party.

iii. Political consideration was one of the criteria for giving advertisements.

iv. Contrary to the policy enunciated by the government on the floor of Parliament, political considerations were taken into account while releasing advertisements.

v. The government utilised its advertising policy as a source of financial assistance to newspapers or denial of financial assistance, etc., in complete variance with the policy which it had enunciated in the Parliament.

III. *Formation and functioning of Samachar*

i. During the Emergency, both the administrative and editorial functioning of *Samachar* (news agency) was supervised by the government.

ii. Accreditation of several correspondents was terminated, with the majority of these decisions being taken as part of a review process.

iii. K. N. Prasad also admitted that, at the instance of the Minister, the character and antecedents of a number of journalists were verified by the Intelligence Bureau.

IV. *Functioning of government media units*

i. The government media units had two main functions during the Emergency. They were at once a source of patronage and they were also used for building up the image of a political party and a few of its leaders.

ii. The D.A.V.P. was used on a large scale for giving advertisements to support the various souvenirs brought out by the Congress Party. Opposition parties were denied any such patronage.

iii. Not merely was the Congress Party given extensive advertising support, but there was an instance when rates per page for souvenirs were increased after they had been agreed upon and the souvenirs printed.

iv. The slant against the Opposition was so obvious that in December 1976, AIR bulletins devoted 2,207 lines to the spokesmen of the Congress Party as against 34 lines to the Opposition.

v. After the change of criteria, three part-time correspondents were appointed to AIR, all of whom were office-bearers of the Congress Party.

vi. A number of films were produced by the Films Division to project the image of Sanjay Gandhi not only as a youth leader, but as a leader in his own right.

vii. A number of multimedia campaigns were launched during the Emergency to coincide with important milestones in Indira Gandhi's career.

viii. The Publications Division was directed to boost the sales of Indira Gandhi's books and to publish informative and interesting sketches with photographs of Indira Gandhi in various journals and periodicals.

Chapter vii – Specific Cases

I. *Case regarding the reversion of Justice Aggarwal of the Delhi High Court*

   i. The order passed against Aggarwal was *prima facie* in the nature of an order of punishment for participating in the hearing in Kuldip Nayar's case and passing an order which tarnished the image of the government in the public eyes.

   ii. A case of misuse of authority and abuse of power is disclosed in this case against Indira Gandhi.

II. *Refusal by Indira Gandhi to extend the term of Justice U. R. Lalit of the Bombay High Court*

   Refusal to extend the term of U. R. Lalit as a Judge of the High Court amounted to subversion of well-established conventions and practices and amounted to abuse of authority and misuse of power by Indira Gandhi.

III. *Deviation from established procedure and irregularities in the appointment of K. R. Puri as Governor of the Reserve Bank of India*

The normal and established procedure in regard to the appointment of the Governor of the Reserve Bank of India was not followed, and the Finance Minister, C. Subramaniam, was virtually compelled to fall in line with the suggestion made by Indira Gandhi. This was yet another case of subversion of established administrative procedure and convention by Indira Gandhi.

IV. *Subversion of lawful processes and well-established conventions in the appointment of T. R. Varadachary as Chairman of the State Bank of India*

i. The Commission gave a ruling that by giving any information before it, Minister of Revenue and Banking Pranab Mukherjee would not be violating either the provisions of the Official Secrets Act or the oath of office taken by him.

ii. In the light of the consistent practice and in the light of the nature of the oral testimony of Sen Gupta and Mukherjee, the Commission is of the view that there was no consultation with the Reserve Bank in this case, as was required in terms of sub-clause (a) of sub-section (1) of section 19 of the State Bank of India Act, 1955.

iii. The normal established procedure in regard to the appointment of the Chairman of the State Bank of India was not followed in this case. Further, it was not in accordance with the provisions of the State Bank of India Act, 1955, which made consultation with the Reserve Bank of India, a condition precedent to the appointment of the Chairman by the Central government. The Commission is of the view that considerations other than strictly professional and totally extraneous have unfortunately been allowed to operate in arriving at the decision to appoint Varadachary. Pranab Mukherjee had violated established administrative conventions and procedures and misused his position in the appointment of Varadachary.

V. *Deviation from established procedure and irregularities in the appointment of T. R. Tuli as Chairman and Managing Director of Punjab National Bank*

i. Before arriving at this decision to appoint the Chairman of a comparatively small bank in the private sector to the senior most position in one of the biggest public sector banks in the country, no effort was made to consider the suitability for this post, of senior managers within the public sector banking system itself as had been done in several other instances.

ii. This is yet another instance where the then Finance Minister, C. Subramaniam, was virtually compelled to fall in line with the suggestion made by the then Prime Minister, Indira Gandhi, and that such compulsion amounted to abuse of authority by the former Prime Minister. It clearly resulted in the subversion of well-established conventions.

VI. *Deviation from the established procedure for the selection of officers for top-level executive posts in public sector undertakings, in the case of Lt. Gen. J.T. Satarawala, as Chairman-cum-Managing Director, India Tourism Development Corporation*

It is not a healthy convention to post an officer as a top-level executive who was earlier interviewed and not considered suitable by the Public Enterprises Selection Board (PSEB) to the exclusion of the names in the panel recommended by the PESB. The better course would have been to request the PESB to suggest a fresh panel of names. By ignoring the recommendations of a statutory body, the government was making an inroad into the relevance and respectability of such a body.

VII. *Deviation from the established procedure for the selection of officers for top-level executive posts* in *Public Sector Undertakings—in the case of Air Marshal H. C. Devon, as Chairman, International Airport Authority of India*

If the person recommended by the PESB, in the present case, was not acceptable for any particular reason, the appointing authorities could well have asked for a fresh panel of suitable candidates. By not doing this and appointing a person who had been interviewed by the PESB, and not found suitable, the government has exposed itself to the charge of, to say the least, injecting into the selection process considerations which may well be extraneous to the requirements of the job. Such a practice does not add to the credibility of established institutions; rather, it impairs it.

VIII. *Misuse of powers and institution of false criminal complaints against four senior officials by the CBI at the instance of Indira Gandhi*

i. The evidence discloses a gross abuse of the authority vested in Indira Gandhi. She had taken into her head to act as she did merely because the officers of the Commerce and Industries Ministries had, in the discharge of their duties, taken steps to acquire information which was likely to affect the interest of Maruti Limited. She pressurised D. Sen to take proceedings for searching their houses and for filing complaints against them under the Prevention of Corruption Act, which were wholly unjustified and which were eventually dropped.

ii. The conduct of Sen shows that he has misused his authority in directing that First Information Reports be filed against all four officers and in starting proceedings against them.

iii. Indira Gandhi was responsible for institution of criminal proceedings against the four officers concerned, having their houses searched and subjecting them to humiliation; merely because they were responsible for collecting information in the discharge of their duties, which would have been prejudicial to the interests of Maruti Limited, a concern in which Sanjay Gandhi, her son, was vitally interested.

iv. It is imperative for the CBI to realise that in setting afoot a series of actions against individuals—whether officials or non-officials—they are irretrievably damaging the reputation and social standing of the individuals concerned. They should not, therefore, be allowed to initiate proceedings against anyone unless it is ensured that the facts on record warrant the type of proceedings that they launch.

v. Now that we have seen that even the man at the top of the CBI with all his seniority and status can still lend himself and his organisation to serve purposes other than strictly legal, constitutional and moral, it has to be ensured that in future no such individual or organisation should be capable of being rendered a helpless and unquestioning tool in the hands of the powers that be. The Commission feels that certain safeguards need to be provided by making the Director CBI accountable to an independent body. Yet another suggestion can be that the Director CBI may be statutorily rendered independent of the executive Ministry, and his term of office may be made subject to a tenure.

IX. *Unlawful detention of Textile/Customs employees under MISA by the Delhi Administration and the institution of false CBI cases against four of them*

i. CBI Director, D. Sen, showed extra keenness to register cases against these four officers, though the material available on record did not warrant the action that followed. On the other hand, when it came to dealing with Bhatnagar and Suri, Sen adopted a different yardstick.

ii. The Commission cannot help feeling that D. Sen applied invidiously different standards in dealing with the two sets of officers.

iii. Going entirely by the facts available on record, it has nowhere been established that these officers were corrupt or had done anything which could even distantly be interpreted as improper or incorrect.

iv. Bhinder, on his own admission, has been the prime mover in the sordid story of these arrests and detentions.

v. The entire action by the CBI under D. Sen was initiated on grounds which were totally inadequate and imaginary. As against this, he let off without any action two officials against whom there was adequate material to warrant prosecution under the Prevention of Corruption Act. He has grossly misused his position as the Director, CBI, and abused his authority.

vi. The Commission feels that Indira Gandhi has abused her authority and misused her power by causing the arrest and detention of these 12 officers without adequate justification and using the CBI to set in motion criminal cases against four of them, all of which had to be abandoned eventually for want of any material.

vii. Bhinder has been the hatchet man, and he went about the arrest and detention of these officers without any justification whatever. He was also responsible, along with D. Sen, to get the CBI to register cases against four of these officials. He has grossly abused his authority and misused his power.

X. *Misuse of powers and miscarriage of justice in saving Sudarshan Kumar Verma, a clerk in the Railways, from legal punishment by the CBI Officers*

i. Normally, the Director CBI handles important cases dealing with high officers, whereas cases involving non-Gazetted officials are dealt with at the Branch level. Neither the Director nor the Joint Director are concerned with such cases. But, in this case, shortly after the case against Verma was registered, the CBI Director, Sen called A.P. Mukherjee, DIG, CBI, Delhi Branch and called for the case papers.

ii. A. P. Mukherjee of the Delhi Branch sent his comments on the representation of Verma. He was of the view that there was no substance in the representation. A.P. Mukherjee had taken a courageous stand even at this stage when he should have been in no doubt about what this superior officer desired.

iii. The circumstances of the case and the evidence given by Sen leave little room for doubt that someone from the Prime Minister's household contacted D. Sen and asked him to arrange that Verma was not prosecuted. Accordingly, contrary to the normal procedure adopted in similar cases, D. Sen himself called for the papers, attempted through his subordinates to retrieve reports from the Railways and having failed to do so, suggested a different line of action according to which Verma should be dealt with departmentally.

iv. It is, therefore, a clear case in which perversion of the normal process by Sen and misuse of power is established.

XI. *Deviation from established procedure, misuse of power and abuse of authority by T.R. Tuli, Chairman of the Punjab National Bank, in allowing a clean overdraft to M/s. Associated Journals Ltd*

i. The bank advancing funds on a clean overdraft would normally try to ascertain the creditworthiness of the borrower and try to ensure whether the amount advanced would be repaid by the borrower on demand. This would be the minimum precaution which a banker could take before advancing even a small amount by way of a clean overdraft. In the present case, however, no precautions which would be normal in advancing money on a clean overdraft account were taken; but solely because of the intervention of the Minister P.C. Sethi, the loan was advanced, disregarding the cannons which would ordinarily govern such a loan.

ii. The Commission is firmly of the view that Tuli, who had permitted the overdraft, had taken it without making the minimum necessary examination of the facts of the case and without exercising a modicum of care or caution. This conduct on his part is attributable to the fact that he was swayed by collateral considerations. Thus, this transaction was not a normal one in the ordinary course of the bank's business. The Commission is of the view that Tuli had subverted established procedure in permitting this overdraft without security to M/s. Associated Journals Limited. He has also misused his powers and abused his authority in so doing.

XII. *Deviation from the established procedure in sanctioning a facility by way of opening of three foreign letters of credit by the Punjab National Bank in favour of M/s. Krsma Chemicals Private Ltd*

This is a clear instance where the Chairman and Managing Director of the Punjab National Bank, Tuli, took a decision and gave directions for its implementation contrary to the normal established procedures in such cases.

XIII. *Concessions by Punjab National Bank in favour of Maruti Ltd*

Taking into account the evidence adduced and the arguments advanced, the Commission is of the view that no subversion of administrative procedures or misuse of power or abuse of authority has been established in this case.

XIV. *Deviation from the established procedure and irregularities in the reconstitution of the Boards of Air India and Indian Airlines Corporations*

i. The normal or established procedure in regard to the appointment of the Board of Directors was not followed, and Minister Raj Bahadur was practically compelled to fall in line with the suggestions made by the Prime Minister, Indira Gandhi. It was only after the suggestion made by her was carried out that the lists submitted were approved.

ii. The role of oral instructions in the transactions of business of the government needs to be defined and definite guidelines set down. To the Commission, this imperative is not only in the interest of healthy administration, but also to protect the junior functionaries acting on the oral instructions of the seniors from the consequences of subsequent denials by the seniors when things go wrong.

XV. *Decision process leading to the purchase of three Boeing 737 aircraft by Indian Airlines*

i. The manner in which this deal was pushed through suffers from several infirmities:

a. The Indian Airlines Management sent a letter to the Ministry for permission to issue a Letter of Intent to the Boeing Company without waiting for the report of the Interline Committee constituted by the Indian Airlines Board.

b. The proposal was sent to the government even before it was approved by the Board of Indian Airlines.

c. No steps were taken to complete the system study suggested by the Planning Commission's representatives.

d. The PIB categorically opposed the proposal pending the completion of the system study. The Secretary's recommendations to abide by the PIB's recommendations were turned down by the Minister, Raghuramaiah, apparently because he had been asked by Dhawan to look into the matter urgently and Raghuramaiah took the suggestion of Dhawan as emanating from the Prime Minister.

e. According to the Finance Ministry, there was no instance of an Administrative Ministry going ahead with the proposal to the Cabinet for a decision against the recommendations of the PIB. This was done in this case.

f. The decision to sign the contract was given on 8 February 1977. On 9 February 1977, the contract was signed. The delivery schedule limit given by the Boeing Company had expired on 7 February.

g. The visit of Rajiv Gandhi to the office of the Chairman of the Indian Airlines, where he was shown the financial projections by the Director of Finance, apparently under the instructions of the Chairman, was a procedure which was totally outside the ordinary course of business.

ii. There has been a certain amount of avoidable haste in rushing through the deal.

XVI. *Detention of Smt. Gayatri Devi, Ex-Member of Parliament and Lt. Col. (Retired) Bhawani Singh under the COFEPOSA Act, 1974*

i. While processing the material that was available with the Deputy Director with the Deputy Director of Enforcement, against the two individuals, certain significant omissions were made in reproducing the information contained in the two letters of the Reserve Bank of India.

ii. In ordering the detention of these two persons under the COFEPOSA Act, the processes and procedures prescribed by the Finance Ministry have not been followed.

iii. It is abundantly clear that in the cases of these two persons, the provisions of the COFEPOSA Act, were not at all applicable, and these were resorted to, to give effect to a pre-determined decision to arrest these two persons.

iv. Pranab Kumar Mukherjee, the then Minister of Revenue and Banking, has misused his position and abused his authority in ordering the detention of Gayatri Devi and Col. Bhawani Singh on wholly insufficient grounds. It is a clear case of subversion of lawful processes and of administrative procedures.

XVII. *Detention of Bhim Sen Sachar and seven others*

i. The practice of issuing warrants of arrest first and obtaining the pre-dated grounds of detentions thereafter had become the general pattern so far as the detentions of persons under MISA in Delhi during the Emergency were concerned.

ii. The story of detention of Bhim Sen Sachar and seven others provides a classic example of the misuse of the provisions of MISA ... This and similar cases, which have come to the notice of the Commission, reveal an undesirable trend in the administration of the MISA. When, as in this case, the Prime Minister felt satisfied about the detention of certain persons, instead of getting the orders issued by the Central Government, small functionaries like the Additional District Magistrates were directed to issue the warrants without they themselves being satisfied either about the need for detention of the individuals concerned or the adequacy of grounds for their detention.

iii. The decision to detain Bhim Sen Sachar and seven others was taken by Indira Gandhi. She has abused her position and misused her power in ordering the arrest of Bhim Sen Sachar and seven others.

XVIII. *Improprieties committed* regarding *Mangal Behari, IAS of the Rajasthan Cadre, and termination of the services of Chandrawati Sharma, Assistant Teacher*

i. Harideo Joshi has conceded that a mistake was committed in the case of Sharma. He thus misused his position, subverted the established administrative procedures and abused his authority in terminating the services of Sharma without observing constitutional provisions.

ii. Indira Gandhi was responsible for (i) causing the termination of the services of Chandrawati Sharma, Assistant Teacher, Government of Rajasthan, in violation of the Constitutional provisions; (ii) the prolonged forced leave on which Mangal Behari had to remain for about 16 months; and (iii) for causing the attendant hardships which ensued as a result thereof. She has thus misused her position, abused her authority and subverted well-established administrative procedures and lawful processes.

iii. The services of Chandrawati Sharma, who was only an Assistant Teacher, was terminated without the slightest fuss or protest … No functionary of the government put up even as much as a note pointing out that the political activities alleged against her were not correct and that she was being kept out of service for no valid and understandable reason. As against this totally indifferent and callous attitude, the manner in which the state government officials rallied to the support of Mangal Behari, an IAS officer, is indeed unique and is in striking contrast to the manner in which Sharma was dealt with. How are we going to ensure that every employee of the government regardless of their rank and status enjoys full security and protection of services? Until this is done, the manner in which these two functionaries of the government were dealt with—one a low-placed Assistant Teacher, and the other a high-placed IAS officer—would be considered as an unpardonable and invidious distinction

iv. Considering the risks involved and the damage that an adverse IB report can cause to an individual, both in terms of his reputation of his career prospects, the Commission recommends that the Government should take steps to ensure that every IB report on the activities and material particulars of the individual is correct.

XIX. *Irregularities in initiating action resulting in search and seizure operations under the Income Tax Act in the case of two trade union leaders*

While the circumstances leading up to the search and seizure operations in these two cases no doubt appear to be somewhat unusual, especially D. Sen's role therein, no subversion of administrative procedure or misuse or abuse of power has been clearly established.

INTERIM REPORT II

Chapter viii

Misuse of Media

I. *Translation of Congress election manifesto by All India Radio and Directorate of Advertising and Visual Publicity translators*

V. C. Shukla has violated the basic norms of administration and has indulged in abuse of authority in getting the translators attached to the All India Radio and DAVP for translating the Congress Election Manifesto. Apart from that, it is also an offence under section 123(7) of the Representation of the People Act of 1951.

II. *Design of election posters for V. C. Shukla by artists of the Directorate of Advertising and Visual Publicity*

V. C. Shukla violated the basic norms of administration and indulged in abuse of authority in getting posters for his election campaign designed by the DAVP artists. Apart from that, his conduct also comes within the mischief of section 123(7) of the Representation of the People Act, 1951.

III. *Harassment of Kishore Kumar, playback singer, by the Ministry of Information and Broadcasting*

Apart from the constitutional responsibility, V. C. Shukla is actually responsible for the various disabilities that were inflicted on Kishore Kumar. This was a clear case of vindictiveness and gross misuse of governmental authority against a film artist of renown, only because the artist did not want to go along with a government-sponsored programme due to certain personal reasons.

Chapter ix

Cases of Misuse of Authority in the Income Tax Department

I. *Baroda Rayon Corporation—Search and Seizure under* Section 132 *of the Income Tax Act,* 1961

i. S.R. Mehta's action in directing Harihar Lal to initiate action under section 132 of the Income Tax Act in this case amounts to subversion of lawful processes and abuse of authority.

ii. As the Head of the Income Tax Department, S.R. Mehta cannot absolve himself of blame for the very grave loss of seized material which should have been returned to the person from whom it was seized by merely stating that he had left the papers on his Minister's desk. The responsibility for the return of these papers to the officers concerned was clearly his and his alone. Mehta's failure or omission in this regard amounts to subversion of lawful processes.

iii. On the uncontroverted statement of S.R. Mehta that these papers were handed over to P. K. Mukherjee. P. K. Mukherjee's action in obtaining and retaining seized documents and subsequent failure or omission on his part to return them to the Chairman of the Central Board of Direct Taxes or to any other duly authorised officers in the Income Tax Department also amounts to subversion of lawful processes and abuse of authority.

iv. Harihar Lal was aware of the illegality of his action. However, in the circumstances then prevailing, Harihar Lal's choice was limited, and he chose to render himself a helpless and unquestioning tool of S.R. Mehta.

v. In spite of a wealth of judicial pronouncements and departmental instructions emphasising the need for administrative restraint and strict compliance with the law, the then Chairman of the Central Board of Direct Taxes, S.R. Mehta, was himself instrumental in unleashing this dangerous weapon of search and seizure, which could unjustly and irretrievably damage the business reputation and standing of the parties affected.

vi. The extraordinary power of search and seizure under section 132 must be exercised strictly in accordance with the law, which provides the necessary safeguards and only for the purposes for which the law authorises it to be exercised.

II. *Search and seizure operation by the Income Tax Department in the case of Bajaj Group of Companies*

i. This case illustrates boldly the prevailing misconception that if an authorising officer has, in consequence of information in his possession, reason to believe that action under section 132 should be initiated in the case of a company or a group of companies, he will be justified in authorising indiscriminate search and seizure at the business or residential premises of all persons connected with the company, however remote the connection may be with these companies or even with their directors and employees. The conditions justifying the exercise of this extraordinary power did not exist in the case of a large number of 120 places searched or surveyed.

ii. The issue of blank warrants of authorisation is not a mere procedural lapse. Such warrants can be misused so as to cause damage to the reputation of any innocent person. If proper implementation of action u/s 132 is not possible, as suggested, then the solution to the problem lies in seeking to amend the law, consistent with the requirements of adequate safeguards and not in flouting the statutory requirements with impunity.

iii. Judicial decisions and departmental instructions brought to the notice of the Commission appear to have been observed only in their breach. Stern action by the Income Tax Department is necessary to prevent such wanton disregard of the law as well as the privacy of the citizens.

iv. Where a blank warrant of authorisation is issued and the authorising officer has acted without any information on which he could have reason to believe that the statutory conditions for the exercise of the power of search existed, such action is clearly unlawful.

v. The inquiry into search and seizure under section 132 of the Income Tax Act, 1961, in the Bajaj & Mukand Group of Companies has revealed several serious irregularities and power was not exercised strictly in accordance with law.

vi. The extraordinary power of search and seizure under section 132 must be exercised strictly in accordance with the law, which provides the necessary safeguards and only for the purposes for which the law authorises it to be exercised.

III. *Special instructions on matters relating to Maruti Limited*

i. S.R. Mehta subverted administrative procedures and abused his authority in giving oral instructions to Harihar Lai, which had the effect of frustrating or, at any rate, inordinately delaying legitimate enquiries relating to benami share holdings in Maruti Limited, which indicated evasion of taxes.

ii. Oral orders or instructions involve the danger of being denied, twisted or misinterpreted by either party to suit their convenience. Hence, these should be obtained in writing immediately. Where it is not practicable to do so, written confirmation should be obtained as soon as possible. In the meanwhile, the recipient should record the oral directions or instructions.

Chapter x

Import of aircraft by Dhirendra Brahmachari of Aparna Ashram

i. S.B. Jain and A.M. Sinha failed to take even the elementary steps and ignored the specific information furnished to them with regard to Brahmachari's proposed trip to New York.

ii. A.M. Sinha has, in not proceeding with the enquiries, failed to discharge his responsibilities.

iii. In this particular case, considering the person involved and the nature of the illegal transaction alleged against Brahmachari, it was a matter for the judgment and direction of a higher functionary than that of the Deputy Director. It was a fit case for the exercise of Jain's discretion and guidance. He has, however, tried to shift the onus to the Deputy Director. His conduct becomes yet more blameworthy in the light of the subsequent note that he recorded in May 1977.

iv. From the evidence, it is quite clear that Brahmachari had obtained the Customs Clearance Permit by misrepresenting that the aircraft was a donation, when it was in fact purchased by him. He also made misrepresentations before the officers in the Office of the Chief Controller of Imports and Exports in the matter of increase in the value of the CCP, which he got increased from Rs 4,00,000 to Rs 6,14,000, when there was no evidence to indicate that the aircraft and spares of the value of Rs 6,14,000 were gifted to him.

v. Brahmachari has fully exploited his association with the then Prime Minister's house in getting the aircraft imported by misrepresenting it as a gift. He has actively subverted the established procedures.

vi. Not only did the issuance of the CCP subvert well-established administrative procedures but even the value of the CCP was also progressively increased in three separate stages by the authority concerned—at the request of Brahmachari—without any documentary evidence to justify the enhancement. There is no explanation, either from any of the witnesses during their deposition before the Commission or in the files reviewed by the Commission, for this unusual and extraordinary procedure. The Commission considers it a clear and unpardonable subversion of all accepted norms and conventions of sound and healthy administration.

vii. It appears that there had been undue haste at various levels in processing the application of Brahmachari for the grant of exemption from customs duty. In the process, enquiries regarding the status of the Ashram were not fulfilled.

viii. While granting exemption from customs duty at the time of the import of the aircraft, the Department of Customs and Central Excise had imposed two conditions:

   a. The aircraft will be used for transportation of the students as well as teachers from the plains to Mantalai Ashram and back.

   b. The Yoga training will be imparted free of charge. From the evidence on record, it appears that both these conditions have been violated.

ix. Brahmachari continued to make misrepresentations for claiming exemption from customs duty on the import of the aircraft. His declaration that Apama Ashram is a charitable institution was also untrue.

x. The evidence before the Commission leads to the conclusion that the initial decision to reject the proposal twice by the Air Headquarters on valid grounds of security and sensitivity of the area was subsequently changed in favour of granting the permission, though with some conditions attached at the instance of the then Defence Minister, Bansi Lal.

xi. It is necessary to place on record that various officers of the Ministries showed extraordinary speed in the processing of this case. For once, the proverbial red tape in the functioning of the bureaucrats was nowhere in evidence. While the expeditious functioning of the government machinery is a desirable objective, in this case, it was not at all motivated by considerations of efficiency, but on account of extraneous considerations. It is evident from the statements of witnesses before the Commission that almost all of them were aware of the standing of Brahmachari in relation to the household of the then Prime Minister. Some of the witnesses admitted that they apprehended harm to them should anyone obstruct Brahmachari's proposals and projects. The apparently effortless manner in which Brahmachari was able to compel the officials of Ministry after Ministry stands out as a classic example of how an entire administrative system can be subverted by an errant individual if only he has the right contacts at the right places.

xii. For Brahmachari, the entire exercise of securing the CCP, "enhancing its value, obtaining customs exemption, and securing landing facilities at Mantalai was effortless." This creates the impression among the general public that rules and laws are meant only for ordinary, law-abiding citizens, while those with influence and authority can bypass them with ease and have their projects pushed through regardless.

xiii. The government may examine whether the administrative systems and procedures can be secured in future from the onslaughts of individuals like Brahmachari.

xiv. To protect against misuse of authority at the decision-making levels, the corresponding responsibility to set out their reasons in writing in every case where a major or even a minor infraction of the procedures and rules are sought to be made, should be insisted upon.

xv. The government must provide for and protect the junior officers from the shifting of the responsibility by the seniors when things go wrong. This salutary principle should not be confined only to the officers but should reach the different levels of Ministers up to the highest.

xvi. While withdrawing papers which have been released earlier as a part of an administrative transaction, definite rules and guidelines should be laid down as to how the papers earlier released can be withdrawn or replaced, if at all.

(a) In dealing with applications for exemption from customs duty, well-defined guidelines should be laid down to enable the decision-making levels to reach the right and uniform conclusions in every case and to safeguard against abuse.

(b) The onus to prove that the exemption sought for will be in the public interest, should be on the applicants.

(c) Where exemption has been given subject to certain conditions, the applicant should be required to furnish evidence periodically that the condition imposed continues to be conformed to.

(d) The conditions under which gifts from foreigners may be received even by institutions should be clearly prescribed.

xvii. Security considerations of the country should not be sidestepped to accommodate the demands of individuals like Brahmachari under any circumstances.

Chapter xi

Arrests and Detentions

I. *Issue of Detention Orders under MISA*

i. An undesirable feature of detentions in Delhi during the Emergency was the misuse of the power under the preventive sections of the Criminal Procedure Code, such as Sections 108 and 151, initially to secure the presence of the persons who were subsequently detained under MISA.

ii. Another ugly feature of arrests and detentions in Delhi during the Emergency concerns the re-arrest of persons released on bail otherwise by the courts.

iii. It also came to the notice of the Commission that some MISA warrants were deliberately kept unexecuted. In fact, directions were issued by K.S. Bajwa and P.S. Bhinder to District Superintendents of Police not to execute certain warrants.

iv. Section 14 of MISA, read with Section 21 of the General Clauses Act, empowers the detaining authorities to revoke an order issued under MISA by the detaining authority. This power was taken away from the District Magistrate/Additional District Magistrates in Delhi.

v. Though the Law Department was associated with the processing of detention orders at the time of confirmation and review, no legal scrutiny was, in fact, done. The initial attempts of the Law Department to scrutinise the grounds of detention and give legal advice were discouraged, and they were made to realise the "futility of finding faults with detention orders".

vi. The evidence of J. K. Kohli, Chief Secretary, S. Chandra, Special Secretary (Home), T.R. Kalia, Deputy Secretary (Home) and Jagmohan, Deputy Secretary to the Lt. Governor, prove beyond doubt the practice of ante-dating the confirmation orders of the Lt. Governor whenever the papers were not received from the detaining authorities in time.

vii. Though Navin Chawla had no position in the jail hierarchy, he was exercising extra statutory control in jail matters and sending instructions on all matters, including the treatment of particular detenus. Chawla had suggested the construction of some cells with asbestos roofs to "bake" certain persons.

viii. Transfer of MISA detenus presents an excess of its own kind. 200 MISA detenus, including some prominent Opposition leaders, were transferred from Tihar Jail to jails outside Delhi during the Emergency. S.K. Batra has stated that the transfer of such persons involved great discomfort to the detenus because of the additional inconvenience and expense it involved to their relatives. He said that such transfers are always considered as penal measures in Jail Administration.

II. *Treatment in Jails*

Political detention is to be basically preventive in character and not punitive. This aspect seems to have been conveniently ignored during the Emergency.

III. *Applications for Parole*

i. No uniform policy was followed by the Delhi Administration in matters relating to the grant of parole.

ii. While some deserving cases for parole were dealt with by the administration in a very callous manner, there were other cases in which the administration was unmistakably indulgent to the detainees. What governed these different considerations in the attitude of the administration can only be inferred.

iii. Grant of parole was used by the Delhi Administration as an incentive to promote family planning in the Tihar Jail.

iv. The attitude of the Delhi Administration was particularly harsh in dealing with the requests from the student detenus for release on parole to enable them to take their university examinations.

v. Though Section 16 of the Delhi Detenus (Conditions of Detention) Orders, 1976 governing the conditions of MISA detenus in Delhi provided that "student detenus may be allowed to appear in examination only with the permission of the Administrator", the discretion was always used against the applicants.

IV. *Attitude of Delhi Administration towards the Ministry Of Home Affairs*

i. In cases where the Lt. Governor did not like to agree with the advice from the Home Ministry, the officials of the Home Department found that invariably the Lt. Governor's views prevailed and the Ministry of Home Affairs had to retrace its stand.

ii. During the Emergency, Bajwa used to furnish material to the authorities concerned and used to issue orders to them asking them "to pick up" the persons named in the list.

iii. P.S. Bhinder, K.S. Bajwa and Navin Chawla exercised enormous powers during the Emergency because they had easy access to the then Prime Minister's house. Their approach to the problems of the period relating to the citizens was authoritarian and callous. They grossly misused their position and abused their powers in cynical disregard of the welfare of the citizens, and in the process rendered themselves unfit to hold any public office which demands an attitude of fair play and consideration for others. In their relish for power, they completely subverted the normal channels of command and administrative procedures.

iv. Krishan Chand, by his various actions and inactions with regard to important and vital matters, appears to have abdicated his legitimate functions in favour of an over-ambitious group of officers like Bhinder, Bajwa and Navin Chawla, with disastrous consequences to the people. He betrayed his trust and committed a serious breach of faith with the citizens of Delhi, and failed to administer the affairs of the territory honestly and justly.

v. Sushil Kumar, in an effort to beat the clock, had also resorted to the issue of a few blank warrants in addition to the warrants that were prepared and issued by him to the police. Since these detention orders were issued without any satisfaction of the detaining authority, the orders were illegal. Since, however, the orders were issued pursuant to the directions of Indira Gandhi, responsibility for the illegal detentions must primarily rest on her.

vi. The Commission has to come to the conclusion that in the light of the evidence on record and without the benefit of knowing Indira Gandhi's version, Indira Gandhi was responsible for directing the arrest and detention of a number of respected citizens without authority of law, motivated solely by a desire to continue to remain in power.

V. *Detention of Mam Chand, son of Malkhan*

i. Both Krishan Chand and Bhinder had misused their position and authority in ordering the detention and continuing in detention a helpless and defenceless individual like Mam Chand.

ii. It was an undesirable act on the part of the administration to have allowed a poor and innocent man like Mam Chand, the only breadwinner of the family, to remain under detention for 19 long months.

VI. *Detention of Dr Karunesh Shukla*

i. The arrest of Karunesh Shukla was a misuse of power by the Lt. Governor of Delhi, Krishan Chand, acting on the advice of Bajwa. As Superintendent of Police, CID, Bajwa apparently wielded enormous authority during the Emergency and often misused it.

ii. Both Krishan Chand and Bajwa misused their authority in the detention of Karunesh Shukla on grounds not covered under the provisions of the MISA.

VII. *Detention of Virender Kapoor*

i. The initial arrest of Virender Kapoor was in the presence of Bhinder. As a Deputy Inspector General, he should have satisfied himself about the necessity of arresting Kapoor. To that extent, he misused his position and abused his authority.

ii. Bajwa has also misused his authority in Kapoor's arrest.

iii. The detention of Kapoor under MISA under the orders of Krishan Chand was in keeping with the general policy of negligence and lack of interest that he displayed in the general run of detentions numbering over 1,000. He has abused his authority and misused his position in this, as in several other cases.

iv. The Commission cannot adequately condemn this type of use of MISA on fabricated grounds. An administration which is impervious to the awareness of the basic norms of liberty and the provisions of law, and a set of functionaries who are willing to do anything at the bidding of their seniors without application of mind and without realising the consequences of their acts, have in them the makings of a totalitarian society. The Commission is of the opinion that the government must make appropriate provision for fixing responsibility on the persons issuing written or even oral orders for every detention.

VIII. *Detention of Vaid Guru Dutt*

Krishan Chand misused his position in ordering the detention of Vaid Guru Dutt. In his anxiety to please the ex-Prime Minister, he seems to have overreacted to a situation which, at best, should have been ignored. It is the arrest of an old infirm and respected individual like Guru Dutt which shakes the faith of the people in the fairness and competence of the administration.

IX. *Detention of Prabir Purkayastha*

The manner in which Bhinder went about the job of arresting Purkayastha, believing him to be D. P. Tripathi, discloses his callous attitude. This was a gross abuse of authority. The story of the arrest of Purkayastha by Bhinder, the manner in which the Magistrate issued the detention orders and the part played by the Lt. Governor illustrate the complete breakdown of the rule of law.

X. *Use of MISA against ordinary criminals*

A large number of ordinary criminals who could be dealt with effectively under the provisions of normal laws were detained under MISA in Delhi during the Emergency. This was in defiance of the specific directions of the Ministry of Home Affairs.

XI. *Detention of juvenile delinquents*

In this category of cases, MISA powers were invoked without adequate grounds and in defiance of the categorical instructions of the Ministry of Home Affairs. Use of the harsh powers under MISA for dealing with such offenders for comparatively unimportant cases, which involved no consideration of the security of the State or larger considerations of public order, amounts to misuse of the powers and undoubtedly results in denial of the beneficent provisions of law relating to juvenile delinquents.

XII. *Use of MISA against violators of the Delhi Administration's (Display of Prices of Articles) Order 1975*

Krishan Chand has misused his position and abused his power by invoking Emergency powers, including MISA, in cases which could well have been dealt with effectively under the normal provisions of law.

Chapter xii

Specific Cases of Misuse of Authority

I. *Requisitioning of Vishva Yuvak Kendra, Chanakyapuri, New Delhi*

i. The building of the Vishva Yuvak Kendra was requisitioned by the Delhi Administration at the instance of Indira Gandhi, in order to pressurise the management of the Indian Youth Centre Trust to agree to reconstitute the Board of Trustees; that Krishan Chand was acting as spokesman of Indira Gandhi in this regard, and that V.C. Shukla was also making determined efforts to acquire a hold over the Vishva Yuvak Kendra with a view to running it in consultation with Sanjay Gandhi.

ii. Indira Gandhi unduly pressurised Krishan Chand, the then Lt. Governor, Delhi, to requisition the Vishva Yuvak Kendra building.

iii. Krishan Chand misused his power and authority, and so did V.C. Shukla in this case.

II. *Appointment of U. S. Srivastav as the Chairman of the Delhi Transport Corporation in 1976*

This case illustrates how established rules and procedures expected to be followed by the appointing authorities were in fact not observed, even though the correct procedures and the problems that were likely to arise from this appointment were pointed out at different levels.

III. *Harassment of the firm Messrs. Pandit Brothers; their arrest and related matters*

i. A series of harassments against the firm of Messrs. Pandit Brothers, including the arrests of the Manager and the two partners, was initiated at the instance of Sanjay Gandhi.

ii. Krishan Chand was the prime mover in getting the raid organised.

iii. It appears that the administration employed the police for a purpose which did not fall within their legitimate sphere of duties and for which they were not equipped. Such misuse of the police force by the administration should be a matter for concern.

iv. The association of J.C. Luther, Commissioner of Income Tax, with this case following his visit to R.K. Dhawan in the Prime Minister's house is also disconcerting. Since no summons under Section 8B of the Commissions of Inquiry Act or notice under Rule 5(2)(a) of the Commissions of Inquiry (Central) Rules were issued to Luther, the Commission refrains from making any observations on his role. Yet, the Commission is constrained to suggest to the government that it must lay down clear rules regarding the chain of command through which alone orders from above should be communicated to the officers in the field. If the process of short-circuiting the chain of command is not frowned upon, the system would be exposed to the machinations of unscrupulous operators willing to jump levels in their anxiety to get close to the seat of power.

v. According to Krishan Chand, the decision to launch the Sales Tax and Price Tag raids against Pandit Brothers was a sequel to the orders that emanated from Sanjay Gandhi. Even so he had a direct responsibility which he failed to discharge. He allowed himself to be used as a willing tool to subserve the designs of Sanjay Gandhi.

vi. Sanjay Gandhi, who wielded such enormous power during the Emergency, did not confine his activities only to the operation of demolition of houses, shops and industrial buildings. He took a hand even in getting some persons, whom either he did not like or who had thwarted him, arrested and detained. In the present case, the evidence brought on record clearly points to him as the source and the motivator of all the harassment that followed the action against Pandit Brothers. On the direct responsibility of Sanjay Gandhi for the harassment that was meted out to Pandit Brothers, the Commission feels no doubt.

Chapter xiii

Demolitions in Delhi

I. *Demolitions in general*

i. After the declaration of the Emergency, demolition operations carried out by the DDA, MCD and NDMC received a spurt. The general policy of caution and concern for the people affected by demolitions gave place to a measure of reckless speed in clearing and cleaning up the areas earmarked. Alternative arrangements to resettle them were not simultaneously made with the same speed.

ii. An impression had been created that Sanjay Gandhi was actively associated with the demolition programmes in Delhi. The affected people went in deputations to Sanjay Gandhi to seek his assistance in several cases. Sanjay Gandhi used to meet these deputationists and deal with them in his own peculiar way.

iii. In their hurry to implement the demolition programme, neither the DDA nor the MCD took the precaution in a number of cases of following even the basic minimum procedures laid down in the Delhi Development Act, Delhi Municipal Corporation Act and other relevant laws. Some of the features of the demolitions are:

    a. No notices as required were issued before the buildings were demolished.

    b. In a number of cases of acquisition of private property, land was occupied even before the proceedings for acquisition were commenced or before the date on which possession could be taken under the law.

    c. In a number of cases, land use prescribed under the Delhi Master Plan was changed without the concurrence or permission of the Union Government.

iv. To ensure that the affected people do not approach the law courts for redress, or political leaders, demolitions were carried out without advance intimation. Stay orders, where these could be obtained, were not respected and demolitions were carried out. Persons who approached the law courts were arrested under Section 108 CrPC on fabricated evidence or threatened with arrest under MISA and compelled to withdraw the proceedings initiated by them.

v. A squad of the police was permanently attached to the DDA, ostensibly for the protection of the DDA officials who used to go on demolition programmes to different areas. Even when the actions were illegal and arbitrary, the police unit attached to the DDA remained present. The squad used to be supplemented by large contingents of both armed and unarmed police from nearby police stations and the police lines with the object of intimidating and terrorising the aggrieved citizens and to prevent them from offering resistance to the demolitions. This affected the image of the police also in the eyes of the public.

vi. When there was public criticism against unauthorised demolitions or some affected people had taken the matter to the court, attempts seem to have been made to fabricate the records or to pre-date orders in an effort to establish that notices were actually issued and served mostly by affixation even when such notices had not been issued.

vii. The demolition operations were carried out like a blitzkrieg in utter disregard to the human problems involved. Alternative accommodation sometimes was provided, but more often only open plots of land were allotted, which were so small that no residential houses could be built on these. Very few built-up quarters were allotted to the affected persons.

viii. A large number of persons whose residences were demolished were making a living by performing some services for the residents living in nearby areas. They belonged mostly to the class of masons, milkmen, domestic servants, watchmen, etc. When alternative sites were given to the persons whose houses were demolished at places far away from their place of work, they had to incur extra expenditure in addition to undergoing additional inconveniences to reach their site of work.

ix. In the matter of allotting alternative accommodation, a standard 25 square yard plot was provided, regardless of the size of the area previously occupied by the affected individuals or the extent of any demolition. The plot was offered at the normal market price, and in many cases, no compensation was offered or paid.

x. In some of the areas of rehabilitation, even basic amenities were wanting. The houses had been constructed back to back in such a manner that there was no ventilation or even passage between the two houses. The rehabilitation areas, in some cases, presented a picture of hasty planning and indifferent execution.

xi. The demolitions undertaken in Delhi during the Emergency did not conform to the established legal and administrative requirements. The Commission recommends that the government may take special steps to redress the grievances of the affected citizens on a priority basis after considering the cases on merit.

II. *Demolitions in Bhagat Singh Market*

i. Ailawadi's contention that the demolitions were purely voluntary cannot be accepted. It, therefore, appears from the documentary and oral evidence that the New Delhi Municipal Committee had carried out demolitions in Bhagat Singh Market and that this was done under the supervision of its Member-Secretary, Ailawadi. (Para 13.79)

ii. After the verandahs had been declared as a public street under Section 171(4) of the Punjab Municipal Act, the Committee could not proceed to remove encroachments or to demolish any structures unless the proper procedure laid down in Section 172(1) of the Punjab Municipal Act was followed.

iii. Ailawadi exceeded his powers and misused his authority in demolishing the shops in the Bhagat Singh Market without observing the provisions of the law on the subject.

III. *Demolitions in Sultanpur Mazra – Occupation of Land in Villages Sultanpur Mazra and Phoot Kalan*

i. The land was occupied by the DDA in spite of protests of the villagers. The so-called consent of the villagers appears to have been taken after the DDA had already occupied the land, and when the villagers had no option but to try and secure the best possible terms from the DDA.

ii. At the time land was occupied, even the proposal for the issue of notification under the Land Acquisition Act had not been signed.

iii. From the statements of witnesses, which have not been challenged by Jagmohan or Ranbir Singh, it is apparent that force was used in removing the residents and demolishing their houses. A contingent of police was present, and bulldozers were used.

iv. After the structures were demolished, the DDA had no legal right to occupy the land on which these buildings were constructed and the action of Jagmohan and Ranbir Singh, Executive Officer of the DDA, was illegal as the land was occupied much before the issue of notification on 2 March 1977.

IV. *Demolition in Sarai Pepal Thala and Jehangirpur Bhulswa*

i. The plea that the entire operation was carried out on a voluntary basis cannot be accepted.

ii. Jagmohan misused his position and abused his authority in ordering the illegal occupation of the land in village Jehangirpur Bhulswa and village Sarai Pepal Thala without proper proceedings under the Land Acquisition Act, and also in ordering the demolition of structures in these villages without going through the procedure laid down in the Delhi Development Act.

V. *Demolition of Arya Samaj Temple*

i. Jagmohan abused his position and misused his powers in ordering the demolition of a building used as a place of worship.

ii. S.M. Dua, the Executive Officer of DDA, seems to have played a part in fabricating the record, and his denial in this regard is not acceptable.

VI. *Demolition in the Turkman Gate area*

i. Jagmohan informed his subordinate officers about the proposed demolition operations in Turkman Gate only on 7 April 1976 and did not give sufficient time to them to go through the records and survey the area by making enquiries from the residents about the status of their property.

ii. H.K. Lal and Jagmohan have shown scant respect for the rights of others and have misused their authority on a massive scale. The demolitions of the unacquired and private properties were done without observing the due processes of law.

iii. Bhinder's action in requisitioning bulldozers to the Turkman Gate area, even before the riots were brought under control, is an indication of the extreme and indecent hurry in carrying out the demolition programme. Bhinder thus showed great callousness to the miseries of the people of the area. He has abused his authority and misused his powers.

VII. *Demolition in Village Samalkha*

i. The Municipal Corporation of Delhi not only demolished the structures but also took possession of the private land in the village of Samalkha without any legal authority. O.P. Gupta, the then Zonal Assistant Commissioner (R), who tried to follow the legal procedure, was harassed and forced to go on leave. Subsequently, he was accommodated in a junior post. The demolition and its illegalities have been admittedly done under the orders of B.R. Tamta. He had misused his power and abused his authority.

VIII. *Demolitions in Village Kapas Hera*

i. Demolitions carried out in this village, allegedly at the instance of Sanjay Gandhi, were unauthorised, and procedures prescribed by law were not followed either by the DDA or by the MCD.

ii. This area was not a development area under the DDA and the DDA had no legal authority to demolish any structures here. However, witnesses stated that it was the DDA which demolished the structures.

iii. The action of demolishing the house of Lt. Col Ram Singh Yadav, a retired Army officer in this village, was, as per B. R. Tamta, taken on the orders of Sanjay Gandhi. He had also to take disciplinary action against his own officers as he was pressurised by Sanjay Gandhi.

iv. Jagmohan, B.R. Tamta, Ranbir Singh and Satya Prakash were all responsible for the demolitions in varying degrees. They all abused their authority and misused their powers in going about the demolitions in a manner in which they did, without observing the requirements of law and procedures.

v. Sanjay Gandhi was responsible for initiating the entire demolition operations in this village, and insofar as demolitions were illegal, he has to take his share of the responsibility for the same.

IX. *Demolitions in Arjun Nagar*

i. Some of the demolitions done by the DDA in the Arjun Nagar area were illegal. Jagmohan, Satya Prakash and Ranbir Singh have all participated in their respective fields and contributed to the illegal demolitions.

X. *Demolitions in Karol Bagh*

The demolitions in Karol Bagh were done at the instance of Sanjay Gandhi. Among other considerations, the political affiliation of the shopkeepers to the party opposed to the Congress was one of the deciding factors which impelled Sanjay Gandhi to order the demolition of the structures in Karol Bagh. The responsibility for these demolitions must rest entirely with Sanjay Gandhi and B.R. Tamta.

XI. *Demolition in Andheria Mor*

i. Action for demolition in Andheria Mor could have been taken by the Corporation only under Section 343(1) of the Delhi Municipal Corporation Act. Admittedly, the procedure laid down in this Section has not been carried out. There is no other law under which the Corporation could have demolished the structures in Andheria Mor. The fact of demolition and its illegality has been admitted by Tamta. The only plea he has taken is that this was done on the instructions of Sanjay Gandhi. This by itself cannot absolve him of his responsibility. He abused his authority and misused his powers.

ii. The demolition operations which took place in Andheria Mor were carried out at the instance and under the directions of Sanjay Gandhi and he was responsible for ordering the properties of the villagers to be demolished. The order was without any authority of law.

XII. *Conclusions*

i. In a number of cases, the normal and established legal processes were not complied with by Jagmohan and Tamta.

ii. It has also very vividly been brought on record that the Delhi Development Authority indulged in falsification and fabrication of records.

iii. Very often the demolitions were undertaken for considerations which were political and not infrequently whimsical.

iv. Though the Lt. Governor was the head of the administration and was also the DDA Chairman, he appears to have been completely ignored by these functionaries, who for all their actions took orders directly from Sanjay Gandhi. The demolitions of places of worship specifically required the prior orders of the Lt. Governor. The requirements were completely ignored when the DDA demolished the Arya Samaj Temple. The lament of the Lt. Governor, Krishan Chand, that nobody consulted him or listened to him and that they used to take orders directly from Sanjay Gandhi has been heard by the Commission with a feeling of disgust. He admitted that he turned a deaf ear and a blind eye to every conceivable piece of illegality and impropriety.

v. B. R. Tamta as Commissioner of MCD had the honesty to admit that he had done wrong things because of compulsions, particularly the pressure on him from Sanjay Gandhi. This by itself cannot be considered an extenuation of his conduct. He has also abused his authority and misused his power.

vi. Jagmohan grossly misused his position and abused his authority. He, during the Emergency, became a law unto himself and went about doing the bidding of Sanjay Gandhi without care or concern for the miseries of the people affected thereby.

vii. Sanjay Gandhi has actually aided and abetted the illegal demolitions undertaken by the DDA and the Municipal Corporation of Delhi, and the evidence on record goes to show that he was the prime mover in the majority of the illegal operations that took place in Delhi.

viii. In the view of the Commission, the manner in which Sanjay Gandhi intervened in the public affairs, particularly in Delhi, is the single greatest act of excess committed during the Emergency, with no parallel and no justification for such assumption of authority or power in the history of independent India. While other acts of the excesses may have been in the nature of acts committed by functionaries having some shadow of authority acting in excess of their powers, here was a case of an individual wielding unlimited authority in a dictatorial manner, without even the slightest legal or constitutional right to do so. If this country is to be rendered safe for future generations, the people owe it to themselves to ensure that an irresponsible and unconstitutional centre of power like the one which revolved around Sanjay Gandhi during the Emergency is not allowed to come up ever again in any form or shape or under any guise.

Chapter xiv

Turkman Gate Firing

I. *Turkman Gate firing–Commencement of demolitions*

i. It is not possible to accept the plea that an operation of the type undertaken in the Turkman Gate locality could have gone on without the intelligence wing of the Delhi Police knowing anything about it.

ii. The uncertainty about the area to be cleared by demolitions and the extension of this area, day after day, contributed in no small measure to the tension being built up and which eventually culminated in the tragedy.

iii. There is confusion about the exact provocation which resulted in the riot. The police placed the responsibility on the public, and the public on the police.

iv. The relevant registers at the police lines did not accurately reflect the actual issuance of arms and ammunition on 19 April 1976. This indicates gross negligence at the concerned levels. These omissions may not be accidental; they could have been deliberate, intended to ensure that the records remain silent in the event of any future inquiry.

v. There is a lot of confusion about the number of rounds that were actually fired in the course of the riots.

vi. The police lines record did not even state the exact number of men detailed for duty in connection with the riot on the relevant day in the Turkman Gate area.

vii. A gross and probably a deliberate effort has been made to cover up the whole incident by not getting even an administrative enquiry made into the events leading to the death by police firing of admittedly six persons.

viii. A report regarding the firing, as required in the Punjab Police Rules, was not drawn up. The report prepared by the Additional District Magistrate and the Superintendent of Police lacked the most important details, such as the exact number of persons who died, the rounds fired, etc.

ix. The magistracy did not fulfil the role expected of it.

x. The bodies of the persons who had died were taken to the police station and not to the mortuary, which was closer to the scene of the incident than the police station.

xi. Enquiries into complaints and molestation of women and looting of property, ordered in a couple of cases, were not pursued.

xii. A police wireless log book had been tampered with.

xiii. All the important documents such as General Diaries of the Police Stations, the documents of the Reserve Police Lines dealing with the quantum of force on the fateful day, the details regarding the arms and ammunition issued to various police parties and even the one and only report that was sent by the administration on the events of the day on April 20, 1976 contain no relevant details. Absence of the relevant details and of these vital documents cannot be regarded as a mere accidental coincidence.

xiv. Investigation of the FIR No. 189 dealing with the riots was entrusted to a very junior officer of the rank of an ASI when almost all the important senior officers of the Delhi Administration were present and were witnesses to the events of the day. Both the Inspector General of Police and the District Magistrate have stated that they were not aware that the investigation of this important case was being done by such a junior officer. It is not surprising that the prosecution staff who scrutinised the investigation of this case sometime in May 1977 have found the investigation full of defects, many of which were of a grave nature.

xv. The prosecuting officer found a number of defects in the investigation which, in a large measure, were avoidable with a little supervision and guidance of the investigation by the authorities at appropriate levels. This neglect of such an important investigation is a part of the design to cover up the events of the day.

xvi. The official communique on the events of the day, prepared at Raj Niwas, issued in the name of Mir Mushtaq Ahmed, sought to give a communal colour to cover up a gross failure on the part of the administration.

xvii. Though the Family Planning Programme may have contributed to the build-up of tension among all the residents of the area, the firing was a direct and immediate sequel to the decision of the authorities to proceed with the demolitions regardless of the resistance of the people and the consequences. The subsequent conduct of the authorities, significant silence of several important and relevant records on material particulars, indicates that this was a part of a design to justify the firing by the police.

xviii. An attitude of vindictiveness by the administration towards the citizens noticed is indefensible.

xix. A pre-dated firing order was not signed through N. C. Ray after pressure was brought to bear upon him by Sanjay Gandhi at the instance of Bhinder.

xx. Bhinder pressurised the magistrates to do wholly improper acts and he got the firing order signed and ante-dated through the intervention of Sanjay Gandhi.

xxi. Sanjay Gandhi intervened on behalf of Bhinder and pressurised the District Magistrate and his colleagues and a junior magistrate to sign and pre-date the firing order.

xxii. It was highly improper and unwarranted interference on the part of Sanjay Gandhi to have called the Magistrates to his residence and ordered them to do a wholly improper and illegal act.

Chapter xv

Observations of the Commission

i. With the Press gagged and a resultant blackout of authentic information, arbitrary arrests and detentions went on apace. Effective dissent was smothered, followed by a general erosion of democratic values. Highhanded and arbitrary actions were carried out with impunity. The nation was initially in a state of shock, and then of stupor, unable to realise the directions and the full implications of the actions of the government and its functionaries. That the primary and not infrequently the sole motivation in the case of a number of public servants, who acted unlawfully to the prejudice of the rights of citizens, was the desire for self-protection, desire for survival, may be regarded as some extenuation of their conduct. Yet, if the nation is to preserve the fundamental values of a democratic society, every person, whether a public functionary or private citizen, must display a degree of vigilance and willingness to sacrifice.

ii. The circumstances in which the Emergency was declared and the manner in which it was accomplished should be a warning to the citizens of the country.

iii. Indira Gandhi did not consult the Cabinet even though she had plenty of time to do so. There is enough evidence to show that Indira Gandhi planned the imposition of the Emergency at least as early as June 22. She had also shared the thought with some of her political confidants as early as the morning of June 25.

iv. In the absence of any explanation which would warrant the declaration of an Emergency, the inference is inevitable that a political decision was taken by an interested Prime Minister in a desperate endeavour to save herself from the legitimate compulsion of a judicial verdict against her.

v. The nation owes it to the present and the succeeding generations to ensure that the administrative set-up is not subverted in future in the manner it was done to serve the personal ends of any one individual or a group of individuals in or near the government.

vi. Censorship of news and the manner in which the media was manipulated should be a lesson to the government and to the people and has serious repercussions on the lives and thoughts of the people.

vii. The state owes it to the nation to ensure that the judiciary will not be subjected to strains which might even indirectly operate as punitive merely because of pronouncements not to the liking of the executive authority.

viii. In selecting its functionaries, the government should not throw to the winds the rules that have been framed for making such appointments. The government, having framed the rules governing its conduct, cannot normally arrogate to itself the discretion to disregard them, unless there are demonstrably compelling reasons and circumstances justifying the sidestepping of those rules.

ix. Forging records, fabrication of grounds for detentions, antedating of detention orders, the callousness with which the request of the detenus for revocation of orders for detention or even parole were ignored should be a warning to every thinking man as to how an Act initially intended to serve an extremely limited purpose to deal with the misdeeds of a special category of persons can be given such a wide and comprehensive application so as to embrace all sections of the population to penalise dissent.

x. The collusion between the police and the magistracy in denying the citizens their basic freedoms by arrests and detentions on non-existent grounds is a matter of anguish.

xi. The government must seriously consider both the feasibility and the necessity of insulating the police from political influence and employing it scrupulously on duties for which alone it is by law intended. Policemen must also be made to realise that politicking by them is outside the sphere of their domain, and the government would take a very serious view of it.

xii. Politicians who use public servants for purely political purposes, and public servants who allow themselves to be so used, both commit a serious disservice to the country.

xiii. The vast majority of demolitions were carried out with a complete disregard for the suffering of persons in very humble walks of life. The government could take immediate steps to remedy the wrong and also to ensure that the conditions in the resettlement colonies are rendered safe, clean and convenient.

xiv. The government has a special responsibility to ensure that extraconstitutional centres of power are not allowed to grow, and if and when located, to snuff them out ruthlessly.

xv. Specific instructions should be issued emphasising that the detenus must be treated with dignity and respect due to them and the restraint imposed upon them will be minimal and consistent only with ensuring the safety of the state or interests of law and order, and that student detenus will be permitted to take their periodical examinations. For female detenus, special provisions should be made for housing them and extending to them appropriate conveniences.

xvi. The practice of appointing retired officers as heads of organisations on a short-term, renewable basis is a pernicious one and often leads to serious abuse of authority.

xvii. Departments like the Income Tax Department, the Intelligence Bureau, the CBI, the Enforcement Directorate, etc., should be led by strong, competent, and self-respecting individuals who are known for their appreciation of values and their concern for the interests of the country and its citizens. Lesser men as heads of such organisations, which play a vital role in the life of the nation, would only be a disaster.

xviii. For the effective and objective functioning of the Intelligence agencies, their activities and achievements should be suitably overseen and evaluated by responsible forums composed of persons specially selected for their integrity and sense of public duty and functioning independently of the intelligence agencies.

xix. The Commission has drawn the government's attention to the guidelines dividing the government servants into three broad categories. Only those who had exceeded or misused or abused their powers or authority for securing personal gains or for securing advantage to other individual(s)/organisation(s) have attracted the critical attention of the Commission.

xx. The Commission would like to reiterate that it would reckon its achievement not by the number or the seriousness of the punitive actions taken against persons who had transgressed the laws, but by the nature and extent of the remedial and ameliorative actions that follow the labours of the Commission.

xxi. If the Commission's observations generate a public debate on some of the vital issues focused on by the Commission with the object of devising corrective machinery and remedial action, the Commission's labour will be amply rewarded.

Chapter xvi

Wrongful confinement and torture of Lawrence Fernandes by the police and maltreatment in the jail

i. The Commission is of the view that the statement of Lawrence that he was taken away from his house and kept in illegal police custody from 1 May 1976 is true.

ii. The Commission has no hesitation in disbelieving the account of Inspector Prameswarappa regarding his visit to the K.G. General Hospital Casualty Ward. His story was false and appeared to have been fabricated in an attempt to shield himself and his colleagues from the likely consequences of the illegal police detention and torture of Lawrence. The cumulative effect of his statements leaves no room for doubt that they are a tissue of falsehoods.

iii. It is established beyond doubt that Lawrence was in illegal police custody from the night of 1 May 1976, and that he was subjected to physical torture, which necessitated his examination by two different doctors on two separate occasions: on the nights of 3 and 7 May 1976.

iv. The account given by the police officers—that Lawrence was arrested on 10 May 1976 at a bus stand in Davangere—bears clear signs of fabrication and falsehood.

v. The circumstances under which Lawrence was reportedly arrested by Visveshwariah, the investigating officer, appear entirely incredible.

vi. The Commission is inclined to accept the testimony of Dr Krishnappa and Dr Nagraj that there was a fracture of the left foot of Lawrence since it is corroborated by the attendant symptoms of severe pain, swelling, inability to stand without support and inability to walk more than a step or two.

vii. On the evidence, the conclusion is inevitable that Lawrence was a physically disabled man when he came into the jail due to the torture and ill-treatment by the police and that within the jail premises Chablani (Senior Superintendent of Jails) colluded with the police by delaying the orthopaedic examination of Lawrance as far as he could and also in keeping him away from the other detenus for obvious reasons. The Commission holds Chablani also responsible for not complying with the order of the court, which had asked for a medical report on the physical condition of Lawrence.

viii. Lawrence was in unlawful police custody from 1 to 9 May 1976, during which time he was assaulted by the police, resulting in multiple personal injuries. Responsibility for this rests with Visveshwariah, Deputy Superintendent of Police, and Inspector Prameswarappa.

ix. Vittal Naik was present when Lawrence was produced before the Magistrate on 20 May, at which time Lawrence complained about being assaulted. Even then, Vittal Naik took no meaningful steps to initiate a purposeful inquiry. He had a duty to ensure that Lawrence had not been ill-treated while in the custody of the police station under his jurisdiction. The Commission is therefore of the view that Vittal Naik bears equal responsibility for what happened to Lawrence in police custody and must share accountability with Visveshwariah and Prameswarappa.

x. The case diaries of the years 1975 and 1976, which were purporting to be a record of investigations conducted in 1975 and 1976, have been found to be written in the forms printed in March 1977. The inference is inevitable that diaries in their original form were found inconvenient and were rewritten on the forms printed in March 1977. Considering the importance and the evidentiary value of case diaries in judicial proceedings, the Commission has no doubt that the original diaries were replaced by fresh diaries and the version of Vittal Naik that he did not initially write the diaries and wrote them only when it was necessary to produce them before the investigating officer is a false statement.

xi. The Commission deems it necessary to draw the attention of the appropriate authorities to the conduct of Vittal Naik, which the Commission regards as reprehensible.

xii. Krishnamurthy Raju, Superintendent of Police, COD, had deliberately ignored the various lapses in the investigation. The Commission is of the view that as Superintendent of Police, he ought to take the full responsibility for everything that happened to Lawrence while in his charge and on account of the activities of his officers. Raju did not take steps to institute an inquiry even when he was told about the allegations that Lawrence had made before the Magistrate. This is a grave omission on the part of a senior and responsible officer of the rank of Superintendent of Police.

xiii. Krishnamurthy Raju's complicity comes out in yet another context. Presumably, he did not think it necessary to publish any item in the Crime and Occurrence Sheet regarding Lawrence because he was already in custody and no further action was indicated in this regard.

xiv. All the four police officers (named earlier) are responsible for the illegal detention and torture of Lawrence Fernandes, the primary responsibility resting squarely with Krishnamurthy Raju, Superintendent of Police, Corps of Detectives, who was the senior most amongst them and with whose knowledge and consent everything else appears to have taken place.

xv. Chablani, the Senior Superintendent Jail, colluded with the police officers in gaining time to let the injuries on the person of Lawrence heal by postponing the medical examination of Lawrence by an orthopaedic surgeon. He also failed to comply with the court's order to submit a medical report on Lawrence. This was a deliberate effort on the part of Chablani with a view to shielding the delinquent police officers. The Commission is also of the view that keeping Lawrence in the corridor of the single cell-barrack was done deliberately with a view to keeping all that happened to Lawrence at the hands of the police a secret from the fellow detenus.

xvi. This case highlights not only the illegal detention and torture of an individual by the police but also a grave subversion of the legal system, including the judicial process, by senior and responsible government officers. The conduct of the police officers involved has set a deeply troubling example for the members of the force they represent. By giving false testimony under oath, they have effectively sought to legitimise perjury. Their actions have not only diminished their own credibility in the eyes of the public but have also inflicted lasting damage on the reputation and integrity of the police force as a whole.

xvii. Highly placed officers whether they belong to the administrative branch or the police branch are the custodians of the ideals of the service to which they belong. When the leadership of the highly placed officers fails, it reflects directly upon those whom they represent and results in the erosion of discipline and performance of the rank and file. Examined in that light, the conduct of the police officers, as disclosed by the investigation of the Commission, is bound to leave a dark spot upon the reputation of this service as an institution.

Chapter xvii

I. *Detention Under MISA of Murali Dhar Dalmia, Chief Advisor, Technological Institute of Textiles, Bhiwani (Haryana)*

i. The detention order against Dalmia, passed on 30 November 1975, was based upon trumped-up charges and the grounds of detention fail to stand the test of scrutiny. According to Parmanand, CID Inspector, his report had to be based on "false and concocted materials".

ii. R. S. Verma, the District Magistrate of Bhiwani, made no effort to satisfy himself on the veracity or the adequacy of the grounds of detention and mechanically passed the detention order.

iii. Parole was granted to Dalmia only when K. K. Birla met Bansi Lal and successfully pleaded with him for this. Bansi Lal agreed to grant parole only on conditions that Dalmia would vacate the house that he was occupying and would be away from Delhi for six months.

iv. This case highlights the highhandedness and arbitrary conduct of Bansi Lal in Haryana during the Emergency. Various functionaries in the government fabricated records and concocted grounds to justify an unjustifiable detention order to fulfil the desire of Bansi Lal regarding the arrest of Dalmia.

v. The Chief Minister employed the authority and the resources of the state to wreck his private grudge against a citizen in an unprincipled and unscrupulous manner. The courts felt compelled to hold that they had no power to grant redress.

vi. Bansi Lal, even though he had ceased to be the Chief Minister of Haryana, and had become Defence Minister, continued to exercise the same authority and power over the affairs of Haryana as he had done when he was the Chief Minister. The power that he exercised and the manner in which he wielded it would rank him with medieval despots. He grossly misused his position and abused his authority as Chief Minister in ordering the detention of Dalmia. He continued to abuse his position even after he had ceased to be the Chief Minister and became the Defence Minister.

II. *Detention of M.L. Kak, Special Correspondent of the Tribune*

i. Kak's detention was a part of the large-scale MISA detention operations that had been mounted all over Haryana on the night of 25/26 June 1975, at the instance of the Chief Minister, Bansi Lal.

ii. Rudra (SSP) has admitted that there was no substantial material against Kak other than the fact that he was generally critical of the government in his reporting. Rudra also brought to the attention of the District Magistrate the crucial fact that there was insufficient material to warrant Kak's detention under MISA. However, Jain, the District Magistrate, has denied that Rudra ever told him, prior to obtaining the detention orders, that there was inadequate material for Kak's detention.

iii. In the MHA file dealing with the detention of Kak, the then Joint Secretary (IS) had noted, "This appears to be a case of misuse of MISA."

iv. In the opinion of the Commission, Rudra's version seems to be more truthful and correct than that of Jain. The position taken by the District Magistrate that he was told verbally by the Senior Superintendent of Police about the grounds of detention, which he believed to be true and genuine, and he based his detention orders on the version of the SSP, is an attempt to evade his responsibility by shifting the blame on to the SSP Rudra.

v. The stand taken by L.M. Jain that he issued the detention order against M.L. Kak only after satisfying himself personally about the grounds for detention does not appear to be consistent with the facts of the situation.

vi. The commission has no doubt that the story of Jain is false.

vii. In his anxiety to save himself, L.M. Jain seems to have taken recourse to shifting the responsibility on the others. The Commission feels that this officer who was holding the important office of the District Magistrate was a party, under the compulsion of circumstances prevailing at that time, to patently illegal acts, had attempted to shirk his responsibility and has in that process invented a story, which cannot be accepted. By his unbecoming conduct, he has done a disservice to the traditions of the service and the legitimate expectations that the people and the government have in the service to which he belongs.

III. *Harassment and detention of Cdr. (Retd.) Pritam Datta of Rohtak*

i. The removal of Cdr. Datta from the membership of the District Soldiers, Sailors and Airmen Board of District Rohtak was not only improper but also a violation of the constitution of the DSSA Board.

ii. Orders for conducting raid on the business premises of Cdr. Datta at Rohtak were given to J. K. Duggal, Excise and Taxation Commissioner, Haryana, by Sham Chand, the then Minister of Excise and Taxation, Haryana, at the instance of Bansi Lal. The raid was ordered by Duggal even though there was no information with him of the commission of any irregularities or malpractices by Cdr. Datta.

iii. O.P. Taneja, Deputy Excise and Taxation Commissioner, acted with alarming haste in initiating action against Cdr. Datta, including the cancellation of his licence and the closure of godown. No proper warrant was issued, and no formal order was recorded in this regard.

iv. On 19 November 1975, Cdr. Datta was detained under MISA, and he remained in detention until December 1975. Mehtani had, on several occasions, informed Deputy Commissioner S.P. Mittal that Chief Minister Bansi Lal was displeased with Cdr. Datta and desired his detention under MISA.

v. S. H. Mohan, SSP Rohtak, has stated that though there were no adverse materials whatsoever to justify Cdr. Datta's detention under MISA, he had to personally prepare a report containing fabricated grounds for detention.

vi. R.C. Mehtani, who had commenced his career as an LDC (lower division clerk) in the Haryana government and had a meteoric rise when he became OSD to the Chief Minister, drawing a salary of nearly Rs 2,300, wielded extraordinary influence and authority in the State of Haryana. His relations stood to gain by getting Cdr. Datta in trouble. Towards this end, he appears to have grossly misused his official position.

vii. Bansi Lal issued verbal instructions to the District Magistrale, Mittal, to detain Datta in a move to help one Ram Chander, who happened to be very close to him. He also acted under the influence of his official assistant, Mehtani, who had a direct personal interest in promoting the business interests of Messrs. Ram Chander and Sons. In the process, he stopped short of nothing, including the detention of Datta on entirely concocted grounds.

viii. An innocent citizen who had given the best part of his life to the service of the nation suffered irreparable damage to his reputation and social standing by the vindictive operations of Bansi Lal and Mehtani. These two persons have grossly misused their position and authority and were responsible for the illegal detention under MISA of an innocent individual for purely personal reasons.

IV. *Detention under MISA of Ishwar Lal Chaudhary, District Employment Officer, Bhiwani (Haryana)*

i. Ishwar Lal Chaudhary, on receiving a message through the DSP, met Chief Minister Bansi Lal at his Bhiwani residence. There the Chief Minister in the presence of various district functionaries as well as members of the public accused Chaudhary of registering names of the people of Rohtak district in Bhiwani Employment Exchange and without giving any opportunity to him to explain his conduct ordered his detention under MISA. Chaudhary was accordingly arrested by the police.

ii. This case reveals a disturbing narrative of power being abused and authority misused, and illustrates Bansi Lal's capricious and highly arbitrary style of administration. A straightforward and honest officer, committed to performing his duties in accordance with the rules, was detained solely for refusing to comply with the irregular requests of Surinder Singh, the son of Bansi Lal. The district authorities, in turn, executed the detention order without question or resistance, despite there being no adverse record against the officer concerned.

iii. The provisions of MISA were misused in a blatant manner because Bansi Lal wanted it.

V. *Harassment and Detention under MISA of Pitambar Lal Goyal*

i. Bansi Lal wanted to prevent Goyal from entering the service and so covert efforts were made at his instance to declare Goyal unfit for selection.

ii. Immediately after the proclamation of the Emergency, orders for the detention of Goyal under the MISA were issued. Nakai, the SSP, has admitted that there were no materials available against Goyal but he fabricated the report against him in view of the clear instruction of the state government.

iii. R. S. Verma, the District Magistrate, admitted that he signed the detention order when there was before him no material whatsoever against Goyal. He has also admitted that in the case of Ram Pratap (father of Pitambar Goyal) detention orders were passed without application of mind.

iv. What Dr Jain (AC) had done was completely contrary to the conduct expected of a senior and responsible doctor and contrary to medical ethics. The Commission is of the opinion that he, as the Chairman of the Medical Board, misused his position and abused his authority in manipulating the medical report on Pitambar Lal Goyal.

v. The evidence of Harnam Singh, SHO, has not been found by the Commission to be reliable.

vi. The Commission does not find R. S. Varma, District Magistrate, responsible for any improper conduct with regard to the verification of the character and antecedents of Pitambar Lal Goyal.

vii. The Commission finds that S. D. Bhambri, the then Chief Secretary in the Haryana government, had no personal grudge against Goyal. The exercise to change the rules was undertaken by Bhambri pursuant to the wishes of Bansi Lal. The Commission cannot be overlook the prevailing conditions in the State of Haryana during the Emergency; given those circumstances, it would have been difficult for anyone to act as a hero. Even so, considering the position of trust and responsibility that Bhambri held at that point of time, his conduct did not conform to the best traditions of the Administrative Service to which he belongs.

viii. The Commission finds the conduct of Bansi Lal in regard to this case reprehensible. For purely personal reasons, he grossly misused his position as Chief Minister and abused his authority. He went after three generations of a family to satisfy his appetite for vengeance. In the process, he got the reports fabricated for the sole purpose of denying a young man an office in the Judicial Service, which would have made his career. He got Pitambar Lal Goyal, his father, uncle and grandfather detained. He appears to have pursued his animosity against the Goyal family even when he was appointed as Defence Minister and got the rules changed so as to disable a detenu and particularly Goyal from taking a competitive examination. There is no evidence before the Commission as to the direct involvement of Bansi Lal, but there is little doubt, on evidence, that Bansi Lal was responsible for the change in the rules.

ix. The Commission notes with amazement the statement of B. D. Gupta to the effect that even as Chief Minister, he stood in constant fear of being detained under MISA by Bansi Lal. This typifies the general atmosphere of fear and uncertainty generated by Bansi Lal in Haryana during the Emergency from the effect of which no one from the highest to the lowest was free.

x. An incumbent to the office of the Chief Minister of a state who should have been the very embodiment of justice and fair play in all public dealings, has descended in this case to a petty vindictive level to satisfy a personal grudge against the members of a family.

VI. *Use of compulsion and force in implementation of the family planning programme in Village Uttawar, District Gurgaon*

i. This raid on village Uttawar was, it appears, planned deliberately by the state officials because of the opposition of the local population to submit to the sterilisation programme of the state government.

ii. All indications on the basis of oral and documentary evidence are that S. S. Bajwa (Police IG - Haryana) was fully aware of what was intended and did happen and agreed with the consequential actions that followed the raid. The Commission accepts his plea that he had been rendered considerably ineffective even in the handling of his officers as it emerges from the letter that he had received from the Home Secretary to the Haryana government (where he was advised not to initiate action against any Superintendent of Police without prior approval of the Chief Minister). The Commission would like to observe that it cannot be expected, on the one hand, the leadership of the Force to function effectively if, on the other, steps are also taken by the government to undermine the leadership.

iii. M. K. Miglani, the then Deputy Commissioner, appears to have used his position as the Head of the District to order the disconnection of the electric supply to the village. He was as much a party to the raid as others were and to everything else that flowed from it. Miglani was interested in fulfilling the family planning target that had been set for him from the State HQ.

iv. Tek Chand, as SSP Gurgaon, was an active participant in the events leading to the raid and following it. The villagers of Uttawar were carried to the sterilisation centre in trucks under police escort.

v. The three officers were privy to the raid which was planned at the behest of the higher authorities. These officers were powerless to resist the express wishes of the government of the time. The Commission, therefore, takes a lenient view of the matter as far as the officers themselves are concerned. This is, however, not to minimise the gravity and illegality of what was done to the people of the village, both in terms of the raid, sterilisation and the cutting of electricity.

vi. Much concentration of power in the hands of the District Magistrates and the Sub-Divisional Officers with regard to the career prospects of officials belonging to the other departments insofar as these were governed by the favourable confidential reports of the District Magistrates and the Sub-Divisional Officers on the work and conduct of these officials appears to have been, in no small measure, responsible for the willingness of a large body of officials to carry out improper or unauthorised directions emanating from the District and Sub-Divisional authorities.

Chapter xviii

In this Chapter, the Commission has set down certain broad aspects relating to abuse of authority and misuse of power in the matter of treatment meted out to public servants insofar as it relates to their service conditions generally and with particular reference to their summary dismissal, compulsory/premature retirements and supersessions.

Chapter xix

Arrests and Detentions

This Chapter deals in a general way with the detentions under the MISA ordered by the detaining authorities of the respective state governments. The discussion is intended primarily to compile and set down at one place, on the basis of the records of the respective state governments, a factual account of the detentions ordered during the Emergency by the different state governments as a record of the times.

Chapter xx

Conditions in jails in India with special reference to treatment of persons arrested

The Commission circulated a questionnaire to all the states seeking information on specific relevant topics. In addition, Commission officers visited jails across various parts of the country to conduct on-the-spot assessments of jail conditions. The information presented in this Chapter is based on responses received and observations made during these visits. Every effort has been made to present the findings factually, with minimal comments, except for a few suggestions offered for the government's consideration.

Chapter xxi

Implementation of the Family Planning Programme during the Emergency

This Chapter examines the manner in which the Family Planning Programme was implemented by the Central and state governments from time to time during the Emergency.

Chapter xxii

Demolitions during the Emergency

The Commission had issued a detailed questionnaire on demolition to all state governments and union territories seeking information on various aspects of the demolition programme carried out in the states. Some general aspects and the salient points emerging from the replies received from the states have been discussed in this Chapter.

Chapter xxiii

Complaints and their disposal with reference to the Issue of Reference

In this Chapter, details have been given regarding the total number of complaints received by the Commission, how these were categorised, classified, investigated and disposed of.

Chapter xxiv

General Observations

i. The one single item which had affected the people most over the entire country was the manner in which the powers under the amended MISA were misused at various levels.

ii. A large number of officers exercising the powers of District Magistrates obediently carried out the instructions emanating from politicians and administrative heads issued on personal or political considerations. Such conduct on the part of responsible officers is not in consonance with the best traditions of the services to which they belonged and of the ethical considerations governing the exercise of such powers.

iii. Some officers did not have the courage to do the right thing during the Emergency: they do not have the character to face the truth now and own up to their past wrongs.

iv. The manner in which the MISA detentions were ordered should be a lesson to the people's representatives in the Legislature as to how a statute, initially well-conceived, may be misused for purposes totally alien to the object and intentions of its framer. It is time that some mechanism is devised to ensure that such enactments are subjected to a periodical review by the framers themselves.

v. In several cases, large-scale fabrication of records has been admitted. Means should be devised to ensure that these concocted records are not used again to the disadvantage or detriment of the individuals concerned.

vi. It is a matter of concern to the Commission that the (then) prevailing acts of impropriety and immorality came to be accepted as a concept of a new propriety and a new morality.

vii. It is necessary to provide certain institutional safeguards to look after the interests of the entire run of officials and particularly those who are involved at the decision-making levels of the government.

viii. Detention of an officer, who had a reputation for integrity, for not carrying out orders which were plainly unwarranted and which amounted to a flagrant and unpardonable misuse of authority by a politician has a very important and telling lesson for the nation as a whole. If this instance is projected on the national scale, a political authority may decide to penalise an officer for tendering advice or faking a decision the operational effect of which, albeit beneficial, transcends the territorial boundaries of the state to embrace the interest of the country as a whole. Public servants are expected to function in the interest of the country as a whole and not subserve a narrow sectarian or regional interest of politicians.

ix. It is imperative to ensure that the officials at the decision-making levels are protected and immunised from threats or pressures so that they can function in a manner in which they are governed by one single consideration—the promotion of public wellbeing and the upholding of the fundamentals of the Constitution and the rule of law.

x. It is hoped that the authorities, both at the Centre and the states, will look at some of the cases in which aberrations have been pinpointed by the Commission in a spirit of honest inquiry and determine what went wrong not only in each individual case but generally and how a similar situation can and should be averted in the future.

xi. Commitment by the public servants means commitment to the policy and programmes of the government in so far as these are in conformity with the rule of law and fundamentals of the Constitution. Public servants have to be politically neutral at all levels and at all times. It is expected of the services that they would tender frank, informed and well-considered advice without getting personally involved in their present position or their future advancement.

xii. The government must encourage its employees to function freely and fearlessly within the framework of established principles, making it clear that deviation from established procedures without justification would be dealt with severely.

xiii. It is necessary for the government to appreciate the need for defining the various functions and powers of the several lower functionaries who are in close proximity to the seats of power. The circumstances under which the personal staff, including special assistants and the private secretaries attached to the Ministers, could convey orders be defined precisely, and safeguards should be provided for checkback in the event of doubt or difference of opinion.

xiv. The trend in democratic governments today is in favour of more and more open functioning. The benefit of experience of such working may be availed of for such action as may be feasible, practicable and desirable in the context of our own peculiar needs and conditions.

xv. It is necessary to devise adequate and appropriate safeguards to ensure that powers available to the government to prematurely retire an employee are not arbitrarily used without any scope for redressal of the employee's grievances.

xvi. What happened during the Emergency was the subversion of a system of administration. To avoid recurrence, the system must be overhauled with a view to strengthening it so that it could work in a free atmosphere and in a spirit calculated to promote the integrity and welfare of the nation and the rule of law.

xvii. The events during the Emergency are merely the tragic culmination of the particular trend that had been identified and condemned from time to time by the

Commissions of Inquiry in the past. The Commission owes it to the citizens of India to emphasise that appointments of Commissions by themselves are not enough if the governments concerned do not follow up and implement such of the recommendations as are avowedly accepted by them.

xviii. If administrative machinery in our country is to be rendered safe for our children, the services must give a better account of themselves by standing up for the basic values of an honest and efficient administration. This alone can resurrect the people's lost faith once again in our services. If a democratic heritage is to be left for future generations, we should want the truth again to be enshrined in its legitimate place in the social, economic and political scheme of things in our country. There is nothing unattainable or profound in this. It is a simple human message.

Chapter xxv

Appendix-I

i. The Commission had to be selective in the matter of hearing of cases in open session not because the Commission did not appreciate the gravity of the allegations made by aggrieved persons but because of the fact that it would have been impossible to do so in all the cases and complete the job within the foreseeable future. The state governments have appointed authorities, and the Commission trusts that the proceedings will be disposed of by them expeditiously, latest by December 31, 1978.

ii. All the officers and staff of the Commission deserve high praise for the single-minded devotion to duty that they have exhibited in the discharge of functions at various levels.

Annexure - II

The Shah Commission Report

General Observations

1. The Commission has dealt with the different heads of the terms of reference relating to the Central and state governments in separate chapters. The observations of the Commission are intended to present a comprehensive picture of the manner in which the various state governments and their employees at different levels functioned during the period of the Emergency. Arbitrariness and reckless disregard of the rights of others and the consequent misery, which characterised a number of actions of the different public servants over a period of nearly 19 months, terrorised the citizens, resulting in a complete loss of faith of the people in the fairness and objectivity of the administration generally.
2. Among the abuses and misuse of authority by the administration, the one single item which had affected the people most over the entire country was the manner in which the powers assumed by the government to detain persons under the amended MISA were misused by the officials at various levels.
3. A large number of officers—District Magistrates and Commissioners of Police, who exercised the powers of District Magistrates ex officio, obediently carried out the

instructions emanating from politicians and administrative heads issued on personal or political considerations. Many of these officers who appeared before the Commission explained that, in the circumstances that prevailed, they had no alternative. In light of the evidence concerning the conditions prevailing during the Emergency, the Commission has generally accepted the plea of helplessness tempered by expressions of regret put forward by the detaining officers. This, however, does not minimise the basic fact that such conduct on the part of responsible officers is not in consonance with the best traditions of the services to which they belonged, and of the ethical considerations which must govern the exercise of powers involving deprivation of liberty, under an order based entirely on subjective satisfaction of the officers concerned without a trial and without affording an opportunity to the person detained or even his knowing what infraction he had, in the view of the official, been responsible for.

4. The Commission has also come across officers who having committed excesses at the behest of others—politicians or higher administrative authorities—have sought to defend patently indefensible conduct by suggesting that they had acted in good faith and in due compliance with the provisions of the MISA. Some of these officers did a series of wrong things, being powerless to resist the pressures in the prevailing conditions and being afraid then of the consequences, if they were not to do what the politicians or higher authorities expected or ordered them to do. They have now sought to justify their wrong conduct again presumably because of the fear of consequences. These officers who could not do the right thing during the Emergency by resisting illegal pressures did not do the right thing even after the withdrawal of the Emergency. Not only that they made no attempt to atone for their past infirmity, they have in fact made vain

attempts to justify their conduct. They could not display courage to face the truth then; they have not the character to face the truth now and to own up their past wrongs.

5. Though at the time of writing the report, Parliament has already taken steps to repeal the MISA, the manner in which the MISA detentions were ordered by the detaining authorities at different levels during the Emergency should be a lesson to the people's representatives in the Legislature as to how a statute, initially well-conceived, may be misused for purposes totally alien to its objects and the intentions of its framers. It is time that some mechanism is devised to ensure that enactments, which confer on public servants powers exercisable on their subjective satisfaction and which interfere with the normal lives and activities of the citizens, are subjected to a periodical review by the framers themselves so that the spirit and motivation behind all such legislations are fully and completely honoured by those invested with power or authority under the Act. An enactment once it comes into the statute book should not be allowed to be forgotten. Its operation should be kept constantly under review. There should be built-in provisions to remind the framers and the public servants exercising authority under the statute for periodical reviews by the legislatures so that the initial aims and objects of the Act are not perverted.

6. In several cases heard by the Commission, responsible officials admitted to the fact of large-scale fabrication of records concerning various individuals and matters to subserve the interests of a few. Considering the manner in which the MISA cases were dealt with by the detaining authorities which often involved large-scale fabrication of records, it is but proper that an effort should be made by the authorities at the Centre and in the states to devise means to ensure that these concocted records are not used again to the disadvantage or detriment of the individuals concerned. This

has necessarily to be done; otherwise the very same records would over a period of time come to be invested with a degree of sanctity and authenticity which they often lack, and these very records may in future be ferreted out of the archives to support or to demolish an individual or a cause.

7. The Commission has referred to the conduct of the officers concerned with the administration, both at the Secretariat and in the field, in Chapter XV, para 20 of the Second Interim Report. In that context the Commission has observed that "imaginary fear of possible and probable consequences for doing the right things have done more havoc than the known consequences that actually may have followed the performance of duties on the right lines by the government servants". The public servants have not infrequently unduly exaggerated the fear under which they were functioning during the Emergency with a view to avoid the likely consequences of a decision which may have been contrary to the express or implied wishes of the political and administrative policy makers. In a number of cases, officials were almost anticipating the wishes of those in authority, however illegal, immoral and incongruous with the basic tenets of administration, such conduct on their part may have been. They have set out the excuse of undesirable consequences that were likely to follow should they have dared to withstand the pressures from their superiors. In the process many of them have also stood to gain, may be even notionally, by being allowed to continue in offices which were to their liking and which may have yielded conveniences or comforts incidental to the office and undoubtedly welcome to the incumbent. It is a matter of concern to the Commission that the prevailing acts of impropriety and immorality were not considered improper or immoral by the authorities. It came to be accepted as a concept of a new propriety, and a new morality.

8. It must, however, be conceded, as it is clear on evidence, that there was an all-pervading fear of consequences among the officials, which in many cases was indeed genuine, which inhibited many officials from acting in the only way which would have been conducive to the health of the administration primarily and of the nation generally. Commandments of good conduct, good behaviour and morality got muted when self-preservation was at stake. Considering the conditions under which the officials had to function in the State of Haryana, and the examples that have been brought on the record of the Commission by way of only a few of the many cases of wanton vindictiveness that were manifest in the actions of the government of Haryana during the period of the Emergency, it is necessary to point out the need to provide certain institutional safeguards to look after the interests of the entire run of officials, and particularly those who are involved at the decision-making levels in the various departments of the government in the states and at the Centre. When unscrupulous and unprincipled politicians and their associates are in a position to harm the public servants refusing to fall in line with wrong and illegal orders, it becomes necessary in the interest of the basic unity and integrity of the country, as also of the fundamentals of the Constitution and the rule of law, to protect the officials who are called upon to function at different administrative levels.
9. The case of Ishwar Lal Chaudhary, Employment Exchange Officer at Bhiwani (Haryana) who was ordered to be arrested on the spot and to be detained under MISA by Bansi Lal when he had gone to Bansi Lal's house to meet him on his arrival there, is a classic example which illustrates how an authoritarian Chief Minister's illegal and indefensible orders for detaining an innocent individual were carried out mechanically at the level of the District Magistrate without even the slightest pretence of satisfaction of the

grounds for detention. It is true that it may have required more than a hero's courage for any District Magistrate to withstand the pressure from Bansi Lal in the circumstances then prevailing. But it must leave an indelible blemish on the administration as a whole. The only fault of Chaudhary was that he was registering for employment applicants who belonged to the districts neighbouring Bhiwani in Haryana. Detention of an officer, who had a reputation for integrity, for not carrying out orders which were plainly unwarranted and which amounted to a flagrant and unpardonable misuse of authority by a politician, has a very important and telling lesson for the nation as a whole. This small functionary, going about his job correctly, truthfully and fairly, was made a victim of the wrath of a politician to whom apparently, the only interest that mattered was his own and that of his son to the exclusion of the interests of the citizens of even a neighbouring district within his own state. If this instance is projected on the national scale, a political authority may decide to penalise an officer for tendering advice or taking a decision the operational effect of which, albeit beneficial, transcends the territorial boundaries of the state to embrace the interests of the country as a whole. It hardly needs be emphasised that the public servants as a class, each in his own place and doing his own job, are expected to function in the interests of the country as a whole and not to subserve narrow, sectarian or regional interests of politicians.

10. The political system that our Constitution has given to our country is such that it contemplates parties with different political ideologies administering the affairs of the Centre and the state governments. It is necessary in the interest of the territorial, political and economic integrity of the nation to ensure that the factors which contribute to such integrity are forever and continuously strengthened and not impaired. One such factor, and a very important and decisive one, is

the body of public servants at various levels and particularly those at the decision-making levels belonging to the different disciplines and functioning in the states and at the Centre. If the basic unity and territorial integrity of the country is to be emphasised at the political level, it is imperative to ensure that the officials at the decision-making levels are protected and immunised from threats or pressures so that they can function in a manner in which they are governed by one single consideration—the promotion of public well-being and the upholding of the fundamentals of the Constitution and the rule of law. The government ought to ensure this, if necessary, by providing adequate and effective safeguards to which the officials may turn if and when necessary against any actual or attempted threats by the political and/or administrative authorities to sway the officials from performance of their legitimate duties.

11. In the light of the overwhelming and disturbing facts that have come on the record of the Commission, to refuse even to look at the administrative failures to the strains of which the nation has been exposed and to pretend that everything has been right with the administrative apparatus save a few minor aberrations by a few wayward officials is to evade the issue. It is hoped that the authorities both at the Centre and in the states will look at some of the cases in which aberrations have been pinpointed by the Commission and many others on which the Commission has got investigations done through its officials and forwarded the reports to the respective governments for further necessary action, in a spirit of honest enquiry to determine what went wrong not only in each individual case but generally, and how a similar situation can and should be averted in the future. It is necessary to face the situation squarely, that not all the excesses and improprieties committed during the Emergency originated at the political level. In a large number of cases, it appears that unscrupulous

and overambitious officers were prepared to curry favour with the seats of power and position by doing what they thought the people in authority desired. The solutions to the various problems that would inevitably get thrown up must, in their nature, be complex, but the right solutions may be found if the exercise is undertaken at various levels with a steadfast desire and determination to reach them.

12. Exhortations have in the past often been addressed by political leaders that public functionaries must be committed servants of the government. These have in no small measure been responsible for some of the serious consequences that had followed certain steps taken by the government servants during the Emergency. The commitment of a public functionary is, however, to the duties of his office, their due performance with an accent on their ethical content, and not to the ideologies, political or otherwise, of the politicians who administer the affairs of the state. Commitment by the public servants, therefore, means only and entirely commitment to the policy and programmes of the government insofar as the policy and programmes are in conformity with the fundamentals of the Constitution. Anything beyond these fundamentals should be construed to mean as falling outside the scope and the purview of the commitment. The nation has given to itself a democratic form of government and the administrative set-up must function in a manner fulfilling the demands of that form of government in the context of our developing society. Public servants of the different departments have responsibilities, special and peculiar to their respective functions and charter of duties, and the orientation of these responsibilities must be to the programme of social and economic change set out by the government, but within the constraints of the rule of law in a democratic society. This orientation should on no account extend to the politics of the party and/or of the individuals in power. But during the

period of the Emergency, the public servants were expected often to orient the performance of their duties not to the rule of law but the desires and dictates of the politicians and the administrative heads. In many cases the administration and administrators ceased to be insulated from politics with disastrous consequences. It may be observed that all the safeguards and lofty principles of administration would be of no avail if the officials concerned are impervious to the sensitivities of established and accepted administrative norms and practices. It is, therefore, imperative that the public servants should adhere strictly only to their commitment to the programme of the party in power which should be in consonance with the provisions of the laws and the Constitution without in any way compromising with the principle that public servants have to be politically neutral at all levels and at all times. Unless the services work for and establish a reputation of political neutrality, the citizens will have no confidence in the impartiality and fairness of the services. It is expected of the services that they would tender frank, informed and well-considered advice without getting personally involved in their present position or their future advancement, however unpalatable such advice may be to the political head of the Ministry.

13. It would serve some useful purpose if the views of the government on this point are set out unequivocally and in a manner which would enable the different government functionaries to function without inhibition, maintaining at the same time the highest standards of administrative propriety. The government's primary responsibility is to guarantee protection to those officials who refuse to deviate from this code of conduct, which should be accepted not only by the officials but also by the political authorities. If there is sincerity at the political level about the need for and the desirability of a non-political and programme-oriented

administrative machinery, the time is ripe for reaffirming these principles and ideals in a manner that there is no ambivalence about the intentions of the government in relation to the government servants. Any dichotomy in this regard is an invitation to the unscrupulous among the officials to ride the bandwagon in the hope of temporary personal benefits or concessions. If the administrative set-up in the country in its largest and most comprehensive sense is to settle down to a spell of clean, efficient and purposeful functioning, the government must encourage its establishment to function freely and fearlessly and yet within the framework of established disciplinary principles, making it clear that deviations from established procedures without justification would be dealt with severely. Such an understanding between the government and the decision-making levels alone would prevent the administrative set-up from being exploited by unscrupulous careerists who lack the patience to wait for their legitimate claim in the services, and place in the scheme of things.

14. The Commission has viewed with concern the evidence relating to the enormous power that was wielded by the lower functionaries like R. K. Dhawan, R. C. Mehtani, Navin Chawla and some others. It is necessary for the government to appreciate the need for defining the various functions and powers of the several lower functionaries who are in close proximity to the seats of power. The Commission views the developments in this regard with great concern, for power came to be exercised by some of these lower functionaries without the requisite authority and the accountability that goes with it. Power and responsibility must generally go together. During the Emergency, the political component of the government in quite a few important cases came to be divorced from the channel of communication. The result was that powers came to be wielded by the Special

Assistants or Private Secretaries in the name of and on behalf of the Ministers, and the people at the receiving end of the orders were left with no option but to carry out their orders without even having any facility or the desire to verify the authenticity and the authority of the orders emanating from the lower functionaries attached to the Ministers. This style of functioning at a higher level of the administration has indeed taken a toll of the liberty and careers of countless people. The government should define as precisely as it is possible, the circumstances under which the personal staff, including Special Assistants and Private Secretaries attached to the Ministers, could convey orders. The government should also provide checks and safeguards to ensure that in the event of doubt or difference of opinion, the levels receiving the orders from the Ministers are in a position to check back and satisfy themselves that the orders in fact had emanated from the source in whose name the orders were issued. Unless every level of the government starting with the political component and going down the line is animated by one and the only desire to function within a democratic set-up with the ultimate aim and object being only to be able to look after the interests of the common man, there is no hope that we in this country will be able to graduate ourselves from mere words to the real core of democracy.

15. The trend in democratic governments today is in favour of more and more open functioning of the government with less and less emphasis on secrecy. It has been established that more the effort at secrecy, the greater the chances of abuse of authority by the functionaries. In this regard, there has been some serious rethinking in certain foreign countries on the Acts and related matters governing the official secrets. It is suggested that the government may take into consideration the present trends in this regard in the democratic countries and avail of the benefit of their experiences for such action

as may be feasible, practicable and desirable in the context of our own peculiar needs and conditions.

16. During the Emergency, 25,962 public servants were compulsorily retired. The Commission had addressed letters to all the state governments and the ministries of the Government of India, requesting them to undertake a review, among other things, of all the cases of compulsory retirement. As a result of this review, 14,187 public servants have been reinstated. The figures speak for themselves. If such a large number of employees could be reinstated following a review of their cases, it only means that in most, if not in all, of these cases of premature retirement, the guidelines laid down for premature compulsory retirement had not been followed strictly and in accordance with the spirit of the rules. The conclusion also follows that if this review had not been undertaken either at the instance of the Commission or otherwise, the unfortunate public servants who suffered injustice for extraneous reasons would have continued to remain under a cloud and consequent ignominy. It is necessary to devise adequate and appropriate safeguards to ensure that powers available to the government to prematurely retire an employee are not arbitrarily used without any scope for redressal of his grievances should the employee feel that he has been unjustly and prematurely retired. Any such safeguard provided should be capable of functioning in a manner that it is able to dispose of the review or appeal within a stipulated time. Adoption of "droit administratif" on the French model is one of the safeguards for looking after the interests of the employees of the government, which may be profitably considered.
17. Interpretation of the happenings during the Emergency merely as an essay in certain unrelated transactions called excesses indulged in by an individual or a group of individuals

would be wholly a misinterpretation, if not a total travesty of facts. What happened during the Emergency was the subversion of a system of administration. The lament of Commander Dutta about the "gutless administration" while referring to the administration in Haryana is an understandable condemnation of the attitude of the government servants contributing significantly to the subversion of the system. If a recurrence of this type of subversion is to be prevented, the system must be overhauled with a view to strengthen it in a manner that the functionaries working the system do so in an atmosphere free from the fear of the consequences of their lawful actions and in a spirit calculated to promote the integrity and welfare of the nation and the rule of law. This will call for considerable heart-searching both at the political and the administrative levels. Both the groups, during the period of the Emergency, sadly deviated from their respective and legitimate roles of duty, trespassing into each other's areas with the consequences that are there for all to see and many to lament. If the officials on the one side and the politicians on the other do not limit their areas of operation to their accepted and acknowledged fields, this nation cannot be kept safe for working a democratic system of government. Unless this realisation dawns upon the government and the people in all its serious implications, especially for the future, the labours of the Commission would be in vain. The Commission has examined the various transactions, not with the primary object of finding fault with the actions therein, not for cataloguing the human frailties, but to extract a lesson for the future. The process of reformation and rejuvenation especially in the field of administration will have to be speeded up bringing it in tune with the ethos of our nation which alone would prevent a recurrence of the type of maladministration and misuse of power and authority as had occurred during the Emergency.

Unless this awareness permeates all strata of our society, even with the best of intentions, possible recurrence of this type of tragedy may not be prevented.

18. The Commission has had the occasion to peruse the findings of the earlier Commissions appointed by the government at the Centre and in the states to probe into the conduct of the Ministers of the state governments—particularly the reports of S.R. Das who inquired into the conduct of late Pratap Singh Kairon, Chief Minister of Punjab (1963–64), Rajgopal lyengar who inquired into the conduct of late Bakshi Ghulam Mohammed, ex-Chief Minister of Jammu & Kashmir (1965–67), Venkatrama lyer who inquired into the conduct of certain Ministers of Bihar (1967–70), Madholkar who looked into the affairs of the Ministry of Mahamaya Prasad Sinha, Chief Minister of Bihar and other Ministers (1968–69), A. N. Mulla, who looked into the affairs of the Ministers of Kerala—M.N. Govindan Nair and T.V. Thomas (1969–71)—and G.K. Mitter, who looked into the Kendu leaves purchases in Orissa (1973–74). The Commission is not aware of the action taken, if any, in response to these reports submitted from time to time in regard to the Minister-Civil Servant relationship. The fact, however, remains that the refrain in all these reports in so far as this concerns the relationship of the Ministers with the civil servants, is the same. One cannot but be struck by the near-unanimity in the observations of the several Commissions on the unhealthy factors governing the relationship between the Ministers and the Civil Servants. Yet nothing seems to have been done, at any rate effectively, to set right such of the aspects of these relationships which, prior to the Emergency, had contributed to the several developments which came in for indictments by the Commissions. In the light of this, it may be easy to conclude that what happened during the Emergency is merely a tragic culmination of the particular trend that had been identified

and condemned from time to time by the Commissions of the past. The Commission owes it to the citizens of India to emphasise that appointments of Commissions by themselves are not enough if the governments concerned do not follow up and implement at least such of the recommendations as are avowedly accepted by the government. Unless the government is prepared to apply the corrective principles in the Minister-Civil Servant relationship effectively and with a determination to produce the desired results at different levels and within the several components of the government, the agonising impact of this unfortunate malaise would be felt by the common man in the streets, in the villages, in the factories and in the far distant corners of this vast country.

19. As borne out by the records of the government and the depositions of several responsible government servants, dishonesty and falsehood became almost a way of official life during the Emergency. As Robert Frost said, "most of the change we think we see in life is due to truth being in or out of favour". If administrative machinery in our country is to be rendered safe for our children, the services must give a better account of themselves by standing up for the basic values of an honest and efficient administration. That alone can resurrect the people's lost faith once again in our services. If a democratic heritage is to be left for future generations, we should want the truth again to be enshrined in its legitimate place in the social, economic and political scheme of things in our country. There is nothing unattainable or profound in this. It is a simple human message.

Annexure – III

Mar Thoma Sabha – The Only Church That Dared to Oppose the Emergency

The Malankara Mar Thoma Sabha, one of the oldest denominations of Christianity in India, was the only religious organisation to publicly protest and directly confront Indira Gandhi over the imposition of the Emergency.

While many other communities and religious bodies, including various Catholic forums, maintained a stoic silence, it was Dr Juhanon Mar Thoma Metropolitan, the then head of the Mar Thoma Sabha, who vehemently opposed the undemocratic move on two separate occasions.

The first instance occurred at a seminar organised by the Christian Institute for the Study of Religion and Society in Bangalore where Dr Juhanon Metropolitan publicly denounced the unjust imposition of the Emergency and questioned the constitutional validity of such a drastic action.

Indira Gandhi, who was present at the seminar, found herself at the receiving end of the Spiritual Head's sharp criticism. He questioned how the daughter of a socialist democrat like Jawaharlal Nehru could ever think of violating democratic norms and imposing her will on the nation in such an impudent manner.

Her mute response to this accusation is vividly remembered by Dr P.J. Alexander, who was the then DIG (Emergency). The retired IPS officer also recalls that it was Congress leader C.M. Stephen who played a key role in his appointment to the post.

Dr Juhanon Metropolitan reiterated his strong opposition to the imposition of the Emergency during a 1976 assembly of the Mar Thoma Church held in Thiruvalla, once again publicly censuring the government's undemocratic actions.

This bold stance was later referenced by former Nagaland Governor and noted liberation theologian Dr M.M. Thomas in his writings, as recalled by Dr P.J. Alexander.

Dr Juhanon Metropolitan's outspoken criticism, particularly against the Emergency imposed under the pretext of "internal disturbance" in the country as visualised by the Indira Gandhi government, infuriated many within the ruling establishment. Jose Kuttiyani, a Congress leader from Idukki and a strong supporter of the Karunakaran group, reportedly demanded the immediate arrest of the Church leader.

Though Dr Juhanon Metropolitan remained under constant threat of arrest, the government ultimately refrained from taking him into custody, clearly aware of the potential repercussions of such an action.

Dr Juhanon Metropolitan's fearless stance during the Emergency is explicitly mentioned by 21st Mar Thoma Metropolitan, Dr Joseph Mar Thoma. His bold declaration—"whether it be the *Poolatheen Aramana*, the then official residence of Malankara Metropolitans, or jail, it is all the same to me"— captures the fearless mindset of a man, reminisces Dr Joseph Mar Thoma.

Dr P.J. Alexander also vividly remembers an encounter during that tumultuous period in which Dr Juhanon told Bishop Kalacherry (of the Changanacherry diocese) that he was already packed and prepared to go to jail at any moment.

Such a stand by the Mar Thoma Church carries historic significance as it stood virtually alone among religious institutions in openly resisting authoritarian rule during the Emergency.

While Sir C.P. Ramaswami Iyer advocated for an independent Travancore, Kerala, as a whole, chose to merge with the Indian Union.

The Mar Thoma Church, along with other regional dispensations, showed solidarity with this decision.

Enraged by this, Sir CP was said to have threatened retaliation, and rumours spread rapidly that the Mar Thoma churches would be demolished. In response, Mar Thoma Metropolitan Titus II remarked, "If they destroy the roofs of these churches made of grass and bamboos, it is all the better. The Almighty sitting above in the sky can easily see and relate with His people on Earth."

Dr P.J. Alexander, who retired in 1994, further recalls that Bishop Titus II fully embraced Indian culture and incorporated it into the day-to-day practices and services of the Mar Thoma Church.

Abraham Mathew
Journalist and short story writer

About the Author

P.S. SREEDHARAN PILLAI: A MULTIFACETED LEADER AND VISIONARY

P.S. Sreedharan Pillai, the Governor of Goa and former Governor of Mizoram, embodies a dynamic blend of leadership, intellect and philanthropy. His illustrious career spans roles as a lawyer, politician, writer, orator and social activist. Renowned for his eloquence, literary contributions and humanitarian initiatives, Pillai's journey reflects his deep commitment to public service and cultural enrichment.

A Distinguished Legal Career

A graduate of Calicut Law College, Pillai distinguished himself early on as an adept legal professional. His tenure as Assistant Solicitor General and CBI Standing Counsel at the Kerala High Court earned him widespread acclaim. Notably, he represented cases with integrity and impartiality, prioritising truth and justice irrespective of political affiliations. His appointment as Special Public Prosecutor by governments across political lines further attests to his legal prowess.

Pillai has also made significant contributions to legal education and community service. As the youngest-ever president of the

Calicut Bar Association and a long-serving legal consultant to the Calicut Press Club for over two decades, his influence on Kerala's legal landscape is profound.

Political Vision and Leadership

Pillai's political journey began with student activism during the anti-Emergency movement, where he rose to leadership in the Akhil Bharatiya Vidyarthi Parishad. His organisational acumen l played a key role in establishing BJP units in challenging regions like Lakshadweep. His two terms as Kerala BJP President (2003–06, 2018–19) showcased his strategic vision and a pragmatic approach.

As Governor of Goa, his flagship "*Goa Sampurna Yatra*" exemplifies his grassroots engagement, personally visiting villages to address public grievances. His innovative financial aid programmes have provided critical support for dialysis and cancer patients. His empathetic initiatives include inviting HIV-affected children to Raj Bhavan on World AIDS Day.

Literary Excellence

A prolific author, Pillai has written over 260 books, spanning diverse genres such as politics, history, poetry, law and travel. His works, translated into multiple languages, underscore his passion for intellectual discourse. Signature literary ventures like the "Heritage Trees of Goa" and "Discovery of Vaman Vriksha Kala" reflect his dedication to cultural heritage and environment love.

Pillai has launched impactful literary initiatives such as the "Nayi Pahel" and "Sargavasantam" schemes to nurture budding writers. His collaborations with eminent personalities, including Presidents, Prime Ministers and Chief Justices of India, demonstrate his literary stature. His book, *Dark Days of Democracy*, was launched by Prime Minister Narendra Modi. Pillai's close association with several

Jnanpith Award recipients further reflects his deep involvement in the literary world.

Awards and Recognition

Pillai's extensive accolades include 32 prestigious awards. In recognition of his contributions to literature, law and public service, he was conferred honorary doctorate degrees by JJT University, Rajasthan in 2020, ASBM University, Bhubaneswar in 2023 and Alliance University, Bengaluru in 2024. His pioneering initiatives, including the creation of a bonsai garden at Goa Raj Bhavan, reflect his creative ingenuity.

A Life Rooted in Values

Hailing from Venmony in Kerala's Alappuzha district, Pillai's personal life mirrors his deeply held values. His wife, K. Reetha, is a lawyer, and their son, Arjun, along with son-in-law Arun Krishna Dhan, are continuing the family's legacy in the legal profession. His daughter Arya and daughter-in-law Jipsa are both practicing dentists. Pillai's commitment to truth, justice and community welfare remains a source of inspiration.

NOTES